Mark McEntire is professor of religion at Belmont University in Nashville. He has authored widely used textbooks, such as *The Old Testament Story*, 8th ed. (2008) and *Struggling with God: An Introduction to the Pentateuch* (2008); scholarly works, *Dangerous Worlds: Living and Dying* [illegible] (2004) and *The Blood of* [illegible] *Plot in the Hebrew Bible* [illegible] Joel Emerson, *Raising* [illegible] *and Fighting Philistines:* [illegible] *Popular Music* (2006).

PORTRAITS OF A MATURE GOD

PORTRAITS OF A MATURE GOD

CHOICES IN OLD TESTAMENT THEOLOGY

MARK MCENTIRE

Fortress Press
Minneapolis

PORTRAITS OF A MATURE GOD

Choices in Old Testament Theology

Cover design: Alisha Lofgren

Library of Congress Cataloging-in-Publication Data is available

Print ISBN: 978-0-8006-9941-3

eBook ISBN: 978-1-4514-2627-4

The paper used in this publication meets the minimum requirements of American National Standard for Information Sciences — Permanence of Paper for Printed Library Materials, ANSI Z329.48-1984.

Manufactured in the U.S.A.

For all of my teachers at
The Southern Baptist Theological Seminary (1986–1992),
especially my doctoral committee:
Gerald Keown
Marvin Tate
Wayne Ward

CONTENTS

List of Tables

Acknowledgments

The story of this book reveals the many people who played a role in its development. It began with an essay called "The God at the End of the Story." I produced a rough draft of this essay as the fulfillment of an assignment I gave myself while the students in my Old Testament Theology class at Belmont University were writing their own papers. I presented the results to the class and sent a proposal to the Theology of the Hebrew Scriptures section at the Society of Biblical Literature, which accepted the paper for presentation at the 2009 annual meeting. The third revision of the paper was then accepted for publication in *Horizons of Biblical Literature*. Thank you to everyone who gave attention to and responded to my work during this stage, and specifically to *Horizons* for its permission to develop the article into what became the first chapter of the book.

I next began work on an essay called "Portraits of a Mature God," which was also accepted for presentation in the Theology of the Hebrew Scriptures section and was presented at the 2011 annual meeting. I was later invited to place a revision of the paper in an issue of *Perspectives in Religious Studies*, the journal of the National Association of Baptist Professors of Religion. The most gratifying aspect of the publication was that this particular volume was a Festschrift for the great Baptist prophet Will Campbell. Again, I received much helpful response to this work along the way, and I appreciate the permission from *Perspectives* to include much of the material from the article in chapter 6 of this book.

Along the way, I was invited to contribute an article to an issue of the journal *Review and Expositor* on the book of Daniel. The production of that work, "The Graying of God in Daniel 1–6," served to expand my thinking about what the final chapter of this book needed to be. Thank you to *R & E* for its permission to include parts of that article in chapter 6.

The final piece of the process was my involvement with Fortress Press. Anyone who has done work in Old Testament theology over the past fifty years knows that our field of study could hardly exist without this resource. My editor, Neil Elliott, was indispensable. His patience and expertise helped to bring everyone involved to a common vision of what this book could be, and his advice and careful work with the manuscript made it better in countless ways. In later stages of the publication process, I have been grateful for the professional assistance of Lisa Gruenisen, Marissa Wold, and others at Fortress.

So, whatever comes of this work, knowing that I am responsible only in part for its achievements but in full for its shortcomings, I humbly offer it to the field of study that has so faithfully fed my heart, mind, and soul for the past quarter century.

Surrounding the specific process of the production of this book, I live with the love of my family, the support of my colleagues, and the energizing presence of my students every day. Thank you.

1

The God at the End of the Story

In many ways, the hybrid field that is often called theology of the Hebrew Scriptures, and its particular expression called Old Testament theology, may be moving closer to consensus in describing its purpose.[1] If I might put that purpose into my own words, it is to describe the character called God in the Hebrew Scriptures and to observe how that character relates to the other characters in the text and to the world in which these other characters live.[2] At the same time, there is an increasing number of ways to go about this purpose, so our approaches are diverging at the same time that our purpose may be converging. One of the most serious problems interpreters face in the contemporary era is that they have developed a keen awareness of the multiplicity of portraits of the divine character within these shared sacred texts. The first concern in this opening chapter is to examine two different ways of attending to this multiplicity and the extent to which these approaches are useful to the enterprise of Old Testament theology.

One approach to this multiplicity proceeds by laying out the many differing portraits of the divine character and allowing them to converse with one another. The result is a canonical debate about the nature of God's character. This approach has been very fruitful, and I will describe some examples more extensively in this chapter. The primary problem with approaches that fall within this category, however, is that, although they would appear to put all biblical texts into play on an even field, some texts inevitably get to speak first and set the agenda. It will become apparent throughout this study, however, that the problems of this practice are often compounded by letting these texts speak last.

The other general type of approach to examining the divine character in the Bible involves putting texts in some order and looking for a sense of development in the divine character. The obvious initial difficulty with such approaches is the choosing of such an order, which establishes a trajectory for the development of the divine character. The discussion in this chapter will identify and analyze examples of some of the potential choices. One significant implication of observing the development of God as a narrative character is that it necessitates more emphasis on the end of such a developmental process and the texts that portray that end. This emphasis contradicts much of the history of biblical theology, which has always given more attention to the divine character in the early parts of the biblical story, where the divine character is more active and more interesting. In the discussion of these two types of approaches, I will illustrate how they bring us to an impasse between a tension-filled but static divine character and a dynamic but receding one. Old Testament theology has paid far less attention to the parts of the Old Testament where God recedes into the background and becomes a subtle influence in various ways, rather than participating in the story as an active character.

Examining Past Trajectories in Old Testament Theology

There is probably no subdiscipline of biblical studies that loves to wallow in its past as much as Old Testament theology. The great difficulty of this tendency is that once one packs up all of the necessary luggage, the weight of it makes forward movement very difficult, and the packing has taken so long that any new path, once visible, may have become obscured. Still, I venture briefly into an aspect of the past with the hope that it will reveal more than it obscures.

The overlapping fields of theology of the Hebrew Scriptures and Old Testament theology have passed through a period of significant disruption and uncertainty during the past few decades. At the core of most, if not all, of the work in these fields has been a desire to develop a synthetic presentation of these related bodies of literature. In the recent past, the framework for such a presentation was often entangled with reconstructions of the history of Israelite religion. Many have become increasingly suspicious of the hypothetical nature of such reconstructions and have understood it as an unmanageable liability of such an approach. This framework relied heavily not just on the observations of the standard historical-critical approaches to using texts but also on their most tenuous conclusions about sources, dates, and the original settings of small literary units. In recent decades, these difficulties have led to an increased focus on the final form of the text and the worlds that it creates, but this move has heightened our awareness of the diversity of the text. It resists synthetic treatment. This resistance can be clearly illustrated in the work of the two giants of the mid-twentieth century, Walther Eichrodt and Gerhard von Rad. Walter Brueggemann has aptly described the similarities and differences in the work of these two figures and the impasse to which they brought the field half a century ago. Eichrodt's goal was to establish the central theme of covenant strongly enough to hold all of the diversity of the Old Testament literature within its gravitational pull. The result was an intense focus upon what Brueggemann called "a constant basic tendency and character to Old Testament Theology."[3] Von Rad, on the other hand, placed his emphasis on the dynamic quality of Israel's faith, particularly as expressed in its recitals of the work of God on Israel's behalf. Brueggemann described succinctly the stalemate created by these two movements: "Eichrodt's accent on constancy makes it difficult, even as he seeks to do so, to allow for historical dynamic in Israel's faith; thus Eichrodt is easily indicted for reductionism. Conversely, von Rad's emphasis on historical dynamic means that in the end, one finds in his work many theologies but no single theological formulation. Indeed, von Rad concludes that such a statement is impossible. The variegated material precludes such a statement without an unbearable cost in terms of reductionism."[4] This situation is analogous to the idea in physics known as the Heisenberg uncertainty principle, which states that an observer cannot measure or describe both the position and velocity of an electron at the same time. Dynamism and constancy are incompatible. Velocity must be measured over time, using change in position. The only theoretical exception to this would be a particle with no velocity. As yet, no such particle has ever been observed, and it seems just as unlikely that the God of a wandering people might stay still long enough to be described fully.

Approaches Based on Biblical Debate about God's Character

I have rehearsed some of the well-known past of the field Old Testament theology in order to consider the possibility that it has reached a similar impasse after nearly a half century of movement away from using a historical framework toward using a primarily literary one. I take it for granted that it is too late for any valid attempt to present the God of the Bible as a simplistic, consistent character and to present the Bible itself as a univocal source on this subject. Once again, constancy and dynamism may function as two helpful categories. If the explication of the literary development of the divine character within the canon is the primary task, then approaches that fit into the "constancy" category are those which present the divine character as one in a state of tension. The primary advantage of these kinds of approaches is that there is no need to place biblical texts along any kind of trajectory. The primary choice is which texts get to speak first, thus establishing a norm. A clear example can be seen in the work of Brueggemann, in his *Theology of the Old Testament: Testimony, Advocacy, Dispute*, where texts in which God is creating, promising, delivering, commanding, and leading get to speak first and constitute the "core testimony." The aspects of God's character that do not fit this core portrait, such as ambiguity, negativity, and hiddenness, receive significant attention in this work. Providing the texts that participate in this development their own legitimate voice is perhaps the greatest strength of Brueggemann's work, but they are framed as "counter-testimony" and thus given a secondary role.[5] Although the result is a creative tension that gives due attention to the many facets of the divine character, the weight of the "core testimony" seems to anchor the divine character to a position that restricts the potential for dynamic character development. Despite this difficulty, Brueggemann's work has been essential in confirming the principle that Old Testament theology must be grounded in the actions God performs as a character presented in the biblical text.[6]

A more recent attempt that moves along similar lines is Karl Allen Kuhn's *Having Words with God: The Bible as Conversation*. Kuhn has argued effectively for a dialogical understanding of Scripture, one that allows for multiple voices to express differing views about the character of God. To support his contention that "Scripture itself embodies and invites dynamic conversation between God and humanity and conversation among believers about God,"[7] Kuhn points to texts such as the discussion between God and Moses at Mount Sinai, in the wake of the golden-calf episode;[8] Abraham's negotiation with God concerning the fate of Sodom;[9] and the lament tradition, which fills so much of the book of Psalms.[10] The usefulness of Kuhn's work on the subject of the theology of the Hebrew Scriptures is limited by his frequent movement into the New Testament, but his dialogical model serves as a useful example of the kind of constant approach I wish to demonstrate here. By adopting a more general conversational model, Kuhn avoids the need within Brueggemann's courtroom model to classify "core testimony" and "counter-testimony." Nevertheless, despite Kuhn's attention to the diverse voices present within Scripture and his acknowledgment that the "story quality" of Scripture is central, he still insists on what he calls a "coherence" that seems to be in control of the story. He does not attempt to place the varying portraits of God along the narrative plotline of the Bible in order to look for linear development of the divine character, so he must look for something other than a narrative coherence. This insistence on a coherence that includes "abiding features of God's character" places a limit on the dynamic development of the divine character.[11] In the work of Brueggemann and Kuhn, the attempted placement of all texts on a level surface in order to allow a creative dispute keeps all of these aspects in a constant tension with each other, but, in the end, texts seem to be assigned different values based upon predetermined theological norms or because they are better or less well suited to this kind of dialogical context.[12] The texts given a more visible position are those which conform to the "core testimony" or the "abiding features."

Another aspect of dialogical approaches is the long tradition of talking about a "dark side" of God. The use of such a term raises some immediate problems but is too common in the discussion of God's character to ignore.[13] This subject was treated extensively at the end of the twentieth century in a two-volume work by Walter Dietrich and Christian Link called *Die dunklen Seiten Gottes*. More recently this work and its subject have been engaged by John Barton in an essay called "The Dark Side of God in the Old Testament." For Dietrich and Link, an unavoidable dark side of God comes with the presentation of a divine character with emotions. Further, because in most of the Old Testament God is understood as the sole cause of everything that happens, a dark side is inevitable.[14] For Barton, these moves by Dietrich and Link are too "apologetic." The dark side of God is portrayed as a necessary by-product of God's positive side. Rejection, for example, is the by-product of election, and vengeance of justice. Such moves are typical of much Christian theology. In many ways, this identifies the "core testimony" as God's primary intent and the "counter-testimony" as the accidental or incidental consequences. Barton prefers to conclude that God is "inscrutable."[15] This is somewhat more satisfying but still appears to place the blame for the problem on the limits of human reason. The implication is that there is some sense of coherence behind God's behavior and if only we had the secret codes, we would be able to perceive that sense. In terms of observing God as a narrative character, this discussion disrupts a sense of continuity by dividing this character's behavior into categories, a move that ultimately leads to a division of the character. Finally, the most telling failure of this theological move is revealed by the tendency not to name the other side, what would logically seem to be the "light side." The implication is that the "dark side" is an anomaly or aberration that must be named, whereas every other part of God's character is the normal or default mode and need not be specifically identified. So, what is being juxtaposed in this language is not God's "light side" and "dark side" but "God" and God's "dark side."

Approaches Based on the Development of God as a Narrative Character

A much different result appears when texts are placed along a trajectory and the divine character is allowed to develop throughout the resulting plot. The simplest way to do this is within a single book, which is limited in size and fixed in order. The most direct and ambitious attempt to do this to date is

W. Lee Humphreys's 2001 work, *The Character of God in the Book of Genesis*. Humphreys made use of models for evaluating the process of characterization in the Bible that had been developed by Robert Alter and Adele Berlin two decades earlier, but Alter and Berlin had applied this model only to the human characters in the Bible.[16] Humphrey's conclusions about the development of God's character in Genesis were quite profound and have significant theological implications. According to his own summary statement, "The movement is from type to full-fledged character to agent, as we move from God the sovereign designer in Genesis 1 to the complex, multi-faceted and changing figure in the bulk of Genesis 2–36, to God as an agent silently shaping the stories other characters tell of him in the latter segments of Genesis."[17] This conclusion begs an important question: Which God does Genesis want its reader to believe in or serve, some hybrid version of all three stages, or the one that the divine character has become at the end of the story? Humphreys's own position on this question is not clear. Perhaps the closest he comes is in passing the question off to the rest of the Bible. In his words, "We also sense that [God] is not complete or full or whole at the end of Genesis. . . . But then Genesis is not an end in itself. It is the Book of Beginnings."[18] It is difficult to imagine, however, that the religious experience of Joseph is not closer to the religious experience of the intended audience of Genesis than is the religious experience of Abraham or Jacob.

One more example of this approach on the scale of a single biblical book may be found in Phyllis Trible's treatment of the development of the divine character in the book of Jonah. Although such a small book of the Bible offers less opportunity for diverse portrayals, the changes in the divine character that Trible observed are profound. Two examples are most noteworthy, and the first has to do with God's actions toward Jonah. A recalcitrant prophet is presented in the scenes narrated in chapter 1, when Jonah flees on the boat, and chapter 4, when Jonah goes out into the desert. The deity who responds in chapter 1 with a violent storm, trying to drown Jonah into submission, becomes one who attempts by argument to persuade the sulking Jonah in the desert in chapter 4. Second, in relation to the Ninevites, the divine character of chapter 3 responds in kind to the Ninevites when they repent by deciding not to destroy them, whereas the God of chapter 4 argues for saving them out of a sense of pity. In Trible's words, God has moved from a "theology of reciprocity" to a "theology of pity." She took this argument one more step and asserted that the book of Jonah seeks to persuade the reader to accept a theology of pity, just as the divine character in the story is attempting to persuade Jonah to do so.[19] This argument comes much closer to a claim that it is the God at the end of its story that the book is promoting, and that the development of the divine character takes part in that process of persuasion.

Moving to a larger collection of literature such as the entire Tanak, rather than just a single book, requires choosing a trajectory upon which to place texts. There would seem to be three basic choices here. The most problematic trajectory would be one based upon the dates of composition of texts. Not only are such dates hypothetical and disputed, but this process would require difficult decisions about how to divide texts into units. Should a supposed original date for a small individual unit be used; or the date of a larger complex into which this unit has been woven; or the date of the final form of the book in which it is found, the composition of which may have involved some reshaping of that individual text? Another possibility is to use a narrative trajectory following the plot of the story the Bible tells. This makes the placement of some texts, such as those in the Pentateuch and the Former Prophets, easy and certain, but what does one do with the parallel narratives in the books of Chronicles, or texts like those in the Psalms and Wisdom literature, which do not fit into the narrative sequence? Most of the problems of these other two types of trajectories are resolved by the use of the canon as a trajectory. Of course, we have more than one canonical tradition, so the interpreter still must make a difficult choice.

It may help to refer briefly to three works that do not quite fit the criteria of a treatment of the narrative development of the divine character throughout the entire canon but that moved the possibility of such a treatment forward considerably. The title of Samuel Terrien's 1978 work, *The Elusive Presence: Toward a New Biblical Theology*, indicates his acknowledgment of the need for a dialectical approach. An elusive figure is one that must be pursued, and pursuit is a dynamic activity. Terrien followed a roughly canonical path for much of the book, but at least two major factors limit the usefulness of his work here. First, his approach is still shaped too significantly by the history of Israelite religion, rather than the narrative development of divine character in the literature of the Old Testament. Second, the whole of his work seems to me to be infused with his desire to get to the New Testament as a resolution of the problem of the *Deus absconditus*. Indeed, Terrien qualified this problem with his phrase *Deus absconditus atque praesens* in order to create a greater sense of continuity between the two testaments of the Christian Bible. Nevertheless, his assertion that, at some point, "God no longer overwhelmed the senses of perception and concealed himself behind the adversity of historical existence" points toward a consideration of a more thorough and precise narrative approach to God's character.[20]

The understanding of God as a narrative character was also moved forward significantly by the 1983 work of Dale Patrick called *The Rendering of God in the Old Testament*. Patrick effectively developed the notion of God as a "dramatis persona," rendered in language.[21] Further, he recognized this character as "dynamic, surprising, [and] occasionally paradoxical," a combination of qualities "requiring of the reader a dialectical process of recognition."[22] Patrick's method required this notion of recognition so strongly that his focus more often became God's consistency of character, which overshadowed a sense of linear character development, but the idea of God as a dramatic character emerged powerfully enough to add substantially to the growing idea of a dynamic narrative character.

Finally, in a work called *Disturbing Divine Behavior*, Eric A. Seibert has raised important theological questions generated by the observation of God's behavior as it is presented in the Hebrew Scriptures. This book has purposes that often take the discussion outside of the realm of narrative to examine historical issues, but it also pays close attention to the possible functions of the portrayal of a character.[23] As the title indicates, Seibert's work also pays attention to the effect a character's behavior has on the observer of that behavior, in this case, the reader.

A more fully developed example of the kind of narrative approach I am describing, one in which the sustained focus is the development of God as a narrative character through all or a large part of the Hebrew Scriptures, is the work of Richard Elliott Friedman. In *The Disappearance of God: A Divine Mystery*, Friedman called attention to a phenomenon in the Bible that has received very little attention in the history of interpretation: a progressive movement of God's character toward hiddenness as the biblical plot progresses.[24] The receding of God's presence is accompanied by a shift in the "divine-human balance." These were not entirely new observations, though. Friedman did not interact overtly with von Rad in *Disappearance*. It may have been most helpful for Friedman to note the observation in von Rad's article that was placed as a postscript on the end of his two-volume *Old Testament Theology*.[25] The full significance of this essay for understanding the direction of von Rad's theology at the end of his career was highlighted by Magne Saebo in his 2000 article "Yahweh as *Deus absconditus*: Some Remarks on a Dictum by Gerhard von Rad."[26] Saebo noted the importance of differing English translations of the key sentence in von Rad's essay, "Ist es Nicht ein Jahwe, der siche von Mal zu Mal in seinen Selbstoffenbarungen vor seinen Volk tiefer und tiefer verbirgt." Saebo's own rendering, "Is he not a Yahweh who from time to time in his self-revelation is hiding himself more and more deeply from his people,"[27] may lean slightly more toward the notion that this hiddenness progresses over time than does the better-known translation of D. M. G. Stalker, "Does he not, in the course of his self-revelation, conceal himself more and more deeply from his people?"[28] Given von Rad's overall framework, if he did observe a progression, it seems more likely that it was historical in nature, rather than canonical or literary, but this sense of dynamism carries over into literary treatment of God as a narrative character.

The work of Friedman is still an apt beginning point, because only he makes any overt attempt to compare the results of a historical trajectory with a narrative one. He does this by delineating specifically eight stages in the disappearance of God and summarizes them as follows:

1. Moses sees God at Sinai.
2. Moses, the one man who has seen God, wears a veil.
3. God tells Moses, "I shall hide my face from the Israelites."
4. The last time God is said to be revealed to a human: the prophet Samuel
5. The last time God is said to have appeared to a human: King Solomon
6. The last public miracle: divine fire for Elijah at Mount Carmel; followed by God's refusal to appear to Elijah at Horeb/Sinai
7. The last personal miracle: The shadow reverses before Isaiah and Hezekiah
8. God is not mentioned in Esther.[29]

The texts to which Friedman connects these stages follow the narrative order of the plot presented in the Bible and are very close to falling in canonical order, with allowance for the problem of parallel passages in the Deuteronomistic History and Chronicles. Friedman's hypothetical attempt to place the texts in the order in which they were written, however, produces rather different results. The revelation to Moses and the story of Esther are still first and last respectively, but God's statement of intent to hide, which is third in the list above, comes from Deut. 31:17–18, a text that he places considerably later than the story of Elijah on Mount Carmel, which is sixth in the list above.[30] The problem this would seem to solve, that stage number 3 in the list above is out of place, may have a relatively simple narrative resolution, though. The speeches of Moses in Deuteronomy frequently project into the distant future, so such a statement need not fit into the "narrative time" in which it is made.

Friedman also goes to greater lengths than any other writer of which I am aware to propose a literary process that could have produced these results. This is a significant challenge, considering that his view of the Bible's composition is far too complex to allow for any kind of deliberate collusion among writers or editors, and he does not seem to hold to the kind of understanding of divine inspiration that would provide magical guidance toward such an end. Instead, this fairly consistent movement in the character of God is the result of a shared experience of the writers and the common assumptions that arise from that experience. In Friedman's words, "Given that miracles and other signs of divine presence were not in fact occurring in any apparent way to them, their perception would naturally be that God's visible interventions in human affairs belonged to a bygone age. Whenever a biblical author lived, no matter how long after the events he or she was narrating, his or her perception would be that God's visible acts had diminished. That is, the placement of God in history, inevitably, meant departure."[31]

At about the same time that Friedman was producing *The Disappearance of God*, Jack Miles was writing his monumental work, *God: A Biography*. Though less deliberately focused on a single theme, like hiddenness, Miles still constructed a similar portrait. Following the basic trajectory of the Hebrew canon, Miles attempted to set aside all general presuppositions about God and to pursue rigorously the divine character presented to us in the pages of this story. Thus, Miles's task was relentlessly narrative in nature. He gave significant attention to nearly every book in the Hebrew canon, and he found a pattern not unlike that which Friedman uncovered. The divine character whom Miles describes early in the canon as creator, destroyer, friend, conqueror, and father is, by the end, described as sleeper, bystander, recluse, and absence. Perhaps two of Miles's conclusions are most significant. First, in describing Ezra-Nehemiah as a resumption of the narrative of God and the chosen people, left off at the end of the book of 2 Kings, Miles notes that "the roles of the two are nearly reversed. In the days of Abraham, Moses, Joshua, and David, the Lord took mighty action on behalf of Israel. In the days of Ezra and Nehemiah, Israel takes energetic action on behalf of the Lord."[32] When, in the eighth chapter of the book of Nehemiah, Ezra reads to the people from the scroll of the law and the people respond by bowing down, the scroll itself has essentially replaced God, just as its public reader has become God's voice.[33] The Bible has managed to replace God with itself, a point to which I shall return later.

Miles's second pertinent conclusion lies in the question that forms the subtitle of his final chapter, "Does God Lose Interest?" In this chapter, he makes one last attempt to resolve the multiplicity of personalities found in the divine character by producing a "polytheistic retelling of the Tanakh," only to discover that this process removes the "diffuse anxiety [that is] the more characteristic mood of the Tanakh."[34] The key to understanding this anxiety is the observation that "the course of the Lord God's life runs not just from omnipotence to relative impotence, but also from ignorance to relative omniscience."[35] God's knowing diminishes God's power, because, in Miles's words, "once God understands what motivated him at the start, his motivation to continue is undercut."[36] Miles's brilliant narrative analysis seems hindered by one presupposition of which he cannot let go, namely, that God is the protagonist of the Bible. This assumption seems at odds with many of his observations, especially those which are so similar to Friedman's. If the divine character is receding, progressively disappearing from the story, then can this description be fitting? Is it not Israel, the character that grows larger and more active as the story progresses, which is best understood as the protagonist? Does this leave God necessarily as the antagonist, and do not those qualities which, in the end of the story, are so ill fitting of a protagonist make for an ideal antagonist? To adopt two of the terms from Brueggemann's countertestimony list, God's character moves toward hiddenness and ambiguity as the story progresses.[37] The work of Friedman and Miles has received little attention from the field of Old Testament theology, a problem that I will attempt to remedy throughout this book.

A decade later, something of a sense of narrative development of the character called God was inherent in the work of Harold Bloom, in *Jesus and Yahweh: The Names Divine*, which appeared in 2005, though it is not developed along clear lines of the Bible's full narrative. Bloom understands the choice of creating as an act of "self-exile."[38] God can make room for creation and humanity only by receding, so creation involves a divine decision to recede. Bloom's reading is idiosyncratic for at least two reasons. First, he is still reading what he understands as the J source, rather than full the text of the Hebrew Scriptures, and he still seems to hold many of the assumptions from his odd work *The Book of J*, from two decades earlier, most significantly a very early date for the J source.[39] Second, as a Shakespearean scholar, he openly reveals that he is reading J's God through the lens of *King Lear*,[40] a move that I personally find powerfully productive but that will cause some to question whether he is doing legitimate biblical interpretation. For Bloom, the development of God's character, God's withdrawal, is inextricably linked to God's initial decision to create: "Yahweh permanently wounded himself very badly in the act of creation. A self-degraded Supreme God, so human—all-too-human, forever will be ambivalent toward everything and anyone, his Chosen People in particular."[41] At times, it is difficult to determine whether Bloom understands this self-exile as an instantaneous act fully congruent with the initial act of creation, or as a narrative progression that continues throughout the story of the Bible, but his constant insistence on reading God as a literary character, illuminated by Lear, makes the notion of character development impossible to escape.

Most recently, the collection of narrative approaches to divine character development has been updated by the appearance of Jerome Segal's *Joseph's Bones: Understanding the Struggle between God and Mankind in the Bible.* Segal is reading the books of Genesis through Joshua, rather than the entire Tanak, so it is easier for him to follow a coherent narrative without having to make any choices of trajectory, and he insists, among other things, that the story of God and humanity in the Hexateuch is a coherent story.[42] Perhaps the key to understanding Segal's work is his discussion of the interplay between God and Moses. This may not contradict the title of the book as much as it seems, given that for the majority of the Hexateuch the bones of Joseph are in the possession of Moses and are under his control. Most important for Segal is determining why God has to kill Moses. It is God's own growth or "evolution" as a character that makes this act necessary. In Segal's words, "God . . . is undergoing an evolution and is finding other tools—indeed the Torah itself is one—that will allow him to interact successfully with the Israelites. He is becoming less in need of Moses, less in need of a human intermediary who will protect the Israelites from himself. What happens is that just as Moses is becoming more problematic for God, he is becoming more dispensable. As these two processes converge, they bring his death."[43] Like Miles, Segal recognized that the Bible ultimately replaces God's more direct presence and becomes God's voice. The competition for this voice is the oral prophet, and none is greater than Moses.

The Place of Divine Character Development in Old Testament Theology

The major attempts to articulate a linear, narrative development of the character of God that I have identified here lie, at best, on the edges of biblical theology. There are, perhaps, a number of reasons for this. The field of biblical theology has typically been more confessional than other areas of biblical studies, and this is to be expected. Though there may be no way to measure such things objectively, works like those of Friedman, Miles, and Segal look and sound less confessional than those of Eichrodt, von Rad, Terrien, Brueggemann, and Kuhn. Those writers who utilize a more strictly narrative approach, whether they have confessional commitments or not, likely view themselves more as literary critics than as biblical theologians, so their work is not overtly oriented in the direction of biblical theology. James Barr's massive 1999 work, *The Concept of Biblical Theology,* formed something of a catalog of the field at the end of the twentieth century; and, although it contains a twenty-two-page chapter on Brueggemann, focused almost entirely on his Old Testament theology, which had appeared just two years earlier, there is no mention of Miles or Friedman, whose books came out in 1995. Perhaps this neglect is best explained by Barr's claim that story itself is not theology but merely the "raw material for theology," because story is "theologically unclear or ambiguous."[44] This claim, of course, betrays an expectation about theology—that it must be clear and unambiguous—a claim that would require serious reconsideration before a focus on character development could qualify as theology. Modern readers are so conditioned to look for and ask for the "moral of the story" that the idea of carefully reading or hearing a story and letting it work on us, trusting a story to do what it will, is an act of patience often beyond our capability.

It is these and other similar observations that continue to drive my question about the compatibility of biblical theology and narrative enterprises that focus on the development of God's character. At least three questions reflect components of this problem and must be addressed:

1. What trajectory of texts do we follow in order to examine this development?
2. What theological significance do we give to the earlier stages of the divine character's development?
3. How do we give appropriate attention to the texts that present the fully developed character, the God at the end of the story?

In response to the first question, the preceding discussion moved toward the necessity of a narrative trajectory, which, for the Tanak, would approximate a canonical trajectory. For the Christian Old Testament, the distance between this trajectory and a canonical one would remain a point of difficulty, but the shape of the Christian canon does provide a possibility. The Old Testament begins by telling the story of God and Israel from creation to the exile, in the books of Genesis through 2 Kings. It then immediately tells us the same story, in a much different fashion, in 1 and 2 Chronicles. This story is continued into the restoration/Persian period in Ezra-Nehemiah. The Protestant Old Testament finds its narrative end there, whereas the Catholic and Orthodox canons continue into the Hellenistic period in the books of Maccabees. Most of the remainder of the Old Testament writings can be connected to this central narrative in some way.

The second question has to do with the relative values we might assign to the various stages of the life of a character who develops through the plot of a narrative. How can a theology of the Hebrew Scriptures cope with a portrayal of a playful, impetuous God who makes a person like a child playing with mud pies,[45] tosses the clay figure over the fence when it will not play as God wishes, destroys the whole earth in a flash of angry regret, and then almost immediately regrets the destructive act; especially when compared to a seasoned, detached, observer God who leaves the humans created so long ago to find their own way in the world, speaking to them only through the indirect majesty of literature? The God at the end of the story is clearly more mature, but the God at the beginning of the story is easily more interesting. In Brueggemann's *Theology,* references to Genesis alone outnumber references to all of Chronicles, Ezra, and Nehemiah together by a ratio of 3 to 1, and the Scripture index of James Barr's *Concept of Biblical Theology* contains not a single reference to Chronicles, Ezra, or Nehemiah. Esther finds no place in either book. The field of theology of the Hebrew Scriptures has always expressed more interest in the earlier part of the narrative about God than in its conclusion. This intense interest in the early part of the divine character's development cannot, and need not, be diminished, but the results of the reading of these passages need to be put in a different place in such a character analysis.

Here, it may help to pause to ask more generally how we understand and describe a narrative character who changes and develops through the course of a plot. What should readers do with the earlier encounters with that character once those have been superseded by later encounters? What relative values do readers assign to the various stages of their encounters with a character? The way one answers these questions will undoubtedly be affected by religious convictions, of course. For many readers, God is not simply a narrative character but one to whom they are related in some way outside of the reading of the text; and even if they follow guides like Miles and Brueggemann in a fairly successful attempt to keep these other experiences away from their reading,[46] these readers cannot keep such experiences from influencing what they do with the results of the reading of the text. So, comparisons to how we value the various stages of our awareness of actual characters that we know, not just literary ones, are apt here. When we know other human beings over a long period of time, we do not let go of our memory of early encounters with them. In some way, we see those early encounters as inextricably bound up in the person's later identity, even if the behavioral traits exhibited early on are no longer expressed. With human characters, we not only accept but even expect a process of change and development. The earlier stages of the development of a person we love are not valued less when we see him or her change and develop. We no longer relate to the earlier version of the person, but we can, along with that person, remember and cherish the experience of those earlier encounters. The difficult question this raises is not just whether we can look at God as a character that changes, with earlier traits and habits receding and becoming subsumed within a more developed version, but whether looking at and describing God in this manner can be a way of doing Old Testament theology.

The third question, the one about the significance of the divine character's final destination, will require another difficult reorientation in the discipline of Old Testament theology: an increased emphasis on the theology of the later literature that forms the end of the story. Surely the firmest ground is found in identifying Ezra-Nehemiah as the target for greater attention. Meir Sternberg's description of the change in mode of narration in Ezra-Nehemiah may illustrate one of the more important ways the divine character has changed by this point. The omniscient narrator of most of the rest of the Hebrew Bible is essentially telling the story from God's point of view. Put more bluntly, God is telling us God's own story in Genesis through 2 Kings, and this is still mostly true in Chronicles,[47] but this is not the case in Ezra-Nehemiah, a point made most apparent by the first-person "memoir" materials.[48] This is another aspect of the disappearance or distancing of the divine character: not only has this character become less interventionist, but one must also now take the word of another voice describing this character. When Nehemiah goes to Judah, he reports that "the hand of my God was upon me" (Neh. 2:8). Whereas Ezekiel uses this phrase to describe the onset of his ecstatic visions, to Nehemiah this is merely an interpretation of his practical success. It explains why "the king granted me what I asked for" (2:8). In 2:12, Nehemiah interprets his desire to rebuild the wall as "What God had put into my heart to do for Jerusalem." Throughout the book, Nehemiah interprets his own planning as God's intent and the successful result as God's blessing. Only in the book's recollections of the distant past did God command (1:8), perform signs and wonders (9:7), and lead the Israelites by pillars of cloud and fire (9:19).

This approach might initially generate the problem so famously produced by von Rad's dynamic approach in the middle of the twentieth century, that is, where to put the parts of the Bible that do not easily fit within its narrative framework. The Wisdom literature is the most obvious point of difficulty here, but a means of including this material in a divine narrative has been sketched by Marvin A. Sweeney in his important work *Reading the Hebrew Bible after the Shoah: Engaging Holocaust Theology*. Sweeney included in this book a chapter called "Divine Hiddenness and Human Initiative in the Wisdom Literature." He seems correct in assigning the Wisdom literature in its canonical form to the end stage of the development of the divine character, regardless of whether some of the material within the Wisdom books might be assigned an earlier date.[49] This is a subject that will be treated more extensively in chapter 6.

Additional difficulties remain, of course. For Christian readers, the divine character is reinvigorated in the moving of the Prophetic literature to the end of the Old Testament canon; and, of course, the extension of the divine character in the figure of Jesus in the New Testament is difficult to keep separate from the reading of the divine character in the Old Testament. For Jewish interpreters of the Tanak, the centrality and ongoing commemoration of the exodus and Passover traditions make the sequestering of the divine action in those events within the distant past difficult.[50] These tensions return us to a question posed near the beginning of this chapter about a possible impasse between the constant and the dynamic. On the one hand, given the diversity of materials in the Hebrew Scriptures, a claim of divine constancy seems incoherent. On the other hand, the dynamic God may be moving to a place that makes doing theology unsatisfying. This is the risk of the readjustment for which this book will contend.

This introduction to the theological examination of God as a narrative character in the Old Testament requires some initial attention to a difficult and often-neglected topic that will arise from time to time throughout this book: God's physicality. Beginning to think about God as a narrative character in a story in which all of the other characters have physical bodies makes this issue unavoidable. The body of God appears sporadically in the Old Testament, but these appearances are far more frequent than many interpreters, especially biblical theologians, tend to acknowledge.[51] This avoidance, or even denial, has been carefully demonstrated by Benjamin D. Sommer in the opening chapter of his 2009 book, *The Bodies of God and the World of Ancient Israel*.[52] The acknowledgment of this tradition, broader and deeper than most readers of the Old Testament recognize, is particularly important in a discussion of the development of the divine character, because embodiedness is an essential component of the way human readers perceive any character. Sommer argued effectively for what he called a "fluidity model," which includes two aspects. The first is the fluidity of divine selfhood, which means that "a deity can produce many small-scale manifestations that enjoy some degree of independence without becoming separate deities."[53] The second aspect of the fluidity model is the "multiplicity of divine embodiment," the idea that God could be present in various ways in multiple places at the same time.[54]

Ultimately, as Sommer went on to demonstrate, strong streams of tradition in the Old Testament, those he labels as "Deuteronomic" and "Priestly," rejected the fluidity model, but they did not succeed in removing it entirely from Israel's sacred texts, nor from the ongoing practices of some Jewish communities.[55]

Through the use of source criticism, these opposing views of God's embodiedness can be set up as an intrabiblical debate, which Sommer did.[56] Such conclusions work well within the dialogical model of Old Testament theology, but a narrative approach will have to ask a different question: When and where in the story does God show up with a body of some kind, and what is the narrative function of that body? We can also observe the characteristics of particular embodiments and how they help to determine the nature of the divine character who possesses them.

On the Act of Reading Biblical Narrative

When biblical scholarship turned its attention to the study of narrative during the last quarter of the twentieth century, it inherited a massive amount of work that had been done on this subject within the fields of philosophical hermeneutics and literary theory. Two of the most influential figures in these areas have been Erich Auerbach and Paul Ricoeur. In 1953, Auerbach published his monumental work, *Mimesis: The Representation of Reality in Western Literature*, in which he began his discussion of narrative theory with a comparison of biblical narrative to other narratives from the ancient world. His primary examples were the story of Odysseus's return home in book 19 of *The Odyssey* and the Akedah ("binding" of Isaac) story in Genesis 22.[57] Though Auerbach was not a biblical scholar, his use of the latter text ensured that his work would receive significant attention within biblical scholarship.

A prominent early figure in the process of incorporating narrative theory into biblical studies was Hans Frei, who moved in a particular direction using some of Auerbach's ideas and brought the problematic phrase "realistic narrative" to the center of the discussion of biblical narrative. Frei defined this kind of writing as "that kind in which subject and social setting belong together, and characters and external circumstances fitly render each other."[58] His next step was to describe such "realistic narrative" as "history-like," in an effort to emphasize what he saw as a connection between biblical story and the "real world," while avoiding a heavy literalism.[59]

The difficulties inherent in Frei's work are best demonstrated by comparing it to the contemporaneous work of the French philosopher Paul Ricoeur.[60] Perhaps the most significant difference between the work of these two is their understanding of the role of the reader. Frei's emphasis on a realistic and "self-referential" text, on the one hand, inevitably led to an exaggerated understanding of the text's autonomy and left little, if any, room for the reader to play a role in the construction of meaning.[61] Ricoeur, on the other hand, argued that texts do not function autonomously but are dependent on the reader to determine the meaning of the language of which they consist.[62] Ricoeur's most overt biblical work was his collaborative volume with André Lacocque called *Thinking Biblically: Exegetical and Hermeneutical Studies*, in which Ricoeur argued for a sense of correspondence between the world of the text and the world of the reader.[63] Although the text must be both the starting point and ending point of Old Testament theology, particularly when operating with a narrative approach, the simplistic idea of a reading experience determined entirely by the text, independent of the experience and identity of the reader, is untenable. Much of Ricoeur's work has focused on the significance of metaphor and symbol, elements that draw deliberately on the active participation of the reader.[64] All of the readings in this book involve choices that I have made, and these choices cannot be entirely separated from my identity and experience. A keen awareness of how the act of reading works will allow us to keep our observations about the divine character presented in the Old Testament as closely connected to the text as possible.[65] Perhaps the best sense of balance on this point is provided by Walter Brueggemann, who at once insists that the "utterance" within the text is the only object of study for Old Testament theology and that the text engages and demands the full imagination of the reader.[66]

A recent study by Greger Andersonn, *Untamable Texts: Literary Studies and Narrative Theory in the Books of Samuel*, raised serious questions about the ways in which biblical scholars have conducted what they have called literary study of biblical narratives. Andersonn seemed particularly bothered by literary interpretations that arrive at conclusions very different from what he called "more conventional readings" of "common readers." He labeled such interpretations as "disquieting" and claimed to find inadequate explanations in the work of biblical literary critics as to why their readings are so different from "common" readings. Andersonn argued that "many critics suggest that . . . common readers misread these texts, whether because they do not have a general ability to understand literary narratives or . . . [because they] have not applied this ability when reading these particular texts."[67] He expressed dislike for the frequently proposed reasons for this misreading: "their unfamiliarity with the specific poetics of the Bible, their misapprehension of the genre of these texts, or . . . [their being] misled by their religious beliefs."[68] It has been my experience, however, from a quarter century of interacting in the classroom with these "more conventional readings," that it is precisely the last of these three causes that is the culprit. Readers come to the Bible with so firm a sense of the character traits of God, given to them by their religious traditions, that they fail to see and acknowledge what is plain on the pages of the Bible. The virtue of any particular poetics is not in its rightness but in its ability to help the reader see what is on the page. Where I find more sympathy with Andersonn is in his identification of some readers' literary interpretations that go another step to replace the preconceptions of common readings with the readers' own, thus "taming" the texts in a different way, by finding hidden meanings.[69]

My own intent is to use a narrative approach not to expose hidden meanings but to help the reader focus on what is on the page. In doing so, I also wish to avoid the common practice of finding a "moral" or "lesson" in a story. Such an approach too often assumes that stories are mere vehicles or packages that contain propositions that can be extracted from them. My own conviction, which I acknowledge can require greater patience and may be less immediately satisfying, is that stories work on their hearers/readers, and the goal of interpretation is to bring more careful attention to narratives while resisting the temptation to explain them or reduce them to pithy maxims.

A study like this one must seek to walk very carefully along a narrow ridge, because there is a constant danger of drifting off in two problematic directions. The first area of potential error involves implying that the God of Judaism or Christianity, a being outside of the biblical text, has been going through some process of maturation. Such an implication is outside the purview of this study and is thoroughly untestable. It is moderately challenging to keep one's thinking about this subject limited to the deity presented as a literary character inside the text, and it is exceedingly difficult to keep one's language inside these boundaries. The second kind of error is to presume a kind of historical development in religious thought that led from a "primitive" understanding of God to a more sophisticated one, and that ancient Israel's course along this path can be charted by tracing the ways of presenting the deity in the literature of the Old Testament along a historical trajectory.

This study will seek to avoid these kinds of missteps and will operate within one basic approach with one assumption. It will proceed by looking at the divine character presented in the pages of the Old Testament and asking how that character behaves in different parts of the story. I am assuming that both the writers of the books that form the narrative end of the Bible and the final shapers of the biblical literature lived in the Persian period, in the late sixth through fourth centuries BCE. This means that the divine behavior described in

Ezra-Nehemiah most closely reflects their own religious experience, and that the divine behavior in the earlier parts of the story reflects the way they thought about the religious experience of their ancestors. I am convinced that it can be clearly demonstrated that the divine character in the literature they preserved about their ancestors behaved very differently from the divine character in the literature that illustrates their own experience. This means that it is possible to talk about this latter portrayal of God as "mature," as long as such a description is used carefully. Most significantly, the God portrayed in these latter texts is the product of a long tradition of theological reflection, which had passed through a long and difficult story of building a society, watching that society be destroyed, being dispersed, and struggling to rebuild or find a permanent way of life in a foreign world. The writers and editors asked hard questions about how their God was involved in that process, and some of their seasoned answers lie in the texts they produced, which were shaped to tell a continuous story and which can be read theologically from beginning to end.

Conclusion

If I might borrow language to which we have become accustomed, at least by way of analogy, have we reached a point of conflict between a diachronic approach to narrative and a synchronic approach to narrative? Do we look at the story of God in the Hebrew Scriptures all at once, seeking language that speaks of that whole story at the same time, or do we follow that character through narrative time, arriving at an articulation of the nature of God's character that has left some aspects behind and arrived at a particular identity? In his sequel to *God: A Biography*, a work primarily about the Christian New Testament called *Christ: A Crisis in the Life of God*, Jack Miles attached an epilogue called "On Writing the Lives of God." In this reflection on his two-volume project, Miles asserted two rules that he followed throughout the process. His second rule was "that conflict in the divine character, rather than being described or analyzed systematically, as in theology, should emerge in the course of the narrative."[70] The accusation about the systematic tendencies of theology, which Miles articulated in this rule, was largely correct up to the time of his writing and remains more or less intact today, even for the field of Old Testament theology, as I have demonstrated in the preceding discussion. Is this way of operating still appropriate, however, or is it time for biblical theology to move away from it at a more determined pace? If biblical theology is to move in a more deliberate narrative direction, it will need to find a way to tend to this impasse, which may involve letting go of the divine character from which the

Bible is trying to lead us away. The dialogical approach has done great service in identifying the multiplicity of voices in the text, but the voice from the earlier portions of the story is still too loud. The voice at the end of the story must eventually be allowed to speak alone, or it will not be adequately heard.

The subsequent chapters of this book will examine stages in the development of the divine character and analyze the ways that Old Testament theology has tended to the stages.

Chapter 2 will open with an examination of the divine character found at the beginning of the book of Genesis and will move from there to look at divine characterization in other creation texts, particularly in Psalms. This being is characterized by power and creativity but also by uncertainty and even naïveté. Biblical theologians have naturally been drawn to this characterization and the parts of the Bible that contain it because of this captivating energy. This is where the Bible begins, and it is a focal point for both Jewish and Christian liturgy and confession. After an examination of what Old Testament theology looks like when these texts and the God they portray are the primary focus, the chapter will end with the question of what we do with these portrayals now that such activity is in the distant past.

Chapter 3 will chart the movement of the biblical story into the ancestral, exodus, and wilderness materials, which present a somewhat different portrayal of the divine being. A more certain voice emerges as God speaks to the ancestors and to Moses, but an inconsistency of behavior emerges ever more clearly. God makes promises to the ancestors but then seems to forget them for long periods of time. The relationship with Israel in the wilderness is complex and hyperemotional. The narrative power of these portrayals has earned them a prominent place in many works of Old Testament theology, but this is not a divine character who fits easily into the later developments of Jewish and Christian religion. Again, an important question at the end of the chapter will concern what we can do with these portraits of God that ceased to be part of the religious experience of writers and readers of the Bible, including ourselves.

Chapter 4 will examine the divine character who builds the nation of Israel. Although this divine project does not have a clear beginning point in the Old Testament, it comes to the forefront in Joshua and the books that follow it. This part of the story presents an active, energetic God, but at the same time this character is busy authorizing and developing institutions that will mediate the divine presence. Because palace/king and temple/priest are included in these institutions, this part of the story still lends itself to a theology of the Old Testament focused upon an active sense of God's presence and work in the world. These characters represent and act for God in a way that is visibly commanding. Nevertheless, the end of the monarchy is a tremendous theological challenge within the Old Testament itself and presents an even greater disconnect between the divine character in the text and later readers of that text.

The part of God's story that turns to a focus on punishment and destruction, which is the subject of chapter 5, is found in much of the books of Kings and Chronicles and is also the primary subject of the Prophetic literature. In what has often been labeled the Deuteronomic view, Israel's failure is blamed on Israel's sin and disloyalty to God. Casting the misfortunes of Israel as YHWH's punishment allows the divine character to remain an active figure in the text, even as the work that this being has accomplished in the earlier parts of the story is being completely dismantled. The work of God becomes, in Jeremiah's words, "tearing down, overthrowing, uprooting, and destroying." Thus, a great deal of attention to this character still fits into treatments of Old Testament theology that presented God as a "mighty actor." The theology of retribution assumed in such treatments, however, begins to become suspect even in the Bible, and it is not a view with which many later readers are comfortable, because of both its harshness and its oversimplifications.

Chapter 6 will examine the narrative conclusion of the Hebrew Bible found in the book of Ezra-Nehemiah, where the portrayal of God is quite different from that in earlier books of the canon. This God moves in the shadows, indirectly influencing events, and does not perform "mighty acts." Such a divine character did not fit well into the Biblical Theology movement of the twentieth century, and, even though that approach has been left behind, some of its habits and tendencies remain. Among them is a relative neglect of biblical literature that does not present an active, energetic, and exciting divine character. Some portions of the Wisdom literature, along with books such as Esther and Daniel, also participate in this kind of portrayal. This chapter will examine these portraits and attempt to move them toward the center of a theology of the Old Testament by allowing them their own voice and their own place to speak that is not drowned out by the claims of mighty acts.

Notes

1. There are two primary reasons that terminology is difficult here. The first is that there is significant overlap between the Tanak of Judaism and the Old Testament canons of various Christian traditions. In some contexts, the hybrid term "Hebrew Bible" partially resolves this problem, but within each of these religious traditions this term misses the mark in various ways. The second problem is that in Christian scholarship Old Testament theology participates in the separate subdiscipline of biblical theology. I will use the term "Old Testament theology," because I

live and write in the context of the Christian tradition and because I think that an entirely separate, self-contained formulation concerning this part of the canon is necessary before entering into the formulation of a biblical theology. Such an approach was espoused, perhaps surprisingly, by Brevard S. Childs, though he may have had difficulty practicing it consistently. See Childs's *Old Testament Theology in a Canonical Context* (Philadelphia: Fortress Press, 1985), 6–10, and *Biblical Theology of the Old and New Testaments: Theological Reflection on the Christian Bible* (Minneapolis: Fortress Press, 1992), 95–102.

2. This general sense of direction is exemplified by a work like Terence E. Fretheim's *God and World in the Old Testament: A Relational Theology of Creation* (Nashville: Abingdon, 2005).

3. Walter Brueggemann, *Theology of the Old Testament: Testimony, Dispute, Advocacy* (Minneapolis: Fortress Press, 1997), 39.

4. Ibid., 39–40.

5. Ibid., 117–44. This development was present in nascent form in Brueggemann's earlier work, which appeared in a pair of brilliant journal articles. These were "A Shape for Old Testament Theology I: Structure Legitimation," *CBQ* 47 (1985): 28–46, and "A Shape for Old Testament Theology II: Embrace of Pain," *CBQ* 47 (1985): 395–415. Again, although both aspects are given a significant voice and a powerful sense of tension between the two is developed, this approach seems to require allowing the "structure legitimation" (core-testimony) aspect to go first and establish the parameters of the discussion.

6. Brueggemann, *Theology of the Old Testament*, 122.

7. Karl Allen Kuhn, *Having Words with God: The Bible as Conversation* (Minneapolis: Fortress Press, 2008), 11.

8. Ibid., 22–28.

9. Ibid., 29–30.

10. Ibid., 33–44.

11. Ibid, 142.

12. Benjamin D. Sommer has recently published a substantial and important article called "Dialectical Biblical Theology: A Jewish Approach to Reading Scripture Theologically." This article is the first chapter in *Biblical Theology: Introducing the Conversation,* ed. Leo G. Perdue, Robert Morgan, and Benjamin D. Sommer (Nashville: Abingdon, 2009). This attempt to articulate a biblical theology compatible with Jewish faith and scholarship is nascent, and where it might situate itself within the landscape of biblical theology is hard to say.

13. Not least among these problems are the potential racial undertones involved in using the language of light and dark as a metaphorical expression of good and bad.

14. Walter Dietrich and Christian Link, *Die dunklen Seiten Gottes: Willkür und Gewalt* (Neukirchen-Vluyn: Neukirchner, 2000), 148–68. This work frequently moves into the New Testament and even the larger discussion of Christian dogmatics, but it does a more than adequate job of isolating the Old Testament presentation of such issues and treating this presentation on its own terms first.

15. John Barton, "The Dark Side of God in the Old Testament," in *Ethical and Unethical in the Old Testament: God and Humans in Dialogue*, ed. Katharine Dell (New York: T&T Clark, 2010), 130–34.

16. See Robert Alter, *The Art of Biblical Narrative* (New York: Basic, 1981), 114–30; and Adele Berlin, *Poetics and Interpretation of Biblical Narrative* (Winona Lake, IN: Eisenbrauns, 1983), 23–42. Of course, Alter had borrowed significantly from a large body of work on characterization in the general field of literary criticism. Humphreys himself points to the classic work of E. M. Forster in *Aspects of the Novel* (London: Edward Arnold, 1927), 65–75.

17. W. Lee Humphreys, *The Character of God in the Book of Genesis: A Narrative Appraisal* (Louisville: Westminster John Knox, 2001), 241.

18. Ibid., 21.

19. Phyllis Trible, *Rhetorical Criticism: Context, Method, and the Book of Jonah* (Minneapolis: Fortress Press, 1994), 216–23.

20. Samuel Terrien, *The Elusive Presence: Toward a New Biblical Theology* (New York: Harper & Row, 1978), 470–71.

21. Dale Patrick, *The Rendering of God in the Old Testament* (Philadelphia: Fortress Press, 1983), 25–27.

22. Ibid., 59–60.

23. Eric A. Seibert, *Disturbing Divine Behavior: Troubling Old Testament Images of God* (Minneapolis: Fortress Press, 2010). Among the important functions of narrative that Seibert presents are "to encourage certain behaviors and beliefs" (138) and "to inspire hope and confidence in the face of powerful threats" (142). The idea that the needs of writers and readers change and grow is not in conflict with the growth of a character. Indeed, they may even grow together.

24. Richard Elliott Friedman, *The Disappearance of God: A Divine Mystery* (Boston: Little, Brown, 1995), 78–89. Friedman does give some attention to the 1983 work of Samuel Balentine, *The Hidden God: The Hiding of the Face of God in the Old Testament* (New York: Oxford University Press, 1983). Although this book does give careful attention to the phrase "hide the face" and the uses of the motif it generates, Balentine did not look for the development of this character trait through a suggested plot of the biblical story.

25. This essay was originally published as "Offene Fragen im Umk einer Theologi des Alten Testaments," *TLZ* 88 (1963): 401–16.

26. Magne Saebo, "Yahweh as *Deus absconditus*: Some Remarks on a Dictum by Gerhard von Rad," in *Shall Not the Judge of All the Earth Do What Is Right? Studies on the Nature of God in Tribute to James L. Crenshaw*, ed. David Penchansky and Paul L. Redditt (Winona Lake, IN: Eisenbrauns, 2000), 44.

27. Ibid.

28. Gerhard von Rad, *Old Testament Theology*, trans. D. M. G. Stalker (New York: Harper & Row, 1965), 2:415.

29. Friedman, *Disappearance of God*, 82–84.

30. Ibid., 85.

31. Ibid., 88–89.

32. Jack Miles, *God: A Biography* (New York: Vintage, 1995), 372.

33. Ibid., 389.

34. Ibid., 398–401.

35. Ibid., 402.

36. Ibid., 403.

37. Brueggemann, *Theology of the Old Testament*, 318–19.

38. Harold Bloom, *Jesus and Yahweh: The Names Divine* (New York: Riverhead, 2005), 200–205. Bloom is very much dependent upon the kabbalistic notion of *zimzum*, or self-emptying, here.

39. Ibid., 116–17.

40. Ibid., 129–31.

41. Ibid., 214.

42. Jerome Segal, *Joseph's Bones: Understanding the Struggle between God and Mankind in the Bible* (New York: Riverhead, 2007), ix–xi.

43. Ibid., 208. The appearance of the word *evolution* in this quotation directs attention to the fascinating work of Robert Wright in *The Evolution of God* (New York: Little, Brown, 2009). Attention to this work does not fit within the primary discussion of this book, because its concern is with the history of Middle Eastern religions, not with the development of a divine character within the narrative of the biblical canon. Still, Wright arrives at some conclusions that are remarkable parallels to this discussion. Particularly, he notes that the deity of Israelite religion ends up as "a remote, even transcendent God, whose presence is felt subtly, but is portrayed earlier in Israel's history as "a hands-on deity" (103). Wright's conclusions are based upon a historically reconstructed text and a great deal of archaeological information.

44. James Barr, *The Concept of Biblical Theology: An Old Testament Perspective* (Minneapolis: Fortress Press, 1999), 354–56.

45. On this aspect of playfulness, see Bloom, *Jesus and Yahweh*, 201–2.

46. Miles explains this as his goal in *God*, 8–10. Brueggemann states this goal in no uncertain terms: "A student of Old Testament theology must pay close attention to the shape character, and details of the utterance, for it is in, with, and under the utterance that we have the God of Israel, and nowhere else. See *Theology of the Old Testament*, 122.

47. Chronicles is much more problematic in this regard. It is universally understood to be later than the Pentateuch and the Deuteronomistic History, but it tells the same story, beginning and ending at the same place. It also sits in two very different places in the two primary canonical traditions. Isaac Kalimi has demonstrated in great detail how the writer(s) of Chronicles develop(s) characters, adapting the material found in the Deuteronomistic History to "render" characters "more significant" or "less significant." See *The Reshaping of Ancient Israelite History in Chronicles* (Winona Lake, IN: Eisenbrauns, 2005), 166–79. Kalimi does not deal specifically with the rendering of the divine character. I would also include here the Prophetic literature, which clearly fits into this part of the story, specifically Haggai, Zechariah, and Malachi. The problem of Chronicles and its relation to Samuel and Kings will be addressed more extensively in chapter 4 of this book.

48. Meir Sternberg, *The Poetics of Biblical Narrative: Ideological Literature and the Drama of Reading* (Bloomington: Indiana University Press, 1987), 86–88. Sternberg refers to these two "models of narration" as "inspirational" and "empirical."

49. Marvin A. Sweeney, *Reading the Hebrew Bible after the Shoah: Engaging Holocaust Theology* (Minneapolis: Fortress Press, 2008), 188–207.

50. In addition, Michael Fishbane has demonstrated the lengths to which early rabbinic interpretation also went to recover a divine personality, particularly using the display of divine emotion. The activities and emotions he identifies—"memory and mourning; sympathy and sorrow; desolation and despair"—seem to be a response to the distinctive lack of pathos demonstrated by the divine character in the pages of the Hebrew Scriptures. See *Biblical Myth and Rabbinic Mythmaking* (Oxford: Oxford University Press, 2003), 160–62.

51. It may well be that Christian theologians have a built-in resistance to this idea, based on a desire to save the embodiment of God for the incarnation presented in the New Testament.

52. Benjamin D. Sommer, *The Bodies of God and the World of Ancient Israel* (Cambridge: Cambridge University Press, 2009), 1–12.

53. Ibid., 38. Examples of this phenomenon are abundant in the Old Testament, as Sommer demonstrates, and include the attachment of YHWH to specific locations and the appearance of God as various kinds of beings, such as the "angel of the LORD" (38–44).

54. Ibid., 44–54.

55. Ibid., 58–79.

56. Ibid., 124–26.

57. Erich Auerbach, *Mimesis: The Representation of Reality in Western Literature* (Princeton: Princeton University Press, 1953), 7–23.

58. Hans Frei, *The Eclipse of Biblical Narrative: A Study in Eighteenth and Nineteenth Century Hermeneutics* (New Haven: Yale University Press, 1974), 13. Here Frei acknowledged the influence of the work of Erich Auerbach on his own understanding of narrative. Most significant was Auerbach's discussion of the Akedah story of Genesis 22 in *Mimesis*.

59. Ibid, 3. Frei's work was influential in what eventually developed into the "Yale school" of hermeneutics. See further discussion of this in Mark McEntire, *Dangerous Worlds: Living and Dying in Biblical Texts* (Macon, GA: Smyth & Helwys, 2004), 3–4.

60. See the very careful analysis of the conflict between Frei and Ricoeur by Gary Comstock in "Truth or Meaning: Ricoeur versus Frei on Biblical Narrative," *JR* 66 (1986): 117–40, and "Two Types of Narrative Theology," *JAAR* 55 (1987): 687–717. Comstock is careful

to give much credit to Frei for the influence of his work on the study of biblical narrative but takes his own position much closer to Ricoeur.

61. Frei, *The Identity of Jesus Christ: The Hermeneutical Bases of Dogmatic Theology* (Philadelphia: Fortress Press, 1975), xiii–xvii.

62. Paul Ricoeur, *Time and Narrative* (Chicago: University of Chicago Press, 1984), 1:77–82.

63. André Lacocque and Paul Ricoeur, *Thinking Biblically: Exegetical and Hermeneutical Studies* (Chicago: University of Chicago Press, 1998), 50–54. On this point, the position of Ricoeur has much in common with the influential work of Hans Georg Gadamer, who used the image of "horizons" to talk about the world of the text and the world of the reader and argued that meaning is formed at the point where those horizons meet, or "fuse." See Gadamer, *Truth and Method* (London: Sheed & Ward, 1975), 269–78. Dan R. Stiver has provided an excellent illustration of the advantages of Gadamer's "fusion" model over Frei's concept of "absorption" in *Theology after Ricoeur: New Directions in Hermeneutical Theology* (Louisville: Westminster John Knox, 2001), 50–55.

64. For more on this element of Ricoeur's work and its implications for the reading of the Bible, see Lewis Mudge, "Paul Ricoeur on Biblical Interpretation," in *Essays on Biblical Interpretation*, ed. Lewis Mudge (Philadelphia: Fortress Press, 1980), 4.

65. On the importance of "self-disclosure" in the practice of Old Testament theology, see Leo G. Perdue, *Reconstructing Old Testament Theology: After the Collapse of History* (Minneapolis: Fortress Press, 2005), 346–48.

66. Brueggemann, *Theology of the Old Testament*, 57–58, 122.

67. Greger Andersonn, *Untamable Texts: Literary Studies and Narrative Theory in the Books of Samuel* (New York: T&T Clark, 2009), 253.

68. Ibid.

69. Ibid., 264–65.

70. Jack Miles, *Christ: A Crisis in the Life of God* (New York: Knopf, 2001), 248.

2

A Creative and Energetic God

A true beginning of Old Testament theology is difficult to locate, but most surveyors of this subdiscipline point to an address by Johann Philipp Gabler in 1787 as a pivotal moment.[1] The primary thrust of this address was the need to separate biblical theology from dogmatic theology. Despite the impact of Gabler's work and more than two centuries of effort by hundreds of others, Old Testament theology has never fully escaped the influence of dogmatic theology, particularly its systematic tendencies. This influence has ensured that creation has always been of some concern to Old Testament theology, though the dominating historical framework pushed it to the margins of concern for much of the nineteenth and twentieth centuries. Not only was creation outside of historical categories, but the tradition-historical approaches of Old Testament theologians such as Gerhard von Rad generally identified Israelite creation traditions as a late-stage attachment to Israel's faith, which was grounded in the exodus event.[2] In a narrative or canonical approach, creating is also the first action we see God performing, if we read the Bible from the beginning, and it is an idea to which the Bible returns from time to time. Thus, creation has received growing attention in the last three or four decades.[3]

The selection of texts for this part of the Bible's narrative about God is difficult, for two reasons. First, though it is obvious that the beginning of the Bible depicts God creating the world, it is difficult to determine when this is finished. Second, there are texts about God's creative activity throughout the Bible, and their relation to each other is not always clear. My answer to the first problem requires some significant explanation, because it depends on a particular understanding of what all of this creating activity is for. If the purpose of the story of creation is to provide the setting in which the story of Israel is to take place, then it seems this activity is not complete until Genesis 11. There are two primary reasons for extending the boundary of creation in Genesis this far, which I shall mention here and support in greater detail later. First, most interpreters agree that the description of the great flood in Genesis 6–8 is a reversal of God's creative activity in Genesis 1. This means that the emergence of Noah's family from the ark is, in some ways, a second start for the world, a re-creation. Second, God's command to the humans in Gen. 1:28 to "fill the earth and subdue it" is not fulfilled until God comes down again and scatters the builders at Babel, who have attempted to gather all in one place instead. Thus, the whole of Genesis 1–11 is bounded by the speaking and forced fulfillment of this command.

In response to the second problem, it is important to observe that all of the creation texts outside of Genesis 1–11 are reminiscences. They speak to their present situations by recalling God's acts of creation in the distant past. An immediate objection that might be raised at this point is that Genesis 1–11 is also narrated in past tense. The distinction here requires the explanation of a concept that will be important at several points within this book. Although the narrative parts of the Bible all seem to be reported to us in past tense, the narrative world being created has a present tense for its own characters. I will call this the "narrative present." Within that narrative present, the characters sometimes recall and refer to events that are in the past for them. I will call that time the "narrative past." Both the narrative present and the narrative past are in the past for us as readers, but only the latter is so for the characters in the story. Two examples may help illustrate this. In Nehemiah 9:6, Ezra stands up before a gathering of Judahites and begins to recite an account of God's work on behalf of Israel, a statement that includes a description of the creation of the world in its first verse. This description is set in the distant past for Ezra and his listeners, so it is the narrative past being recited in the narrative present. Creation is also the subject of Prov. 8:22-31. In this case, the narrator of the book has introduced a female character called Wisdom, and this character talks about her participation with God in the work of creation "long ago." Again, this is a recital about the distant past for the characters in Proverbs, so its events are in the narrative past.

These texts and others like them will be treated in this chapter, but it is vital to keep in mind that the divine character depicted within them may not match the divine character as it is experienced by the human characters in the narrative present of these texts. The creative and energetic God is a God remembered in such texts, not necessarily a God experienced in the narrative present. A text such as Psalm 44 makes this difference explicit:

> We have heard with our ears, O God,
>   our ancestors have told us,
> what deeds you performed in their days,

in the days of old: (v. 1)
Rouse yourself! Why do you sleep, O Lord?
Awake, do not cast us off forever! (v. 23)

This psalm has received significant treatment from David Blumenthal in *Facing the Abusing God: A Theology of Protest*, in which he argued forcefully against the exclusion of abusive texts. He highlighted in particular verse 17 of this psalm, which makes a claim that stands almost alone against the weight of biblical tradition:[4]

All this has come upon us,
yet we have not forgotten you
or been false to your covenant.

The religious experience of the Israelites had changed since the period of the earlier writings, and parts of the Old Testament seem to assume that the feeling of abandonment resulting from this change was deserved; but other voices, like this one, went another direction and protested a sense of change while placing more direct divine activity in an earlier time. This issue is foundational to the entire Old Testament and will reappear periodically in this book, most significantly in chapter 5.

God of Creation

The opening chapters of the Bible have long held great fascination for many kinds of readers, but they are problematic for Old Testament theology, for a number of reasons. One of these is that the world depicted in these texts has an uncertain connection to our world and to the world of the initial readers of the Bible.[5] One of the first differences readers may notice is the lack of a clear geography: Where is the garden of Eden? Where does Cain kill Abel? Where does Noah build the ark? Even the geographical identifications provided, such as the land of Nod (Gen. 4:16), Mount Ararat (8:4), and the land of Shinar (11:2), are vague at best. A second odd feature of Genesis 1–11 is its sporadic attention to the passage of time. There is no indication of how long Adam and Eve are in the garden of Eden before they eat from the tree of knowledge, nor any indication of the ages of Cain and Abel at the time of the first murder. Even the references to time that are present, such as the life spans of the human characters in the many hundreds of years, tend to be far outside of the experience of readers, both ancient and modern. These are two features among many that give this "primeval" setting an otherworldly feel. This setting must be taken into account when examining how God acts in these texts.

The world of Genesis 1–11 also assumes a direct connection between heaven and earth. The divine character walks in the garden with Adam and Eve (3:8), talks to Cain (4:6) and Noah (6:13) with no theophanic fanfare, and comes down to deal with the builders at Babel (11:7). There are many other differences between the narrative world of Genesis 1–11 and the narrative world of the rest of Genesis,[6] but this one is the most significant for the central question of this chapter: How is the divine character portrayed in the earliest events of the story the Old Testament is telling? This direct connection also allows the presence of God on the earth to be sporadic. God comes and goes and, as readers, we usually come and go with God. Asking when and why God arrives on the human scene in Genesis 1–11 will be an important part of examining how God is portrayed in these texts.

Genesis 1 is a strange way for a story to begin. Although this text is typically presented in prose format, it comes very close to being poetry. Its rhythmic patterns are impossible to miss. The text also possesses a sense of self-contained isolation, like a poem, and it is limited in its ability to develop and present narrative characters. Jack Miles has asked and answered a very important question about the divine character at the opening of the Bible: "What makes God God-like?"[7] Miles identified at least two important answers to this question. One is that the God of Genesis has no "private life." The reader gets to see only God's actions directed toward the created world.[8] The other answer involves God's lack of a past. The biblical story must have a starting point, but there is nothing offered, even in retrospect, about God's life before the beginning of creation in Genesis 1. In these ways, God is unlike the human characters that will eventually emerge in the book. In Genesis 1, God is the only character. Even the human beings, finally created at the end of the sixth day, do not become narrative characters. We are not told how many there are or what any of their names are. The closest they come to being identifiable characters is the point when God speaks to them, in verses 28-30, but there is no indication of whether they listen or respond in any way.

Mark S. Smith identified three models of creation in the texts of the Old Testament and paired each with a text from the book of Psalms that exemplifies that model. Psalm 74 represents creation by "divine power." In this text, God must overcome powerful opponents, like Leviathan. This is likely a remnant of the mythic divine conflicts that are characteristic of Mesopotamian creation accounts.[9] The model called "divine wisdom" is represented by Psalm 104. Though it contains some elements similar to those in Psalm 74, pointing toward divine skill and prowess, verbs such as *crushing* and *rebuking* are absent, as there is no opponent to be defeated. The third mode, "divine presence," can be located in Psalm 8, where the divine–human relationship moves to the fore. Genesis 1 contains some elements of all three of these models but does not fit any of them completely. Perhaps one of its functions, at the beginning of the Bible, is to unify these different perspectives within the biblical tradition.[10] The verbs of which God is subject are ones such as *created, said, saw, named, divided, made, placed,* and *blessed*. God exhibits power and skill in this text with a rhythmic certainty. There is no conflict, though, and readers are not aware of the exertion that all of this activity requires until we get to the seventh day and find that God needs to rest. The constant declarations of goodness and complete lack of awareness that anything could ever go wrong with the creation also provide God's character with an innocent naïveté.

At the end of the opening creation account, which extends to Gen. 2:4, God is finished and resting, and it would be difficult to say where this story might go next. There is nothing left for God to do, and, although there is a vague sense of a human presence in the world, there are no characters for us to know or care about and to follow. What would appear to be an entirely separate story that comes after this one allows for the Bible to keep going, however, and the genius of the combination of these texts will become apparent later.

Interpreters have noticed for a long time not only that the divine character beginning at 2:4b is named differently but also that it acts very differently. Some of the verbs of which YHWH God is the subject are *formed, breathed, planted, said, took, placed, commanded,* and *said*. The primary point of overlap with Genesis 1 is God's speaking activity, but this is a more embodied deity who touches in the act of creating, and this is also a character that is far less certain. YHWH God seems surprised that the man he has created is alone and goes through a very strange process of failed attempts to form a suitable mate, before finally discovering that such a mate cannot come from the dirt but must be formed from a piece of the man. Unlike the story in Genesis 1, where the divine character created only what was good, here there is also something at least potentially bad, the "tree of the knowledge of good and evil" (2:9). In Genesis 1, we are given no hint of God's motive in creating the world, and this seems largely true in the garden of Eden story, too, but what is new is that the reader is provided a reason to be suspicious of God's motives. The divine character does not fully retain the innocence found in Genesis 1 but seems at least as naive. In terms of Smith's models delineated earlier, the story beginning in Genesis 2:4b seems to fit within the "divine presence" category. YHWH God exhibits neither overwhelming power nor a keen sense of skill, and deliberately and overtly plants the possibility of failure in the created world.[11]

This may be as good a place as any to raise the issue of the gendered portrayal of the divine character in the Old Testament generally, and specifically here in its opening chapters. The classic treatment of this issue is Phyllis Trible's groundbreaking work *God and the Rhetoric of Sexuality*. Although Trible acknowledged that "the patriarchal stamp of scripture is permanent,"[12] her work leads to the discovery that the portrayal of the divine within the Bible is more diverse in every way, including gender, than a casual reading might reveal or assume. Moreover, the possibility of feminine dimensions to God's activity, which Trible grounded in Genesis 1–3,[13] reveals that some of our resistance to portrayals of God that are less power-oriented may be the result of viewing the text through the lens of our assumptions about gender.[14] This issue poses a difficult challenge for a discussion of the narrative portrayal of the divine character in the Old Testament, who is often presented in distinctly male language. My own approach will not be to remove gendered language about God but to limit such usage to places where God's maleness seems essential to the text.[15]

The garden of Eden story in Genesis 3 is perhaps more well known than any other story in the Old Testament. It is clearly connected in the text to Genesis 2, but in popular consciousness it has become a separate entity. The behavior of the divine character, still YHWH God, is entirely strange to modern readers when they actually read the story. The notion of a connected but separate heaven and earth is still a necessity for this account, as God is away while the woman and man interact with the talking snake.[16] The divine character must come to the garden for his daily walk in order to discover that something has happened. This deity is characterized as a speaker here, but in two starkly different ways. He begins, in 3:9, as a conversation partner, to whom the humans respond with their own lines of dialogue, but at verse 14 the mode of speaking changes entirely. YHWH God speaks not to but at the snake, then the woman, then the man. Most contemporary translations appropriately signal this change by casting verses 14–19 as poetic lines, and there are two aspects of this speech that are most important to observe in terms of how it shapes the divine character. First, this is speech to which there is no way to respond, and none of the three characters to whom it is addressed attempts to do so. Their speaking is finished. Second, as Miles has noted, it is an "emotional outburst" that in no way matches the act that has led to it. The result is that, "as a character, the Lord God is disturbing as anyone is disturbing who holds immense power and seems not to know what he wants to do with it."[17] This is an impulsive and reactionary deity for whom obedience is an all-or-nothing matter.

Though the creation accounts in Genesis 1 and Genesis 2–3 have different origins and very different styles, they are brought together in 3:23, when the man and woman leave the garden and enter a world that can be understood only as the one created back in Genesis 1. This is confirmed in 4:1, when the first thing Adam and Eve set about doing is fulfilling the command of God in 1:28 to "be fruitful and multiply." The problem of a lack of characters to connect with and follow at the end of the Genesis 1 account has been resolved, because readers will want to know what happens to Adam and Eve when they exit the garden. Two things happen rapidly in the text, which the humans characters in the story interpret as divine action. First, in language that is very difficult to decipher, Eve acknowledges divine involvement in the birth of her first son, Cain. Next, the narrator indicates that the relative successes of Cain and Abel are a reflection of divine favor or disfavor concerning the offerings they bring.[18] The subsequent divine actions in the text are God's conversations with Cain. The divine character still seems to come and go from the scene and speaks to Cain both before and after the killing of Abel. The divine behavior here seems more stable but is still mystifying in ways. The first mystery is the lack of any divine dialogue with Abel. In light of the warning given to Cain in 4:7, the absence of any warning for Abel is especially striking. God's interaction with Cain after the murder is reminiscent of the divine interaction with his parents earlier in chapter 3, as God questions Cain, then banishes him for his act, but two of the features of Genesis 3 noted earlier are missing. This time, the banishment falls short of fitting the crime, rather than being an overreaction, especially when God softens the effect by putting the protective mark on Cain. Along with that, the mode of the divine speech remains conversational, and Cain continues to respond to God.

It may be somewhat outside the scope of this study to note the absence of Adam and Eve from Genesis 4:2-16, but one of their sons has murdered the other, and they are nowhere to be found. This highlights a significant feature of Genesis 1–11, however, which is that the interaction between human characters is very limited. The vast majority of the dialogue is between the divine character and the human characters.[19] The result of this and other literary features is that readers generally come and go with God, usually visiting the human scene when God does. The human characters are flat, and none of them appear in the narrative in a sustained enough manner to hold the story together around them. Thus, God is the central character of Genesis 1–11 and has no serious contender for this status.

In terms of divine characterization, the genealogies in Genesis 1–11 offer very little other than their literary role of connecting the major stories. It is possible to understand the genealogies as the playing out of God's choices by narrowing each generation to just one person, but this selection process is carried out largely in silence.[20] God does appear, however, at two significant places in the genealogical material: the notice concerning Enoch in 5:21-24 and the description of Nimrod in 10:6-8. Although these divine references appear primarily to play the role of elevating the reputation of the human being involved, the claims that Enoch "walked with God" and that "God took him" provide the deity with a presence in the long "book of the *toledoth* of Adam" (Genesis 5) and remind the reader of God's power over humanity. Nimrod is an enormously powerful figure in the biblical text, even though he is present only momentarily, and he seems to encompass the entire world and two archetypal identities. He is associated with both Cush, the biblical designation for Africa beyond Egypt, and Mesopotamia, so he spans the entire world known to the ancient Israelites. He is a "mighty hunter before YHWH" (10:9) and a city-builder (10:11), like Cain and the people of Babel.[21] In fact, Babel is listed as one of the cities he builds. Nimrod is a human being large enough to straddle the entire known world of the time, but his Mesopotamian city-building activity is ultimately subject to God's disapproval in Genesis 11, and his African hunter identity must be authorized by God's presence.

The flood story in Genesis 6–9 is the site of perhaps the greatest success of source criticism, the force that ruled over nearly every facet of Old Testament study for at least a century. Attention to the alternation of divine designations, other vocabulary, and the details of the text enabled source critics to separate the nearly incoherent final form of Genesis 6–9 into two separate, easily understandable flood stories. What this approach was unable to accomplish, however, was to explain why the author of the final form would have combined the two narratives in such a way. One of the results of the combination is the presentation of two different divine motives for flooding the earth. In 6:5-8, YHWH sees the wickedness of human beings and is sorry for making them, so YHWH decides to blot out everything. In 6:11-12, God sees that the earth is corrupt, so God confides in Noah that he has decided to "make an end of all flesh." Miles has appropriately identified an internal divine motivation in the former text and an external motivation in the latter.[22] The result of the combination of accounts results in not just an incoherent story but a confusing divine character. What the two accounts seem to agree upon, in 8:21 and 9:11, is the deity's apparent regret for this destructive act, once it is over, and a promise never to do it again.

Many interpreters have recognized that some elements of the flood narrative reflect the creation account in Genesis 1, except that they happen in reverse.[23] God does not do the work directly but commands Noah to make a microcosm of the creation inside the ark. The language of 7:13–17 is specifically reminiscent of the variety of animals created in Genesis 1. The eruption of water from below and the pouring down of water from above, through the "windows of heaven" (7:11), undo the vertical separation of waters on the second day in Gen. 1:6–8. The covering of even the highest mountains (7:19) cancels the horizontal separation of waters to expose dry land on the third day in 1:9–10. The result is that the ark, a seed of the original creation, moves along "on the face of the waters" (7:18) much like the divine spirit in Gen. 1:2. The key point in the story is when "God remembered Noah" in 8:1 and once again sent the creative wind or spirit to begin to put all of the water back in place.

On either side of the flood narrative, there is a striking connection between the garden of Eden episode in Genesis 3 and the tower of Babel story in Genesis 11. Both stories highlight God's concern about human abilities and accomplishments.[24] In 3:22, YHWH God is concerned that the humans have taken a step toward being "like one of us" by acquiring knowledge. The threat that they might take the additional step of attaining immortality is the reason for banishing them from the garden, so that they will not have access to the tree of life. In 11:6, YHWH is concerned that there are no limits on human accomplishment, so YHWH must scatter the humans and confuse their language. Within the narrative world of Genesis 1–11, this concern is incoherent. It looks like nothing but an insecure need to control lesser beings. Why did God create a world in which human beings had such potential, if God was unwilling to tolerate its realization? God's concerns about violence and corruption in the Cain and Abel story and the flood story are much more understandable, but the solutions to this problem are insufficient. The banishment of Cain leaves him and his descendants, such as Lamech in 4:23–24, with the potential to commit further acts of violence, and the human world after the flood appears to be just as violent and corrupt as the one before it. There is an attempt to connect these divine concerns, however, as Cain, the first murderer, becomes the first city-builder in 4:17. He is the precursor to the builders at Babel. The mysterious Nephilim, who play a part in the violence and corruption that lead to the flood make a name for themselves in 6:4 just like the people of Babel.[25] They are also a threat to the distinction between God and humans, like Adam and Eve and the people of Babel, because of their mixed divine and human parentage.[26] Making sense of this part of Genesis requires placing it within the context of the entire book, a task that leads into chapter 3 of this book.

Bits and pieces of an understanding of what Genesis 1–11 is doing on a literary level appear in the preceding pages, but a clear summative statement is necessary here, because it must precede an effort to draw theological conclusions. The literary features I have demonstrated, along with many others, serve to construct a narrative world in Genesis 1–11 that is strikingly different from the world of the reader, both ancient and modern. When combined with the remainder of the book of Genesis, these features help create a literary work that functions brilliantly to move the reader from that strange and distant world into a more recognizable one. By the time one gets to the stories of Abraham, Sarah, Hagar, Isaac, Rebekah, Jacob, Rachel, and Leah, these characters are living in a world where space and time function in expected ways, in which human characters are living relatively familiar kinds of lives, for much closer to normal life spans, in places that the original readers of Genesis would surely have recognized. This is vital to keep in mind because of the tendency to impose later theological categories on these texts. This phenomenon will be explored further later in this chapter, but one important example should be noted here. The idea that the early chapters of Genesis portray a "fall" of humanity is often supported by observations about the declining life spans in Genesis 1–11,[27] but this decline happens far too gradually in two separate genealogies in Genesis 5 and 11 for readers to make such a connection to Genesis 3, unless the idea of the "fall" is already imposed on the text. Moreover, the frequent connection to the notion of limiting life spans in 6:3 glaringly contradicts the attribution of much longer life spans in Genesis 11 all the way down to Abraham's father, Terah, who lives for 205 years.

When all of God's behavior in Genesis 1–11 is put together and evaluated, one conclusion becomes clear enough. God wants the human beings God has created to behave in a certain way, and when they do not, God intervenes. God banishes, destroys, and scatters because God does not want human beings to be like God, to commit acts of violence, to make a name for themselves, or to gather in one place. What remains entirely unclear in this part of the Bible is why God wants things this way and how human beings are supposed to know about it. The one episode in which God tries to be instructive, the conversation with Cain before the murder, ends as a failed attempt. The world that God created so powerfully and declared to be good in Genesis 1 has one component, the human beings, that will not behave as God wants it to, but there seems to be no attempt in the text to understand why there is such a great distance between expectations and reality. The story simply moves forward with no pause for reflection. It has done its work of building the set for the story of the ancestors of Israel, even though it has left behind a divine portrait as scattered as the human community at the end of Genesis 11.

Creation Texts outside of Genesis 1–11

Identifying texts to be included in a section like this one provides some methodological problems. A purely lexicographical approach—for example, looking for the word "create" (*br'*)—will not suffice, because it misses important creation texts like Psalm 8 and Job 38–41 while pointing toward texts such as Amos 4:13, which mention creation in passing while addressing another subject. Any attempt to be exhaustive in selecting texts is almost sure to fail, so I have selected for the discussion here a collection of texts that give sustained attention to the divine character's activity of creating the world. These are as follows:

- Isaiah 40, 45, 51
- Psalms 8, 74, 89:5-14, 104
- Job 38–41
- Proverbs 8:22-31
- Nehemiah 9:6

It is important to recall, as is mentioned earlier, that each of these texts has a later context in the story being told by the Old Testament, so they are reminiscences of God's creative activity long ago. The final text in this list may seem out of place because of its relative brevity, but it is vital here for two reasons: The first is the role this text will play in the final chapter of this book, which seeks to negotiate between the recalling of God's creative activity in the past and the religious experience of its present. The second reason is that this is the key text that joins creation with the story of God's covenant with, and deliverance of, Israel.[28]

Isaiah

The appearance of creation texts in Isaiah 40, 45, and 51 requires some attention to context. Creation language and ideas appear in numerous places in Isaiah 40–55. The prevailing understanding of this part of the book of Isaiah is that it addresses the experience of release from exile in Babylon in the sixth century BCE. This is confirmed in concrete fashion by the reference in 45:1 to Cyrus, the Persian king who defeated Babylon and released the Israelites from captivity. It should probably not be surprising that in this moment, when many new possibilities were opening up for Israel, creation imagery would emerge.[29] It is also important to acknowledge at this point, though, that the experience of exile and release from captivity was not the experience of the majority of Israelites in the sixth century. The Golah group, composed of those returning from Babylon to rebuild Jerusalem, dominates the book of Ezra-Nehemiah, and their experience seems to give shape to much of the Old Testament.[30] The field of Old Testament theology has played along with this dominance by using the language of "exile" and "restoration" somewhat uncritically. This bias has been most clearly identified and evaluated by Jill Middlemas, particularly in her book with the conspicuous title *The Templeless Age*. The awkward nature of this title reveals the difficulty of naming a more heterogeneous set of experiences. The common denominator of all of those experiences was the absence of the temple for most of the sixth century. Whether the Israelites stayed in a badly damaged Judah, escaped to Egypt, or were taken into captivity in Babylon, the loss of the temple as the center of their religious experience was experienced by all of them.[31] Thus, the idea of a new creation may have appealed to all of these groups, but it probably spoke most clearly to the "returners." This points once again to the essential recognition that creation texts outside of Genesis are recollections of the distant past, which the writers struggle to connect to their present.

Isaiah 40 introduces a new voice to the book. The previous chapter ended with the enigmatic visit of the Babylonian envoys to Hezekiah in the late eighth century BCE. The bizarre tour given to these visitors, in which they are shown everything Hezekiah has, followed by Isaiah's brief prediction in 39:7 of the invasion to come a century and a half later, seems to be the closest this book can come to describing the defeat and destruction of Judah and Jerusalem. A gap opens up between chapters 39 and 40 so wide that the latter can be perceived only as a new beginning. The desire for salvation in the present is bolstered by distant recollections of YHWH's creative activity, in the form of questions that evoke a sense of skill and mastery:

> Who has measured the waters in the hollow of his hand
> and marked off the heavens with a span?
> Enclosed the dust of the earth in a measure,
> and weighed the mountains in scales
> and the hills in a balance? (40:12)[32]

YHWH's mastery over the hills and mountains in the past connects with the desire for deliverance and return in the present expressed in the image of hope that "every mountain and hill be made low" (v. 4), a metaphor for a smooth return back to Judah.

Isaiah 45 contains only a brief reference to creation in verse 7, but it is a startling and controversial one. Translation of this text is difficult for a number of reasons. The division between verses 6 and 7 seems to be in an awkward place, and verse 7 contains only participles, with no explicit subject, unless one is carried forward from verse 6. In addition, the Isaiah scroll from Qumran contains one very important word change. The Masoretic text of verse 7a reads something like, "[I] form light and create darkness, make peace and create evil." The first part of this line appears to be connected to God's first act of creation in Genesis 1. The Qumran text replaces "peace" with "good," thus causing the second line to reflect YHWH God's planting of the "tree of knowledge, good and evil" in the garden of Eden. In the face of a developing sense of dualism in Israel, this text reasserts YHWH as the source of all things, a vital claim in the context of the identification of Cyrus, the king of Persia, as YHWH's anointed agent.

Perhaps the most stunning creation text in this part of Isaiah appears in 51:9-11, where the prophet reaches even beyond the creation language of Genesis:

> Awake, awake, put on strength,
> 　　O arm of the LORD!
> Awake as in days of old,
> the generations of long ago!
> Was it not you who cut Rahab in pieces,
> who pierced the dragon?
> Was it not you who dried up the sea,
> the waters of the great deep;
> who made the depths of the sea a way
> for the redeemed to cross over?
> So the ransomed of the LORD shall return,
> and come to Zion with singing;
> everlasting joy shall be upon their heads;
> they shall obtain joy and gladness
> and sorrow and sighing shall flee away.

Psalms

A full discussion of the preceding passage from Isaiah will be aided by simultaneous consideration of the closely related Psalm 74:12-17:

> Yet God my King is from of old,
> working salvation in the earth.
> You divided the sea by your might;
> you broke the heads of the dragons in the waters.
> You crushed the heads of Leviathan;
> you gave him as food to the creatures of the wilderness.
> You cut openings for springs and torrents;
> you dried up ever-flowing streams.
> Yours is the day, yours also the night;
> you established the luminaries and the sun.
> You have fixed the bounds of the earth;
> you made summer and winter.

The context of Psalm 74 is also the aftermath of the Babylonian invasion. Within the psalm itself, lines such as "Your foes roared within your holy place" (4a) and "They set your sanctuary on fire" (7a) are unmistakable references to this event. In the book of Psalms, this poem is near the beginning of book 3, which reflects the experience of defeat, destruction, and exile.[33] Both Isaiah 51 and Psalm 74 use images of ancient divine conflict with monstrous dragons and a chaotic sea, which Genesis seems determined to avoid. In fact, these texts appear to use the creation imagery of their enemies and captors the Babylonians.[34] The point in Psalm 74 seems to be to illustrate the vast difference between the powerful acts of God in the distant past and the Israelites' own beleaguered situation. The book of Isaiah speaks of the present experience of its community using metaphors of long ago. Thus, these poetic expressions of creation point forward to the narrative of Ezra-Nehemiah as much as they point back to the story of God in Genesis.

Psalm 8 begins and ends with a well-known refrain about YHWH in verses 1 and 9, but the remaining seven verses at the center of this psalm have the role and place of human beings in creation as their primary focus. Smith has proposed that this psalm, which he uses as his primary example of the "divine presence" model, is "unique in the Bible" because of the way it praises the divine being specifically for the creation of human beings.[35] Psalm 8 has strong connections to Genesis 1, sharing the language of a divine assignment to humans of "dominion" over the rest of creation, but Psalm 8 goes even further, insisting that YHWH has made humans "a little lower than God(s)." This elevation of human status points back to the refrain that forms the framework of the poem in verses 1 and 9:

O LORD, our Sovereign,
how majestic is your name in all the earth.

The reference to the "name" of God as that which inhabits the earth is another signal of a withdrawal of divine presence. God has put humans in charge of the works of creation, which were established long ago.

Psalm 89 is a massive and powerful poem. It sits at the end of book 3 of the book of Psalms, and it portrays the end of the Davidic dynasty in the most brutal terms.[36] The typical order of a lament poem is reversed as the first thirty-seven verses recall and celebrate the glories of the ancient Israelite monarchy, and then the final fifteen verses plunge into absolute despair over its destruction. This poem is included in this discussion because verses 5-14 use the language of creation to help establish the divine authority of David's throne. Two aspects of this section create an archaic feel. First, it operates from a polytheistic framework:

For who in the skies can be compared to the LORD?
Who among the heavenly beings is like the LORD,
a God feared in the council of the holy ones,
great and awesome above all that are around him? (vv. 6-7)

Second, like Psalm 74 and Isaiah 51, it evokes the image of conflict with the monsters of chaos:

You crushed Rahab like a carcass;
you scattered your enemies with your mighty arm. (v. 10)

The narrative present of this text is the Babylonian captivity, as revealed in the language of destruction and defeat in verses 40-41, so the goal of the powerful creation imagery and the portrayal of God that it develops is to accentuate its distance from the present experience of the singer(s).

All of the psalms addressed here speak of creation in various ways. Patrick Miller has contended, however, that Psalm 104 may be the only one that speaks "wholly" and "extensively" of God's creation. In the other psalms, including those discussed here, "the praise of God's creative power is a feature of a larger whole that encompasses other concerns."[37] There are many connections between Psalm 104 and the early chapters of Genesis, especially Genesis 1, but there are distinct differences as well. Smith has cited Psalm 104 as the primary example of the "wisdom model" of creation.[38] Miller identified "order and purpose" as the primary idea of Psalm 104.[39] This lengthy poem struggles to speak of creation in its own present in places like verses 20 and 30:

> You make darkness, and it is night,
> when all the animals of the forest come creeping out.
> When you send forth your spirit they are created;
> and you renew the face of the ground.

But these descriptions pale next to the recollections of past acts like verses 5, 9, and 19:

> You set the earth on its foundations
> so that it shall never be shaken.
> You set a boundary that [the oceans] may not pass,
> so that they might not again cover the earth.
> You have made the moon to mark the seasons;
> the sun knows its time for setting.

This last line reveals the difference between past and present, from the time when God was making great things to the present day, when these things operate on their own, even if based upon the nature that God gave them long ago.

Miller may be right about the internal focus of Psalm 104 on creation, but externally it serves a larger purpose, too. Recent attention to the book of Psalms has identified a distinct shape to the book. The section designated as book 3, Psalms 73–89, appears to be a reflection on the experience of exile and all of its losses, including the monarchy. Book 4 (90–106) and book 5 (107–50) point toward restoration and the renewal of worship in the rebuilt temple. Near the end of book 4, Psalm 104 addresses this experience using the language and imagery of creation. One of the most noticeable differences when compared to Genesis is the appearance of architectural metaphors in a creation text, such as in 104:5, perhaps revealing a more overt connection between creation and the temple.[40] Again, this language points forward as much as it looks backward.

Proverbs

Proverbs 8:22-31 is a remarkable creation text in many ways. It is the only such text in all of the Old Testament in which the divine character has a partner in the creative process. Moreover, this partner is female, and it is she who speaks. Once again, however, it is important to recognize that the words are a recollection of a distant, narrative past, and that they have a purpose greater than simply describing the creation of the world to the reader. In 8:1, the narrator has introduced the female character called Wisdom, and she speaks of her own personality and virtue in 8:2-21. The poem that begins at verse 22 would appear to be an additional attempt by this character to establish her credentials as a divine representative. The purpose of this authorization becomes clear in Proverbs 9, when Wisdom shares the stage with the "foolish woman," and both attempt to entice the young person to whom the book is addressed into their respective houses. In 8:22-31, God is a skillful creator, operating in the wisdom model. The primary focus is on architectural metaphors, and Wisdom herself exhibits the playful characteristics (vv. 30-31) that were sometimes displayed by God in Genesis. In their recent work *God of the Living: A Biblical Theology*, Reinhard Feldmeier and Hermann Spieckermann called attention to this text and the Bible's avoidance of the divine life prior to creation. Wisdom presents herself as the first act of creation, who then assists in the remainder of the project. Feldmeier and Spieckermann translate the difficult *'mwn* of 8:30 as "darling" and describe her task as "putting God in a creative mood," which "influences YHWH to do his creative work with desire and love."[41] In a larger sense, the role of Wisdom seems to be the replacement of God as an active, energetic force in the world.[42] The larger discussion of this sense of replacement will have to wait for chapter 6 of this book. At this point, it is important to note the use of the Wisdom character to put distance between the narrative present of the book of Proverbs and God's energetic engagement of the world in the past.

Job

The other major presentation of the creation tradition in the Wisdom literature is found in Job 38–41. It is neither incidental nor accidental that this text is bewildering, for this is exactly the intent it has in the narrative flow of the book—to bewilder Job. The divine character summons Job to a battle of words in 38:3 and must surely know that it is not a fair fight.[43] It is little wonder that Miles gives his chapter on the book of Job the title "Fiend" and includes the description "Few speeches in all of literature can be more properly called overpowering than the Lord's speeches to Job from the whirlwind (Job 38–41). . . . The Lord refers to absolutely nothing about himself *except* his power. . . . Might makes right, he thunders at Job."[44] As in the other cases presented here, the creative actions depicted are far removed from the narrative present of the text. Typical of the wisdom understanding, as in Proverbs 8, the creative work of long ago set up an order that continues to grind away on its own, only now with Job caught in its teeth. The barrage of questions that review God's creative work in the past offer Job no real comfort, but they help him to recognize in 42:6 that he has no choice but to get up out of the dust and go on.[45] Even God recognizes the weakness of his overpowering response when he acknowledges twice in 42:7-8 that Job has "spoken straight of me."

Nehemiah

The grand recital of Israel's faith, placed in the mouth of Ezra in Neh. 9:6-37 will receive major attention in the last chapter of this book, but a brief reflection on its first verse is in order here. There is not much in this short statement, but it is the first time that any such statement has been attached to a narrative recital of Israel's past. As the preceding survey demonstrates, creation is attached to certain other parts of Israel's story numerous times in the poetry of the book of Psalms. Here in Nehemiah, the statement about creation serves to introduce the story of Israel. Its central assertion is that Israel's God is the source of all life, whether in the sky, on the dry land, or in the sea.

The position of this recital of faith reflects the use of creation traditions in the texts discussed here from Isaiah, Psalms, Proverbs, and Job. These other texts are all poetic in nature, and it seems fitting that Israel speaks of creation long ago in such forms. These references to creation typically relegate such divine activity to a distant past and draw contrasts to divine behavior in their own present. The brief mention of creation at the beginning of a long recital of Israel's story in Nehemiah 9 affirms this tradition but keeps it in its place, in Israel's distant past, a great distance from the experience of the struggling fifth-century Judahites listening to the recital within the book of Nehemiah. The Israelites and their reflective texts do not deny that YHWH created the world, but this kind of divine work is unlike anything they observe in their own day, and these texts can even serve to draw contrast between these differing modes of divine behavior.

The God of Creation in Old Testament Theology

In the history of Old Testament theology, discussion of Genesis 1–11 has been dominated by attention to a cycle of sin, punishment, and redemption. This is one of the most significant examples of a later biblical concept being pushed back into an earlier part of the story. The idea of sin does not adequately identify the problems that arise in Genesis 1–11. The divine character wants the creation to behave in certain ways, and neither this character nor the writer seems to understand why it will not. God's responses to this realization are erratic, unpredictable, and largely ineffective. As was stated earlier in this chapter, it is common within the field of Old Testament theology to understand the exodus story as primary and normative. Thus, the divine character of these more understandable and palatable categories is placed over top of the earlier character.[46]

The imposition of later categories of sin, punishment, redemption, and salvation cannot tame this strange divine being, however. Terence Fretheim adequately demonstrated that the "words for creation are also used for God's salvific work," especially in Isaiah 40–55. He went on to identify a relationship between creation and salvation.[47] The problem with this argument is that the sharing of language moves in only one direction. As I have established, the context of creation texts in Isaiah 40–55 must be understood as Israel's need and desire for deliverance from captivity in Babylon. This desire is expressed not just in creation language but also in the language of other venerable traditions in ancient Israel, such as exodus (Isaiah 40:3-5). The language characteristic of deliverance and salvation is absent from Genesis 1–11, however.[48] The language of deliverance in the Old Testament typically revolves around the verbs *nṣl*, *yšʿ*, *yṣʾ* (in *hipʿil* forms), *ʿlh* (in *hipʿil* forms), and *gʾl*.[49] These verbs appear nearly one thousand times combined in the Tanak, and almost three hundred of these occurrences are in the Torah. Only about thirty-three are in the book of Genesis, though, and of those only four are in Genesis 1–11. Moreover, none of those four instances has the divine character as the subject. The two Hebrew words most commonly used for sin, *ḥṭʾ* and *ʿwn* (often translated as "iniquity" because it appears in parallel with *ḥṭʾ*), appear only once each in Genesis 1–11, and their uses here, both in Genesis 4, are far from usual. In 4:7, *ḥṭʾ* seems to be an entity lying in wait for or coming after Cain.[50] In 4:13, Cain laments to YHWH that his *ʿwn* is "more than he can carry"; therefore, many English translations often render *ʿwn* here as "punishment." Regardless of how the questions about usage of these two words is resolved, the important point is that they are rare in Genesis 1–11, and when they do appear they do not designate an act of disobedience, which is their typical meaning elsewhere. The primeval texts in Genesis do not contain the standard biblical language of sin, redemption, salvation, and deliverance. This set of observations points to the possibility that it is readers of those texts who have carried these ideas, found in abundance in later parts of the Old Testament, back into those texts. This would also indicate why literary critics, attempting to read the story of God from the beginning, do not tend to see this kind of system within the portrayal of divine behavior in this part of the text. In his classic *Theology of the Old Testament*, Walter Eichrodt looked at creation in the Old Testament through the lens of a fully developed theological system centered on the ideas of covenant, sin, redemption, and salvation, and he declared, "Where Yahweh was acknowledged as Creator, it was inconceivable that the creation should be based on impulsive caprice, or the unpredictable and aimless sport of kindred or hostile divine powers; the sovereignty of God experienced in the present meant that it could only have been transcendent rationality and moral force which determined the character of the created order."[51] It is little wonder that those approaching the Old Testament as a narrative in which the divine character is being developed through a portrayal of the character's actions have had difficulty fitting into the tradition of Old Testament theology. These readers would have to look at a statement like this from Eichrodt and wonder even whether they are reading the same Bible.

These observations illustrate some of the difficulties of an Old Testament theology grounded in narrative character development. It is not easy to allow the earlier texts in this trajectory to speak for themselves, on their own terms, when we know the texts further along so well. There is a constant impulse to tame the divine character in the early chapters using the categories of later portrayals. This problem has a converse as well, which will become clearer as this study progresses. It is the inability to let go of earlier portrayals as later ones develop. Even in more recent, synchronic attempts to do Old Testament theology, which often recognize so keenly the difference between the portrayals of the divine being, there is still an effort to hold such portrayals together in a system of static tension. Rolf Knierim, for example, made a great start at the beginning of his 2000 work, *The Task of Old Testament Theology*, with this argument:

> In the history of the discipline of Old Testament or biblical theology, the ever-increasing awareness of the plurality of theologies, as well as the danger of the Old Testament's theological disintegration and atomization implied in that plurality, has been met with attempts to identify holistic dimensions. . . . The implication seems universal that as soon as the holistic dimension can be discerned the plurality of theologies in the Old Testament can be regarded as an enriching phenomenon rather than as a critical problem. . . . This implication is indefensible.[52]

But several pages later, Knierim was outlining a "systematic" task that would "identify those components which are fundamental and, thus, to which all others are accountable." The fundamental components that he identified, "the theology of creation and dominion of the world" and "the theology of justice and righteousness," are clearly important and broad in scope within the Old Testament.[53] Nevertheless, it is not clear in his work how this is substantially different from the identification of "holistic dimensions" that he criticized earlier. In contrast to this, treating the divine being as a developing narrative character allows certain portrayals to be examined and left behind as new portrayals emerge.

It is very tempting for us to want to think of creation as an ongoing process, and this way of thinking certainly has its place in the theology of the religious traditions that embrace the Hebrew Scriptures as sacred text. The Old Testament, however, seems to be doing something else with the active, energetic God of creation. The creative work of this deity is placed back at the beginning of the story. Though it is remembered frequently, it is just that—remembrance—and when this activity in the distant past is placed alongside God's activity in the narrative present, it is typically done to demonstrate a sense of contrast rather than continuity.

Notes

1. The original address and its title were in Latin. The title is often translated as something like "On the Proper Distinction between Biblical and Dogmatic Theology and the Specific Objectives of Each." For a more thorough analysis of the context, content, and impact of this work, see the account in John H. Hayes and Frederick Prussner, *Old Testament Theology: Its History and Development* (Atlanta: John Knox, 1985), 2–5.

2. Gerhard von Rad, *Old Testament Theology*, trans. D. M. G. Stalker (New York: Harper & Row, 1962), 1:136–51. See also Werner H. Schmidt, *The Faith of the Old Testament: A History*, trans. John Sturdy (Philadelphia: Westminster, 1983), 170–74. For more on the attention to creation in Old Testament theology, see Hayes and Prussner, *Old Testament Theology,* 273–76.

3. Old Testament theology is also influenced by its social and cultural contexts, and growing interest in environmental issues has directed more attention to the biblical portrayal of creation. See, for example, Carol J. Dempsey and Mary Margaret Pazdan, eds., *Earth, Wind, and Fire: Biblical and Theological Perspectives on Creation* (Collegeville, MN: Liturgical, 2004).

4. David Blumenthal, *Facing the Abusing God: A Theology of Protest* (Louisville: Westminster John Knox, 1993), 85–110. The theological implications of Psalm 44 will be discussed further in chapters 5 and 6.

5. On the effects of this phenomenon, particularly as it relates to cultural memory, see John W. Rogerson, *A Theology of the Old Testament: Cultural Memory, Communication, and Being Human* (Minneapolis: Fortress Press, 2009), 42–48.

6. For more discussion of these differences, see Mark McEntire, *Struggling with God: An Introduction to the Pentateuch* (Macon, GA: Mercer University Press, 2008), 45–47.

7. Jack Miles, *God: A Biography* (New York: Vintage, 1995), 85–95.

8. There is a possible exception to this observation, depending upon how one reads the two uses of divine first-person plural in Genesis 1:26 and 11:6-7. The uses in question seem most likely to be a reference to the heavenly court, the supernatural beings surrounding God, including those who would have participated in the mysterious events of Genesis 6:1-4. If this is true, then these characters are nearly invisible. Another possibility is that this type of speech is "divine self-deliberation." On both of these possibilities, see the discussion of divine speech in Genesis 1–11 in Joel S. Burnett, *Where Is God? Divine Absence in the Hebrew Bible* (Minneapolis: Fortress Press, 2010), 83–84. In either case, the conversation is entirely about the human beings on earth, so the sense of a divine "private life" is minimal.

9. See the discussion in Jon D. Levenson, *Creation and the Persistence of Evil: The Jewish Drama of Divine Omnipotence* (San Francisco: Harper & Row, 1988), 7–12.

10. Mark S. Smith, *The Priestly Vision of Genesis 1* (Minneapolis: Fortress Press, 2010), 11–37.

11. It is no surprise that some interpreters are uncomfortable with this type of description and the notion of divine naïveté that I have presented here. As Terence E. Fretheim indicated, some may be more comfortable speaking of God as an experimenter, or as doing creation by "trial and error." See Fretheim, *God and World in the Old Testament: A Relational Theology of Creation* (Nashville: Abingdon, 2005), 56–57.

12. Phyllis Trible, *God and the Rhetoric of Sexuality* (Philadelphia: Fortress Press, 1978), 202.

13. Ibid., 5–22.

14. Ibid., 200–201.

15. In my own speech and writing about the being of God outside of the biblical text, it is my practice to avoid gendered language.

16. See the discussion of a divine–human relationship "negotiated often in spatial terms" in Burnett, *Where Is God?* 176–77.

17. Miles, *God*, 35.

18. It is notoriously difficult to determine what it means for God to "look upon" Abel's offering but not to "look upon" Cain's. See the discussion in Mark McEntire, *The Blood of Abel: The Violent Plot in the Hebrew Bible* (Macon, GA: Mercer University Press, 1999), 19–20.

19. There are perhaps only two true exceptions to this tendency. Lamech speaks the vengeful little poem in Gen. 4:23-24 to his wives, and the unnamed characters at Babel speak to each other about their building plans in 11:3-4. Three times humans speak when it is not clear to whom they are talking, if indeed they are talking to anyone in particular. These are Eve in 4:1 and 4:25, and Noah in 9:25-27. I think the latter case is best understood as Noah speaking to God, requesting divine curses and blessings on his sons. In two cases, 4:8 and 9:22, human characters are reported to speak to one another, but no dialogue is provided. In the former case, tradition has inserted a line of dialogue for Cain and Abel, which is absent from the Masoretic Text. See the discussion of this in Mark McEntire, "Being Seen and Not Heard: The Interpretation of Genesis 4.8," in *Of Scribes and Sages: Early Jewish Interpretation and Transmission of Scripture*, ed. Craig A. Evans (London: T&T Clark, 2004), 1:4–13.

20. For an extensive discussion of the literary and potential theological functions of genealogies, see Matthew A. Thomas, *These Are the Generations: Identity, Covenant, and the "Toledoth" Formula* (London: T & T Clark, 2010), 83–95.

21. On this double identity, see Yigal Levine, "Nimrod the Mighty, King of Kish, King of Sumer and Akkad," *VT* 52 (2002): 350–66, and Modupe Oduyoye, *The Sons of God and the Daughters of Men: An Afro-Asiatic Reading of Genesis 1–11* (Maryknoll, NY: Orbis, 1984), 91–97.

22. Miles, *God*, 43.

23. This idea has formed the framework for the recent volume on Genesis 1–11 by Joseph Blenkinsopp. See particularly his description of the flood narrative in *Creation, Un-Creation, Re-Creation: A Discursive Commentary on Genesis 1–11* (London: T&T Clark, 2011), 137–42.

24. On this connection, see W. Lee Humphreys, *The Character of God in the Book of Genesis: A Narrative Appraisal* (Louisville: Westminster John Knox, 2001), 77–78.

25. This feature is typically obscured in English translations by the rendering of the final phrase in 6:4, literally "men of a name," as something like "warriors of renown" (NRSV).

26. See the discussion of the *bny 'lhym* and the threats they pose in Oduyoye, *Sons of God and the Daughters of Men*, 23–25.

27. See, for example, the discussion in Fretheim, *God and World in the Old Testament*, 70–72. That this has not always been, and is not necessarily now, the only or most obvious way to read Genesis 2–3 has been amply demonstrated by Elaine Pagels. See her survey of the history of interpretation of these texts in *Adam, Eve, and the Serpent* (New York: Vintage, 1988), 3–31.

28. See the discussion of this accumulation of elements from a tradition-critical perspective in Gerhard von Rad, *Deuteronomy: A Commentary*, trans. Dorothea Barton (Philadelphia: Westminster, 1966), 157–59.

29. Walter Brueggemann has stressed the idea that the central claim in all of the creation language in Isaiah 40–55 is that YHWH is stronger than the gods of Babylon. See Brueggemann, *Theology of the Old Testament: Testimony, Dispute, Advocacy* (Minneapolis: Fortress Press, 1997), 149–51.

30. For a thorough description of this group and its contexts, see Daniel L. Smith-Christopher, *A Biblical Theology of Exile* (Minneapolis: Fortress Press, 2002), 27–74.

31. Jill Middlemas, *The Templeless Age: An Introduction to the History, Literature, and Theology of the "Exile"* (Louisville: Westminster John Knox, 2007), 1–7.

32. Smith, *Priestly Vision of Genesis 1*, 13–14. Smith places this text in his list of those that display the "divine wisdom" model of creation.

33. The idea that the final form of the book of Psalms follows the plot of the story of Israel has been developed in a number of studies. See particularly Gerald Wilson, *The Editing of the Hebrew Psalter* (Chico, CA: Scholar's Press, 1985); and Nancy deClaissé-Walford, *Reading from the Beginning: The Shaping of the Hebrew Psalter* (Macon, GA: Mercer University Press, 1997).

34. See the excellent discussion of these two texts and their mythic backgrounds in Levenson, *Creation and the Persistence of Evil*, 7–12.

35. Smith, *Priestly Vision of Genesis 1*, 28–29.

36. The centrality of kingship will give this psalm a larger place in chapter 4 of this book.

37. Patrick L. Miller, *The Way of the Lord: Essays in Old Testament Theology* (Grand Rapids, MI: Eerdmans, 2004), 178.

38. Smith, *Priestly Vision of Genesis 1*, 23–27.

39. Miller, *Way of the Lord*, 178.

40. Many interpreters have argued that even in Genesis 1 this connection is present. See, for example, Joseph Blenkinsopp, "The Structure of P," *CBQ* 38 (1976): 275–76. Blenkinsopp uses common language patterns, such as what he calls the "solemn-conclusion formula" and the "execution formula," to connect Genesis 1 with the building of the tabernacle in Exodus 25–40 and the drawing of tribal boundaries in the promised land in Joshua 13–22. Thus, these parts of the Old Testament seem to look at the construction of the world, the construction of Israel, and the construction of the tabernacle/temple through the same lens.

41. Reinhard Feldmeier and Hermann Spieckermann, *God of the Living: A Biblical Theology*, trans. Mark E. Biddle (Waco, TX: Baylor University Press, 2011), 253.

42. See the discussion in William P. Brown, *The Ethos of the Cosmos: The Genesis of Moral Imagination in the Bible* (Grand Rapids, MI: Eerdmans, 1999), 272–73. There is an extensive debate about the meaning of some of the words in verses 30-31. For a full explanation, see Michael V. Fox, *Proverbs 1–9: A New Translation with Introduction and Commentary* (New York: Doubleday, 2000), 285–89. The debate typically comes down to whether the image of Wisdom is skillful co-creator or playful companion. The point I make here fits with either set of images. Even if Wisdom was predominantly playful in this ancient recollection, she has become a skillful divine partner in the present.

43. See the characterization of this "fight" in Gustavo Gutiérrez, *On Job: God-Talk and the Suffering of the Innocent* (Maryknoll, NY: Orbis, 1987), 69–70.

44. Miles, *God*, 314.

45. See the discussion of this verse in Gutiérrez, *On Job*, 86–87. This text will receive more extensive treatment in chapter 5.

46. For a typical example of this phenomenon, see Bernhard W. Anderson, *Creation versus Chaos* (Philadelphia: Fortress Press, 1987), 35–36.

47. Fretheim, *God and World in the Old Testament*, 10–11.

48. Such observations and the implications drawn from them need to be made with care, of course. The absence of specific vocabulary does not necessarily mean the absence of the idea it is typically used to convey.

49. On the language of salvation in the Old Testament, see Brueggemann, *Theology of the Old Testament*, 173–76.

50. On the problem of translation caused by complicated grammatical issues at this point, see Ellen van Wolde, "The Story of Cain and Abel: A Narrative Study," *JSOT* 52 (1991): 30–32.

51. Walter Eichrodt, *Theology of the Old Testament*, trans. J. A. Baker (Philadelphia: Westminster, 1967), 2:98.

52. Rolf P. Knierim, *The Task of Old Testament Theology: Method and Cases* (Grand Rapids, MI: Eerdmans, 2000), 2–3.

53. Ibid., 16.

3

A Commanding and Delivering God

The commanding and delivering God who dominates the Bible from Genesis 12 through Deuteronomy 34 is difficult to resist. This deity acts decisively to give his people what we all need and want. Though the process of human liberation may seem accomplished for many and, thus, pushed aside, the continuing desire for such a powerful deity among human beings still in need of deliverance from oppression is well demonstrated in works like Elsa Tamez's *Bible of the Oppressed*, Jorge Pixley's *On Exodus: A Liberation Perspective*, and Robert McAfee Brown's *Unexpected News: Reading the Bible with Third World Eyes*.[1] When we examine the Bible carefully and look for the divine character who exhibits this kind of behavior, however, we find a pattern similar to that described at the end of the previous chapter. This deity is confined to stories at the beginning of the Bible, about Israel's distant past. The diminishing nature of this deity is not presented in a straight line of development, though, so it is necessary to follow the plot of the Old Testament carefully in order to discern the pattern.

The previous chapter already gave some attention to the abrupt shifts in narration that take place at the end of Genesis 11, when the story moves from the primeval world into the world inhabited by the great Israelite ancestors. It will be helpful, however, to delineate the emerging features more thoroughly at the beginning of our discussion of this section. Genesis 12–50 will be the central text with which we begin this discussion, and a coherent expression of how God is behaving in this part of the biblical story will require a precise understanding of the settings in which the deity acts. The first essential feature is the change in the way Genesis deals with geography, because this feature develops the spatial locations in which God acts. Beginning in Genesis 12, every event occurs in a place that can be identified on a map, and that we can assume would have been familiar to the ancient readers of Genesis. This stands in sharp contrast to the missing or fuzzy geography of Genesis 1–11, where the deity is never connected to a place, other than the ethereal garden of Eden.

Second, the human characters in Genesis 12–50 become highly developed as we follow their lives in fairly continuous fashion over a long period of time. In contrast, the characters in the first eleven chapters of Genesis are very limited in development and transitory in nature. Readers are shown one or, at most, a few events in their lives, and then these characters vanish. God still comes and goes from the human scene in Genesis 12–50, but as readers we continue to follow the human characters even during lengthy divine departures. As the book of Genesis develops, the connection between heaven and earth diminishes and the divine presence recedes, until it is represented only by the symbolic dreams of Joseph. The effect of these developments, along with other features, such as the decline in human life spans to a recognizable length, is to create an ancestral world and a kind of religious experience that it seems reasonable to assume would have been familiar to the first readers of Genesis. The settings of these stories have been shaped in such a way that they are at least close to the settings of the lives of the implied readers, even though we must acknowledge that for modern readers there is still a great distance between these narrative worlds and the worlds of our experience.

God of the Ancestors

The first glimpse of the divine being in the ancestral material looks familiar to readers who have made their way through Genesis 1–11. God comes to Abram in a manner similar to earlier approaches to Adam, Eve, Cain, and Noah. The initial difference is that this encounter is in a specifically named place, but the divine address to Abram in Haran is quite different in another way, because it is not simply a response to a past or pending event, such as the eating of the fruit, the rejection of Cain's sacrifice, the murder of Abel, or the flood. Instead, God gives Abram a promise and a set of instructions that point toward an entirely new life, not just for him but also for his descendants to come. This difference is reflected in the ongoing narrative, as the story stays with the human characters and as readers watch those characters' lives unfold even when the divine presence has departed. The next several stories about Abram and Sarai are all the more striking because of the divine absence within them. Despite the promises to Abram, he and his family are left to fend almost entirely for themselves in a dangerous world.

The pattern of divine behavior yields puzzling texts. It seems strange enough that God directs Abram and Sarai to a new land that they must leave so quickly because of its lack of fertility. This departure leads to the strange set of events in Egypt in Gen. 12:10-20, which are ultimately resolved by powerful divine intervention, but it seems so poorly timed. The plagues inflicted on

Egypt would have been unnecessary had God stepped in to reassure Abram of divine protection, or simply to inform Pharaoh that his pending marriage to Sarai was inappropriate. Indeed, these incongruities in the story may be one of the reasons that a similar story has to appear again in 20:1–18. In this second story about the interaction of the ancestors with a foreign king, Abimelech of Gerar is informed by God in a dream that Sarah is a married woman, so he gives up on his designs to marry her, but not before he successfully convinces God in the dream of his innocence in the matter. Outside of the dream, Abimelech repeatedly berates Abraham for his dangerous and thoughtless deception, to which the great ancestor can respond only with his feeble claim that the lie about Sarah's identity is half true (20:12–13). In Genesis 12, Pharaoh seems quite willing to respond appropriately to new information and hardly needs the roughing-up inflicted upon him and his household, and this observation is confirmed by Abimelech's obedience in Genesis 20,[2] but this is a deity who seems to have something to prove and who will increasingly demand proof of loyalty from his primary client.

The actions of all the characters, YHWH included, are inexplicable in these early ancestral stories, and readers are left to watch in bewilderment. W. Lee Humphreys has concluded that the voice of YHWH "does not address the moral concerns raised by the other characters within the story." Perhaps more challenging is his conclusion that God's plans for Abraham "stands outside matters of motive and morals, beyond any concerns for good and evil."[3] To what do we attribute this absence of morality? Is YHWH a character who is not yet morally formed? These are questions to which the text of Genesis deliberately returns repeatedly.

The kidnapping of Abram's nephew, Lot, in Genesis 14 is a story that reveals much about the divine character and his relation to human beings. This is another problem that Abram is left to solve entirely on his own. However, we discover at 14:14 that YHWH has made a covenant not with one individual named Abram but with a relatively large company of people. With 318 men of fighting age, it is not unreasonable to envision the clan of Abram as a group numbering one thousand or more. The effect of keeping this formidable number obscured in the background, though, is to highlight the childlessness of Abram and Sarai as individuals. This sad element of their lives contradicts the promise given to Abram by God and is a matter of continuing concern to the narrative.

It is in Genesis 15 that something entirely new happens, when a human being, Abram, takes control of a human–divine contact. Old Testament theology has typically placed great emphasis on the promises that make up the covenant tradition, but comparatively little on the divine failure to keep those promises. Abram himself makes this point in 15:2-3, and God responds by reaffirming the promise, but there is still no immediate fulfillment. The ancestors are again left by their deity to find their own solutions to the lack of fertility of both land and womb. The latter initiates a remarkable pair of stories, split apart in Genesis 16 and 21, involving Hagar, Abraham's Egyptian slave-wife, and each of these stories elicits divine action. The behavior of God in the first story is notable because it is a conversation with a non-Israelite woman and because it is wrought with ambiguity. The status of Hagar is uncertain throughout the story. As a member of Abram the clan, is she a recipient of God's covenantal promises? Having secured the divine promise of offspring in chapter 15, Abram now goes about solving his problem of childlessness without divine assistance, and Hagar is caught up in the triangle of frustration and failure. Is she Abram's second wife or the slave of Sarai? Phyllis Trible has carefully identified the ambiguity of God's interaction with Hagar in 16:6-12. Although the divine appearance to such a woman might appear to elevate her status, this is counteracted by the command to return to Sarai and submit to her harsh treatment. God comes to Hagar not to liberate but to reenslave her. Though she is promised a son in return for this act of submission, the promise is muted by the predicted character of this son's life (16:11-12).[4] One is left at the end of the encounter wondering why God has even bothered to find her and send her back. The presence of Hagar and Ishmael in Abram's household serves no purpose other than to make the second story about them possible, and the divine behavior concerning Hagar continues to be perplexing in Genesis 21.[5] After going to considerable lengths to send Hagar back to Abraham in Genesis 16, in 21:12 God supports Sarah's intent to send her away again. Following the dialogue between God and Abraham in 18:23-33, in which Abraham convinces God to take a different course of action, the reversal here is striking. God convinces Abraham to banish Hagar and Ishmael, against Abraham's own wishes. The end of Hagar's story leaves the portrait of the divine character in a condition of remarkable instability. God is present with Hagar and even helps to keep her and her son alive by indicating the presence of the well. But for what is she rescued? Trible finds in Hagar "a symbol of the oppressed." Hagar's story reveals much about the story of God and Israel to come: "This Egyptian slave woman is stricken, smitten by God, and afflicted for the transgressions of Israel. She is bruised for the iniquities of Sarah and Abraham; upon her is the chastisement that makes them whole."[6]

The character named Lot fades from the scenery of Genesis for some time after his rescue, as the text of Genesis addresses the continuing childlessness of

Abraham and Sarah as its primary issue. These two subjects come together in Genesis 18, however, when Abraham and Sarah receive strange visitors. This odd story requires significant attention, because one of the three men who appears to Abraham and Sarah is understood to be divine. Esther Hamori has identified this text (18:1–15) and Gen. 32:22–32 as the only two occasions in the Hebrew Scriptures in which God appears fully embodied as an ordinary human being. She has called these two texts examples of the "*'sh* theophany," because God is described in both using the ordinary Hebrew word for "a man."[7] In this first instance, both the appearance and the interaction are puzzling. God has communicated with Abraham numerous times already, but never in this human form. Sarah's response would seem more than reasonable to most readers, given the situation, but God seems perplexed or offended by it, and this part of the story ends abruptly on this note, as the narrative moves on to the account of the destruction of Sodom.

If readers wondered earlier about the moral formation of the divine character, this issue comes into full view in Gen. 18:22–33. Jack Miles has suggested that Abraham's childlessness is still at play in his startling conversation with God about Sodom, and that this is what gives Abraham the boldness to "come forward" in God's presence:[8] "'Will you indeed sweep away the righteous with the wicked? Suppose there are fifty righteous within the city; will you then sweep away the place and not forgive it for the fifty righteous who are in it? Far be it from you to do such a thing, to slay the righteous with the wicked, so that the righteous fare as the wicked. Far be that from you! Shall not the Judge of all the earth do what is just?'" (18:23–25). This text is central for those who work with a dialogical approach to biblical theology.[9] Abraham has taken the initiative in dialogue with God before, but the conversation in this story goes one step further when he successfully alters God's behavior. However, the true concerns and motives of the divine character are impossible to determine from this sparse text. Is God testing Abraham's sense of righteousness? To what extent does concern for the fate of Lot, Abraham's nephew who lives in Sodom, lie in the background of this conversation? Is God trying to prove some point to Abraham? The divine plan here invites immediate comparison to the flood narrative in Genesis. Is God acknowledging the failure of that prior effort to deal with human wickedness and inviting input or counsel from Abraham this time?[10] Walter Brueggemann connects this story to a larger debate about "Yahweh's capacity for unmitigated rage." His conclusion is that "wonderment about Yahweh's lack of restraint is near the surface, even though it is not fully allowed in the narrative."[11] Whether this is still an open question about the deity at the end of the biblical story is an issue to which this study will return.

Trible's conclusion about the Hagar story highlights the extent to which texts in Genesis are always pointing forward. Every episode in the story of Abraham and Sarah is pointing forward to Genesis 22, the Akedah story. The writer of Genesis reminds readers of this with the curious beginning of the narrative, "After these things . . . " The impact of this story is so powerful, however, that it seems to explode out of the text, reducing to forgotten rubble everything around it. Therefore, it requires great effort to push it back into the overall narrative and pay careful attention to what it is doing in its literary context. This is the climax of the Abraham and Sarah portion of the book of Genesis; nobody is the same after the bewildering event is over, and the narrative barely has the energy to carry on. Sarah, who is conspicuously absent from the Akedah story, dies immediately after it. Abraham moves on, acquires a wife for Isaac, takes a new wife for himself (Keturah), and produces numerous children. This time, however, the family is of no real significance, as if Abraham is just any other person now. The dynamism of his character and of his interactions with the divine character are over, and he dies at the beginning of Genesis 25. Isaac never achieves significant stature as an adult, and his one encounter with the divine character, in 26:23-25, is perfunctory. Perhaps a more definitive divine-human interaction in this part of Genesis involves another character who represents the diminished Isaac. In Genesis 24, Abraham sends a servant back to his old home place to find a wife for Isaac, because he does not want him to marry a Canaanite woman. Richard Elliott Friedman has drawn careful attention to this episode, because in it a human being requests a specific divine action, and it is immediately granted. In 24:12-20, Rebekah speaks and acts as the servant of Abraham as requested. Friedman has found in this story an indication of a new direction in divine-human interaction: "Thus the element of uncertainty in human control will diminish and humans will more clearly and specifically determine the form of divine action."[12] The book of Genesis is ready to move on to Jacob, and God has begun to interact with human beings in new and different ways.

The most striking example of this shift in divine behavior is Jacob's famous dream at Bethel in Gen. 28:10-17. This is the first unambiguous dream theophany experienced by any of the Israelite ancestors in the Bible.[13] This type of divine interaction was exhibited earlier with a foreigner, King Abimelech in 20:3-7, so it seems odd for the central ancestor to have such an experience, but Jacob has other divine encounters that are not presented as dreams. This experience is also different because of the way Jacob bargains with YHWH in its aftermath. Compared to the promises YHWH made to Abraham, Jacob's requests are meager. He asks in 28:20-22 only to be kept alive until he returns to his father's house. Still, as Miles has noted, this is unlike anything preceding it in Genesis, because Jacob names the terms of his bargain.[14] Human initiative has replaced divine initiative.

The middle portion of the life of Jacob, the fourteen-plus years in the area of Haran, is essential for his own character development. The fugitive who eventually returns to claim his right of power is a theme that dominates great literature both inside and outside the Bible.[15] Jacob's years outside of Canaan also raise important questions about the character of the God of the Israelite ancestors. This deity has already spoken to Jacob's grandfather, Abram, in this place (12:1), so we would not expect him to be absent in this part of the text, but Humphreys has identified a very different type of divine presence in the account of Jacob's Haran years. Aside from God's brief instruction to Jacob in 31:13 telling him to return to Canaan, the character of God is constructed in the words of the human characters in the story. Humphreys concludes:

> But we must note that God seems largely to have left the scene of action, and left himself to be present only as constructed by others as a rhetorical figure in their give-and-take. . . . Thus even as they speak of God's authority and control, his ability to shape events so that Jacob's rights and those of his wives are justly affirmed, God's authority and control are called into question for the reader as we recognize that this is an image of God constructed by other characters who have their own agendas and intentions.[16]

The next significant divine act occurs when Jacob is traveling back southward, returning to his father's house. Jacob is still in control in 32:9-12 (HB 32:10-13), defining God's relationship to him by making requests and promises. His requests made long ago at Bethel have been more than fulfilled, as he comes with four wives, many children, servants, and livestock. Yet it is only when he is alone, having sent everybody and everything else ahead to appease the anger of Esau, that the divine visit comes, and it is the most striking theophany in all of the Bible. This is the second of only two examples of the "*'sh* theophany" identified by Hamori. The strangeness of the text of 32:22-32 sparks an incredulity that has led to many different interpretations of the text that seek to avoid the identification of the divine presence.[17] In the narrative flow of Jacob's life, this event is the mirror image of the dream at Bethel, which may tempt the reader to construe it as a dream, but nothing in the text allows such an escape. The wrestling match on the bank of the Jabbok is the return of the divine initiative, which Jacob seemed to have taken away during this period of his life. Perhaps the greatest theological challenge is not the wrestling match itself but the result. At best, the match is a draw, but some, including Stephen Geller, perceive it as a defeat for God: "Jacob's defeating God is blasphemous; his defeating a man is meaningless."[18] This event has far too much gravity to be the attack of a mugger, or Esau, or even a river demon. And in the end it is far more than just a physical stalemate. Friedman has described the end of a trajectory here that demonstrates an increase in human initiative: "Adam disobeys God. Abraham questions God. Jacob fights God. Humans are confronting their creator and they are increasing their participation in the arena of divine prerogatives."[19] Jacob gets what he wants from God, a name and a blessing, but he also pays a heavy price, as he walks away limping. Like his grandfather departing Moriah, Jacob is diminished by this encounter, and this becomes more apparent in the stories that follow. Perhaps his inability to respond in any vigorous way to the situation of his daughter, Dinah, and his failure to control the response of his sons, Simeon and Levi, is the clearest illustration of this diminished capacity. The divine character seems equally diminished. God makes another appearance to Jacob in Genesis 35, first instructing him to return to Bethel (35:1). Following the vague sense of divine terror that protects Jacob and his family as they travel to Bethel (35:5), God appears to Jacob for a longer conversation, but it is entirely a reiteration of the past, the changing of Jacob's name to Israel (35:10) and the listing of the contents of the covenant with the ancestors (35:11-12). The book of Genesis is prepared to move on to the God of Joseph, a very different sort of divine portrayal.

The book of Genesis allows space for this change in character by drawing attention away from the deity almost entirely. The two primary divine designations, YHWH and Elohim, are not present in Genesis 34, 36, and 37.[20] YHWH makes a reappearance in 38:7-10 in the explanations of the untimely deaths of Er and Onan, then vanishes again until Joseph is in Egypt in Genesis 39, the point at which the Elohim designation also reappears. When God reappears in the Joseph story here, it is to "bless the house of [Potiphar] for Joseph's sake" and to be "with Joseph" in a vague, unspecified way. Joseph does not encounter the divine being like his father or his great-grandfather did.[21] Instead, he receives symbolic dreams and he is able to interpret the dreams of others, both of which are understood to be divine gifts, and they help accomplish two larger goals. First, they bring Joseph success in the Egyptian court and, second, they put him in a position to ensure the survival of his family.

When Joseph constructs God with his language, most poignantly in the scene in which he reveals his identity to his brothers (45:4–14), he understands all of this, even the evil deeds of his brothers, to be part of a providential plan. Such observations lead Humphreys to describe God at the end of Genesis as "Joseph's Silent Patron."[22]

The instability of the divine character in the ancestral material of Genesis is reflected in the way this character is named. Two collections of data, presented in tables 3-1 and 3-2, make this point apparent.

Table 3-1: Divine Designations in the Pentateuch

YHWH	1,820 times
Elohim	813 times (in various grammatical forms)
YHWH Elohim	Used in combination 21 times (12 in Genesis 2, 8 in Genesis 3, and 1 in Exodus 9:30)
El	34 times
Elyon	2 times (Numbers 24:14 and Deuteronomy 32:8)
El Elyon	4 times (all in Genesis 14)
El Shaddai	6 times (5 in Genesis, 1 in Exodus)
El Ro'i	1 time (Genesis 16:13)
El Olam	1 time (Genesis 21:33)
Yah	2 times (Exodus 15:2 and 17:16)

Note: Word counts of this sort are most easily obtained using Francis I. Anderson and Dean A. Forbes, *The Vocabulary of the Old Testament* (Chicago: Loyola Press, 1993). The high counts are frequently off by a small amount, but not enough to affect the resulting observations. It is more difficult to obtain them from a source such as Abraham Even-Shoshan, *A New Concordance of the Bible* (Jerusalem: Kiryat Sefer, 1990). The large numbers in this table will not match exactly in these sources because of textual problems and the difficulty of counting so many occurrences, but they are easily close enough to serve the points of comparison made here.

Table 3-2: Divine Designations in the Books of the Pentateuch

Book	Elohim	YHWH
Genesis	188	165
Exodus	65	398
Leviticus	5	311
Numbers	11	396
Deuteronomy	15	550

Two important conclusions emerge from this data. First, Genesis is the most evenly balanced of any book in its use of Elohim and YHWH, and it contains the majority of uses of the former in the Pentateuch. Second, the rare designations for God, such as the combined "YHWH Elohim" and the various "El" names, appear primarily in Genesis. The discussion of the divine character up to this point reveals a search for identity that is reflected in both behavior and naming. More significantly, there is a directional nature to this development. In the work of readers such as Humphreys and Karen Armstrong, a clear conclusion about the divine character in the first book of the Bible has emerged: "Genesis traces God's gradual disappearance from the human scene."[23] Jack Miles has described this disappearance in more precise terms: "The Lord God in [Genesis 1–11] is maximally powerful and minimally kind, whereas the God mirrored in Joseph is maximally kind and minimally powerful."[24] The differences between these two descriptions is telling, because they reveal assumptions about what it means for God to be present. Such assumptions, and the ways in which biblical theology has typically attended to them, are a subject to which we will return at the end of this chapter, and again in the final chapter of this book.

The God of the Ancestors outside of Genesis

Like the theme of creation in the previous chapter, the work of God with Israel's ancestors is a subject that arises at many places in the Hebrew Scriptures. One of the frequent uses of this tradition is as an identifier for Israel's God, who often refers to himself as "the God of your fathers, the God of Abraham, Isaac, and Jacob" (for example, Exodus 3:15; 4:5). This deity is remembered as the one who called, commanded, and made promises to these great figures in Israel's past. Abraham, for example, appears in other parts of the Hebrew Scriptures, as is illustrated in table 3-3.

Table 3-3: Abraham outside of Genesis

Exodus	9 appearances, all in 2–6 and 32–33
Leviticus	1 appearance (26:42)—note the order of Jacob, Isaac, Abraham!
Numbers	1 appearance, referring to promise of land
Deuteronomy	7 appearances, all in the "Abraham, Isaac, and Jacob" covenant formulation
Joshua	2 appearances (24:2, 3), both referring to Abraham's polytheistic origins
Kings	2 appearances: "God of Abraham" in 1 Kgs. 18:36 and a covenant reference in 2 Kgs. 13:23
Chronicles	7 appearances: three genealogical references, two "God of Abraham" descriptions, and two references to covenant
Psalms	4 appearances: Israel named as "seed of Abraham" in 105:6 and three references to covenant
Isaiah	4 appearances: YHWH as "redeemer" of Abraham in 29:22, Israel as descendants of Abraham" in 41:8, and a reference to covenant in 51:2 and 63:16
Jeremiah	1 appearance, Israel as "descendants of Abraham" in 33:26
Ezekiel	1 appearance, a reference to covenant in 33:24
Micah	1 appearance, a reference to covenant in 7:20
Nehemiah	1 appearance, a reference to covenant in 9:7

Of the thirty-two references to Isaac, all but two include Abraham and Jacob in the immediate context. Of these thirty, four are genealogical in nature, whereas the other twenty-six involve the list of the three great patriarchs, either to identify their God or to recall the covenant. This leaves Amos 7:9 and 7:16 as the only isolated references to Isaac, where his name is used as an odd poetic parallel to Israel, apparently referring to a specific portion of the northern kingdom, perhaps the region around Shechem.

Jacob's name appears by far the most often outside the Pentateuch, but this is deceiving, because it is used frequently to designate the nation of Israel, rather than as a recollection of the character in Genesis. When these names are used together in parallel, as they are about forty times in Psalms and the Prophetic literature, they serve as a reminder of that ancient, impenetrable moment on the riverbank, and recall a divine character unfathomable in any later context.

Although Old Testament theology has given adequate attention to the absence of the ancestral material and the exodus tradition in the Wisdom literature, it has rarely, if ever, asked why this is the case. Why is this material, unlike the creation traditions explored in the previous chapter, of no use to the wisdom tradition? Could it be the uneasiness and unpredictability of this deity that is the problem? Perhaps it is too easily assumed that the international character of the Wisdom literature does not match such a narrow national story. Rather, might the Wisdom literature, Job notwithstanding, require a system that is simply undone by the kind of deity who haunts the ancestral traditions? Such a presence fits only in a long-ago world.

God of the Exodus

Reading the Hebrew Scriptures as a continuous narrative yields a big surprise. The God who has been so carefully withdrawn from the human story in the book of Genesis roars back into action at the beginning of the book of Exodus. This newly emerging divine character functions in two significantly different ways, however. First, the divine actions are in response to human behavior of two very different kinds. Second, this deity needs a partner who can function as an intermediary between him and the larger human community. Much of the beginning of Exodus is spent bringing these two aspects of the divine character together. In the "narrative of oppression," which dominates the first chapter of Exodus, God has no direct response to Pharaoh's attempt to control the Hebrew people. The only act God performs is the rewarding of the midwives for their defiance of royal power.[25] In the rapid story of Moses' birth and childhood, God is never mentioned, and Moses looks much like Joseph, in whose story God was also a withdrawn character. Moses finds a place within the Egyptian palace in a process that is, at most, assisted by an unseen, providential hand.[26]

The divine reinvigoration begins in what at first seems a mere summary notation in Exod. 2:23-24: "God heard their groaning, and God remembered his covenant with Abraham, Isaac, and Jacob." If we read this behavioral description of a character about whom we had no preconceptions, we would probably take the idea of "remembering" very seriously. Because of the theological dissonance created by the idea of a God who forgets, this act of remembering is often reinterpreted. Moreover, what God remembers, the covenant made with Israel's ancestors, is often understood to be the list of things God promised to them: offspring, land, and prosperity. If we take the act of remembering by this character more seriously, however, then we might also consider the content of that memory to include the way this deity used to act in relation to those ancestors. This notice sets a tone for a feature that will dominate much of the Pentateuch. The so-called murmuring tradition is problematic in many ways, which will be explored in this chapter, but here at its starting point it must be acknowledged that this deity typically responds only to human complaint. Had the Israelites not groaned, would YHWH have remembered and liberated them? Lyle Eslinger proceeded one step further, arguing that it is precisely the fulfillment of God's promise of prolific progeny to Abraham that causes the suffering of the Israelites in Egyptian bondage.[27] This God both caused and ignored their plight, until they groaned.

Exodus 2 is composed primarily of a rapid report of the life of Moses, from his birth until the birth of his first child in Midian. The selection of elements in this sparse account seems specifically designed to recast Moses, the Egyptian prince, as a worthy leader of the Hebrew people. Who better to use as a model than Jacob? Thus, Moses flees his home, afraid for his life, meets his future wife at a well, and takes a job tending the sheep of his father-in-law.[28] The use of Jacob's story as a template for converting the fugitive, whom Zipporah and her sisters describe to their father as "an Egyptian" (2:19), into the Hebrew who will lead his people through the wilderness invites comparisons between the theophanic experiences of these two characters. The famous burning-bush episode in Exodus 3 marks the formal reappearance of this deity in a manner recognizable to anyone who has read Genesis 12–36. Not only does the voice from the bush identify itself using the names of the three great patriarchs (3:6), but it also speaks in a manner reminiscent of those earlier events. The divine name that is famously revealed and explained in this text has long been the subject of debate. It is important to remember that this deity had previously refused to reveal his name (Gen. 32:29), so Moses moves beyond the status of Jacob by receiving it. The earlier refusal perhaps makes the cryptic nature of the response here not surprising. Is the *'ehyeh 'asher 'ehyeh* really a name, or is it an evasion? Miles has argued that the phrase connects God's being and God's action, so that "I am who I am" might be rendered "I am what I do."[29] This would not be strange in light of the deity's identification in relation to Abraham, Isaac, and Jacob. This text also begins a rather lengthy negotiation about the task of Moses and the way he will mediate between this God and the Israelites.

The other reemergence here goes back to even earlier parts of Genesis. Not only does the deity in Exodus appear to humans and speak directly to them, but he also has some control over nature and uses nature to punish and manipulate human beings. The plague narratives in Exodus 7–12 recall the kind of power and control demonstrated in the flood story, the tower of Babel episode, and the destruction of Sodom and Gomorrah. At the same time, it should not be ignored that the God of Genesis never did control nature to help anyone. Even God's chosen few were forced to move out of the promised (but not so promising) land repeatedly because of famines, and they did not even question why their patron deity was unable to change these situations. In the early part of Exodus, God again has massive power, but it can be used only in a coercive manner toward Pharaoh. The use of God's power over nature to provide will have to wait until the Israelites are in the wilderness, where the problematic issues will be the timing and extent of God's helpfulness.

A God this powerful and personal is ultimately unsustainable, however, and perhaps the first sign of this in the book of Exodus is one more event that is a mirror image of an element in the life of Jacob. After his conversation with God, Moses gathers his family to return to Egypt from Midian, and Exod. 4:24-26 reports: "And it happened on the way at the lodging place that YHWH met him and sought to kill him, but Zipporah grabbed a flint and she cut off the foreskin of her son and she touched his feet. She said, 'For you are a bridegroom of blood to me.' Then he left him when she had said, 'a bridegroom of blood by circumcision.'" In many ways, of course, this text is impenetrable. On a literary level, it is not difficult to see how it completes the parallel pattern between Jacob and Moses. Still, the divine behavior here is even more perplexing than the attack and wrestling match in Genesis 32. Whereas God injured Jacob in order to escape his grasp in the earlier text, we are told in this story that he intends to kill Moses from the beginning. Whereas Jacob boasted, "I have seen God face to face and yet my life is preserved," Moses makes no such claim. Close contact with a being this powerful is dangerous, a realization that will continue to develop throughout the life of Moses.

The plague narratives bring with them a significant negotiation between divine and human power and initiative.[30] Miles has noted three aspects that are new about God's behavior in the first part of the exodus story. One of these is God's use of an intermediary, Moses. In addition, "never has [God] offered his action as a response to human skepticism." This appears most clearly in Exodus 4, when God performs a series of signs to convince a recalcitrant

Moses and offers to call Aaron as Moses' spokesperson. A final new behavior is God's exercise of "dominion over the human mind and heart."[31] The hardening of Pharaoh's heart is a tradition involving divine action that demands careful examination. This idea first comes to the surface in 4:21, in the divine forecast of the plagues, and it reappears in the prologue to the plague narratives in 7:3. It then appears in various ways within all ten of the plague accounts. The grammar and vocabulary of the appearances of this tradition, however, take three quite different forms, which vary in their assumptions of divine involvement. These three forms are described below in table 3-4.

Table 3-4: The "Hardening" Tradition

- Ten times there is an active verb with God as subject. Exod. 4:21, 7:3, 9:12, 10:1, 10:20, 10:27, 11:10, 14:4, and 14:8 all have "I [YHWH] hardened Pharaoh's heart." In 4:17, YHWH hardens the heart of the Egyptians.
- Three times there is an active verb with Pharaoh as subject. Exod. 8:15, 8:32, and 9:34 have "Pharaoh hardened his heart."
- Six times there is a passive verb with Pharaoh's heart as subject and no true agent. "Pharaoh's heart was hardened" in Exod. 7:13, 7:14, 7:22, 8:19, 9:7, and 9:35.

These three types of texts use three different verbs to express the idea, each of which may carry a different nuance of meaning.[32] When Pharaoh hardens his own heart, the verb literally means "make heavy." This type of expression appears in plagues 2, 4, and 7, a group that has other features in common.[33] This verb also appears in one case in which God is the subject (10:1) and in one case in which there is no agent (9:7). In most of the other texts, the verbal root literally means "make strong."

The puzzling nature of this divine behavior has caused many interpreters of these texts to construct defenses of God. The simplest type of defense involves the claim that the divine prerogative is simply not subject to human, moral evaluation. Such a claim, however, is inconsistent with the biblical text itself, in places such as Genesis 19, as presented earlier. When Abraham says, "Shall not the judge of all the earth do what is right?" what "right" can he mean other than right in the eyes of Abraham? God tacitly agrees with Abraham's objection. A related, but more sophisticated, argument is that the story has a purpose that lies outside the bounds of morality. Dorian Coover Cox, for example, has argued that "if the Lord had not hardened Pharaoh's heart, readers would know less about Pharaoh and less about the Lord."[34] Such an argument is obviously true, but it ignores the conclusion that the "more" we have learned about God is repulsive. Could we not have learned a different, less disconcerting "more"? Arguments that this is just a figure of speech, that it is just a way of saying Pharaoh was stubborn, ignore the observations that there are multiple ways of talking about this phenomenon in Exodus, as table 3-4 demonstrates, and that the second and third categories create no serious theological problems.[35] It is the first kind of statement that is most difficult to resolve with common understandings of God outside the text, and with presentations inside the text that we will examine at a later point.

In light of this hardening-of-the-heart tradition, it is difficult to escape the conclusion that God is deliberately prolonging the plague conflict. There are a number of places within this part of the narrative (9:14-16, 10:1-2) that indicate that one purpose of these episodes is for Egypt, Israel, and all other nations to see a demonstration of God's power and, thus, to learn their proper place in the order of things. This is the position of David Gunn, who argued further that "Egypt/Pharaoh must be made an example of, spectacularly, so that Israel, and the whole world may freely come to recognize that [YHWH] is indeed master."[36] Arguments like this go only so far, because they presume that the lesson would stop once Pharaoh had learned it. Indeed, Gunn claimed that Pharaoh had a chance to repent after each plague.[37] This conclusion ignores God's apparent prevention of such repentance ten times. More significantly, this argument fails to explain why this particular kind of demonstration of power was necessary. All attempts to explain or soften the hardening tradition ultimately fail in the harsh light of Exod. 4:23: "Then you shall say to Pharaoh, "Thus says YHWH, 'Israel is my firstborn son. I said to you, "Let my son go that he may worship me." But you refused to let him go; now I will kill your firstborn son.'" The final plague, the original Passover event, was always to be the end of the story, raising this question: To what extent is the purpose of the plagues liberation, and to what extent is it revenge? This text seems unaware of the first nine plagues, and it creates a sense of inevitability about the sequence of events. The clearest narrative sense of the variation in the language of hardening is that in the cases where the first type of language in table 3-4 is used, Pharaoh was going to repent and God had to act to stop it.

Any thorough theological understanding of the plague narratives must extend itself to include one more event, the crossing of the Red Sea by the

Israelites, followed by the drowning of Pharaoh's army. Eslinger uses the framing of the poetic account of this event in Exodus 15 as the centerpiece of his argument that the narration of the exodus story produces a sense of "existential and temporal distancing" between the reader and claims like those expressed in the Song of the Sea, in Exodus 15.[38] This poem has received perhaps an inordinate amount of attention for at least three reasons, not least of which is its dramatic position in the text. In addition, the perceived majesty of the poem as a piece of literature combines with the common conclusion that it is an ancient composition that reveals something of the origins of Hebrew poetry, and thus it is placed at the core of many discussions of Israelite religion.[39] The Red Sea tradition presents the same theological problems as the plague narratives, because the pursuit into the wilderness is caused by the first type of description indicated in table 3-4: "God hardened the heart of Pharaoh" in 14:4 and 14:8. The event at the sea in Exodus 14–15 is also part of the wilderness narrative, and its purpose there will be discussed later in this chapter. Perhaps one function it performs for the book of Exodus is to connect the two sets of stories, Israel in Egypt and Israel in the wilderness, and to provide a sense of continuity in a divine character who seems so discontinuous at this point.

God of the Exodus outside the Book of Exodus

The discussion of this subject presents problems for a reason that has been mentioned in passing a few times already in this study. If there is any tradition or story that lies at the foundation of all other biblical texts, it is the exodus. Psalm 90 illustrates well the importance of this foundational story. This psalm, which stands at the beginning of book 4 of the collection, is the only one that names Moses in its title. Psalm 89 ends with a devastating description of the end of the Davidic monarchy and the destruction of Jerusalem:

> But now you have spurned and rejected him;
> you are full of wrath against your anointed
> You have renounced the covenant with your servant;
> you have defiled his crown in the dust.
> You have broken through all his walls;
> you have laid his strongholds in ruins. (vv. 38-40)

At this juncture in the book of Psalms, the Israelites are defeated, dispersed, and taken captive by the Babylonian Empire, and the book of Psalms makes a stunning and dramatic move by employing the voice of Moses in Psalm 90 to inaugurate a new exodus from this captivity:[40]

> Turn O LORD! How long?
> Have compassion on your servants!
> Satisfy us in the morning with your steadfast love,
> so that we may rejoice and be glad all our days.
> Make us glad as many days as you have afflicted us,
> and as many years as we have seen evil. (vv. 14-15)

The sound of the voice of Moses and the recollection of his ability to summon God's deliverance remain at least a poetic reality, but whether they can be any more than that is a live question.

The reference to the exodus in 1 Samuel 4 is fleeting but telling. It appears in the Philistine response to the arrival of the ark of the covenant in the Israelite camp after the first battle of Ebenezer/Aphek, a decisive Philistine victory. This is not a description of an actual Philistine reaction, of course, but an Israelite's perception of an appropriate Philistine response. In the eyes of the Israelites, the recollection of YHWH's defeat of Pharaoh should terrify Israel's enemies. The text recognizes, however, that this is not the effect, and the Philistines easily overcome their fear and go on to inflict an even more resounding defeat against the Israelite army.[41] This defeat, and the accompanying capture of the ark, becomes part of the argument for an Israelite monarchy and a standing professional army capable of competing with the Philistines. Old stories of the divine warrior may have some symbolic power, but they no longer bring victory in the rough-and-tumble world of Iron Age Canaan.

Finally, the prophetic tradition was capable of recalling and making use of the exodus tradition. Isaiah 40, like Psalm 90, seems to cast a potential return from exile as a recurrence of the exodus motif, though the connections are vague. Much more specific is the reference in Hosea 11:1-5, but here it has a surprising double-edged quality. The voice of God both reminds the audience that God led the Israelites out of Egypt and threatens to send them back into that servitude. Although the certainty of deliverance has vanished, the recollection of it has persistent rhetorical power, particularly in this mode of reversal, which functions as a threat.[42]

God of Mount Sinai

The arrival of the Israelites at Mount Sinai in Exodus 19 is a moment of massive cognitive dissonance. The deity they encounter there lives on the mountain and requires them to come there to meet with him, but this deity somehow defeated Pharaoh in Egypt to set them free and has provided for them in the wilderness. The spatial aspect of divine presence is a subject that has been recently advanced in the work of Joel S. Burnett. In *Where Is God? Divine Absence in the Hebrew Bible*, Burnett first explored the nature of the relationship between God and Israel, noting some of its spatial characteristics, particularly its "mountainous aspect," a notion that Israel seems to have inherited from its West Semitic environment.[43] He developed this subject further in his consideration of "cosmic and terrestrial realms of divine presence and absence," by describing "structural divine presence." It becomes obvious in this discussion that there is no singular understanding of such concepts in the Old Testament, but the composite result might best be described in terms of degrees of intensity of God's presence.[44] God's intense presence at Sinai allows for lesser degrees of presence elsewhere. This understanding accounts for the differing roles of Moses, who serves as God's proxy—or even replacement, if one takes Exod. 7:1 as more than just a crude figure of speech—but who may emerge as a mediator of the intense divine presence at Sinai.

Thus, Exodus 19 is a textual juncture in a variety of ways. Source critics have strained mightily to unravel the complexities of this chapter, which is obviously composite in nature, but there has been no consensus on this point. However the text arrived in this condition, though, the end result of the confusion is an uncertainty about who can approach God, and when and why. One purpose of this uncertainty, and the danger it presents, is to establish the continuing need for Moses as an intermediary. Now that the Israelites are free from Egypt and have been successfully led to the mountain, his role might seem uncertain. Can God function without Moses from this point forward? This question will be answered with a resounding no at the conclusion of the Decalogue in Exodus 20, but even the divine character is baffled about how to proceed in 19:20-24, and Moses must guide him. It is difficult to escape the problematic theological conclusion that the divine being is acquiring a new sense of self-awareness here. This being has destroyed most of the earth once and two entire cities another time, and has twice attacked and injured or nearly killed a specifically chosen human partner. God seems aware of the danger in 19:23 and succeeds in keeping an appropriate distance from the people, if regretfully.

The legal material that fills the middle of the Torah is the first ongoing example of a principle illustrated by Moses himself: the mediation of the divine character. The need for such mediation is declared in a most straightforward manner in Exod. 20:18-21. This deity is far too dangerous and unpredictable for direct contact with ordinary human beings. Walter Brueggemann thoroughly charted this move from unmediated to mediated or "embodied" presence, with its focus in this part of the book of Exodus, describing "a prompt move to mediation."[45] Brueggemann went on to provide an extensive analysis of the five major mediators of divine presence in the Old Testament, with Torah in the first position.[46]

The juxtaposition of the three entities—God, Moses, and the Israelites—is entirely unclear in Exodus 20. In 19:25, Moses has gone down the mountain to report a divine message to the people; then, suddenly, God is speaking in 20:1. The content of this speech is what is traditionally understood as the Ten Commandments, but there is no indication of who is listening. At the end of the collection, there is a description of what the people hear in 20:18, but it is only a repetition of the theophanic fireworks from 19:16-19. Even this is enough, though, to lead to the final resolution of the matter in 20:19-21: "And [they] said to Moses, 'You speak to us, and we will listen; but do not let God speak to us or we will die'" (20:19). What the people understand so clearly, God and Moses come to accept, but not until Moses utters one of the most nonsensical lines in all of the Bible: "Do not be afraid; for God has come only to test you and put the fear of him upon you so that you do not sin" (20:20). Can Moses really be this puzzled by the people's reaction, or is this Moses expressing the thoughts of a divine character who is still not fully aware of the effect he has on human beings?

Much has been made of the apparent differences between the so-called Abrahamic covenant and the Sinai covenant. The difference that has received the most attention is probably the lack of conditionality in the former compared to the latter.[47] The narrative development of the divine character in relation to humanity might account for this difference more clearly than attempts to chart changes in the development of ancient Israelite religion. The move at Mount Sinai is one from an individual or family following a deity to whom they have direct access, to a society following a deity to whom they have only mediated access. The piling up of legal material not only provides the shape for this society, it also helps build the mediating distance between it and a dangerous deity. The law is not so much a theological condition as a narrative necessity.

In the midst of the legal material that makes up the second half of the book of Exodus lies another baffling story of divine behavior, the golden-calf episode in Exodus 32–34. It is a great temptation to search this narrative, find its secrets, and reshape them into a coherent episode of interaction between Israel and its God. Success in such a task, however, would surely be a false accomplishment. An appropriate understanding of this portion of the divine character development demands the embrace of its incoherence. God has commanded and engineered the deliverance of the Israelites and told Moses to bring them to this mountain, but now seems remarkably uncomfortable in their presence. God has been dangerous to the Israelites ever since their arrival, and there seems to be no reason for it, but the golden-calf episode provides God the excuse to be dangerous that God has so desperately needed.

The golden calf also functions as a point around which to organize the building of the tabernacle. The repetition in this part of the book of Exodus is astounding. The divine command of much of Exodus 25–31 is simply converted to a narration of construction in Exodus 35–40, by changing second-person verbs into third-person verbs. This has the feel of textual stalling, and perhaps this is the strategy, because monumental shifts are taking place that should not pass quickly. The tabernacle signifies an important transition in the development of the divine character. The completion of the tent allows the deity to move off of the mountaintop and into a structure at the base of the mountain. Aside from saving Moses a lot of climbing, this move domesticates the divine character. At the end of the book of Exodus, God moves in the form of a cloud and takes up residence in the tabernacle. Throughout the book of Leviticus that follows, Moses will go in and out of the tent to perform his mediating work. Brueggemann has placed additional emphasis here on the significance of the divine movement into the midst of Israel. There is a sense of availability and accessibility, as Brueggemann states, and this idea fits comfortably into his insertion of the tabernacle building into a full discussion of the temple cult.[48] But when this construction project is placed back at Sinai in the midst of the divine fireworks on the mountain and the harrowing experience of the Israelites in the wilderness, with the golden-calf event, including the slaughter of three thousand Israelites (32:28) and a deadly plague nearby (32:35), it looks more like a dangerous deity is being wrapped in layers of separation from a people he cannot keep from harming.

The multiplying of mediating institutions as the narrative progresses here is reflected in the layering of the text. Although the actual ordination of the priests will wait for Leviticus 8–10, their existence is presumed here in the ordination instructions and in the inclusion within the tabernacle construction of the fabrication of priestly garments and equipment. The tabernacle is a precursor to the temple in Jerusalem, of course, and the priesthood is an indispensable part of this structure that will be not only the divine dwelling but also the place to which the people will come to interact with God's mediated presence. Therefore, it is difficult for any part of the complex to come first chronologically, for all of the aspects—structure, personnel, implements, and processes—are part of an intricate and interdependent system. Developing this system under the harsh gaze of a demanding deity will be an ongoing problem.[49]

Up to this point, I have been treating Exodus 32–34 as a unit I call the golden-calf episode, and there are significant ways, as I have described, that these chapters function as a cohesive unit in this part of the book of Exodus; but there are two elements of Exodus 33-34 that require more careful, individual attention. The fascinating theophany in Exod. 33:17-23 has been the focal point of Howard Schwartz's work on the embodiment of God. In this text, in which Moses requests and is granted an opportunity to see YHWH, the divine character has a hand, a back, and a face. During the experience, the divine hand covers Moses while YHWH passes by, and Moses is allowed to see the back but not the face. This passage contains virtually all of the difficulties inherent in analyzing this issue of embodiment or anthropomorphism. There are many texts in the Hebrew Scriptures in which God's face and hand are used purely metaphorically, to represent presence and power respectively, so they do not represent true embodiment. It is also unclear to what extent this experience is a vision or its opposite, something that exists materially within the world of ordinary human experience. Schwartz has brought two additional issues into clearer focus in his discussion of this text. The first is the challenge of understanding figurative language that comes to us from a very different culture. It is difficult in these cases both to distinguish figurative language and then to determine its meaning, because our frame of reference is so different from that of the writers.[50] The second problem is that there are clearly competing traditions in the Hebrew Bible concerning the ability of human beings to see God.[51] However these issues are resolved, this text stands apart from those in Genesis that I have discussed, because it is not a normal human interaction. Moreover, the ability of God to cover Moses with a hand implies a body of greater than normal human size. Like earlier texts, this one gives no indication of the age of this body. In these and other ways, this embodiment does not fit in our modern experience.

The second element that requires closer attention is the famous creedal statement in Exod. 34:6-7. This text will receive further treatment at various points in this study, because it is repeated in whole or in part in numerous texts outside of the book of Exodus. The powerful, descriptive statement of the divine being comes from YHWH's own mouth, so it may be the most important self-disclosure of God's character in the Bible:

> The LORD, the LORD,
> a God merciful and gracious,
> slow to anger,
> and abounding in steadfast love and faithfulness,

keeping steadfast love for the thousandth generation,
forgiving iniquity and transgression and sin,
yet by no means clearing the guilty,
but visiting the iniquity of the parents
upon the children
and the children's children,
to the third and the fourth generation.[52]

The most striking aspect of this statement is its conflicted nature. The statement functions as the core of Brueggemann's discussion of the use of adjectives to talk about God in the Old Testament.[53] This is not only because of the relative dearth of adjectives used to describe characters, including God, in the Hebrew Scriptures but also because of the summative and synthetic power of this particular text. The passage is ideally suited for dialogical approaches, because it seems to debate itself when moving from its first half to its second. Brueggemann notes that the reuses of this text tend to focus upon the "positive" first half of the utterance.[54] Following the narrative approach of this study requires an acknowledgment that the divine character says all of this as a statement of self-disclosure at a single time. The virtue of this statement is that it matches the depiction of the divine character throughout the exodus–wilderness–Sinai drama. This character is so conflicted as to be unpredictable; indeed, in the end, this statement functions as a divine confession to Moses, that the God who has chosen and commissioned him is thoroughly unpredictable, a reality that Moses has already experienced and will see repeatedly in forty years to come. A large part of Moses' task will be to manage and mediate this unpredictability.

A lingering set of questions about Moses himself, the answers to which will say something important about the God for whom he works, finally come to some resolution here. Exod. 34:29-35 is somewhat difficult to interpret and has a checkered history, but it clearly says that Moses' physical appearance has been changed. This change limits his ability to interact with humans freely and directly, and is a reflection of the divine character's need for mediated presence. The separation of Moses from the human community of the Israelites is fully recognized here, but he never really fit into this group. In retrospect, this quality of Moses has something to do with his being chosen in the first place. YHWH is a deity who, in the biblical story thus far, has come to the Israelites as an uneasy stranger. YHWH encounters the Israelites in odd ways and struggles to be a usable deity for them, at least as much as they struggle to be a usable people for him.

The construction of the tabernacle has been addressed, but its reuse to close the book of Exodus merits a moment of reiteration. The way in which this text is wrapped around the terror and struggle of Exodus 32–34 is a reflection of the wrapping of the temple cult around the dangerous presence of YHWH. The cloud of smoke that descends from the mountain in 40:34-35 as a visual representation of this presence reminds the reader of so many clouds before, not least the one that seemed to swallow Moses in 20:21, when the Israelites first arrived at Sinai, encountered this deity, and realized their need and desire for distance. The fearful gap is bridged by the character of Moses. Miles has captured this in his stunning observation that "the volcano has come to live in the tent because the tent was built by the volcano's friend."[55]

The nature of the book of Leviticus raises significant questions about the divine character and how it is being portrayed within the narrative flow of the Old Testament. The opening words of the book set the tone for its entirety: this is a book that is dominated by the divine voice, largely disembodied. Given this feature of the book, it would be easy to understand it as a pause in or retraction from the divine story. Stephen K. Sherwood has emphasized the very different operation of time in the book of Leviticus. Because the book is made up almost entirely of divine speech, what is understood as narrative time is almost the same as the narration time.[56] The result is that the passage of time virtually disappears in the book. The recognition of this feature will force great emphasis onto the one episode in the book that varies from this pattern: the ordination of the priests in Leviticus 8–10.

Wilfred Warning has produced the most significant attempt to provide a sense of structure and development to all of this divine speech. Warning divided Leviticus into a series of thirty-seven divine speeches, which can be identified by the "And YHWH spoke . . ." formula.[57] The vast majority of these divine utterances take place in the tabernacle, with Moses as the audience. I will examine some of the individual components of this massive collection, but if it is taken as a whole, it is difficult to escape the feeling of being overwhelmed by divine speech. It is important to remember at all times that, as readers, we are placed inside the tent with Moses, listening to divine speech. The assumption of the book is that Moses eventually emerges from the tent and repeats all of this speech to the Israelites, but Leviticus does not show us this aspect. If it did, then the book of Leviticus would be nearly twice as long and would share the redundant quality of the tabernacle-building in Exodus 25–40. This literary design allows the reader to encounter the divine voice safely, as the written text now does for us the work of mediation that Moses does for the characters inside the story.

The book of Leviticus opens with seven chapters of instructions for priests concerning the offering of sacrifices. In the context of this study, this so-called Manual of Sacrifice forces questions about what such ritual does to, and says about, the divine character. Sacrificial ritual is, of course, a significant part of the mediation of divine presence. The various offerings are significantly different in their purposes, and the ways in which they mediate divine presence cannot be understood as all the same. Perhaps the most significant difference is between offerings that are regular in nature and are, therefore, part of maintaining the relationship between God and the Israelites, and those which are responses to specific problems. This latter type includes the "sin offerings" described in Leviticus 4–5,[58] and it continues to emphasize the dangerous nature of the deity. In both Exodus and Numbers, we see a God who is constantly on the verge of breaking out against the Israelites. The Manual of Sacrifice reveals that, ordinarily, this threat can be kept at bay by a regular practice of ritual offering. James Watts has argued that the final form of Leviticus 1–7 has a distinct rhetorical purpose that explains its repetitive style: it is designed to be read aloud in order to convince its audience of the authority of the Torah over sacrificial ritual.[59] An important part of this argument is the distinction it makes between literary descriptions of sacrificial rituals and the ritual acts themselves. The final form of Leviticus is literature intended for theological persuasion rather than a cookbook-like set of instructions for priests. This view need not be denied in order to insist further that this literature plays a role in developing the divine character who speaks it and is presumed within it.

Leviticus 8–10 comprises the only large narrative section of the book. The internal development of this section, its relation to other ritual texts, and its place in the history of Israelite religion have all been the subject of significant scholarly discussion. The primary concern in this study is the divine behavior in this text, which points toward one feature that connects 8–10 with the rest of Leviticus: the refrain "according to the command of YHWH," which appears thirteen times in these three chapters. The effect of this repeated reminder, which is present in both narration and the speech of Moses and Aaron, is to remind the reader and the audience inside the story that the human actions presented here are the result of divine intent, expressed in the divine speech that dominates the entire book. Lest the divine character fully disappear behind layers of mediation, here is a reminder of a potentially aggressive presence. This aggression erupts in the story of Nadab and Abihu, the two sons of Aaron, who are killed by God in Leviticus 10. Watts is likely correct when he argues, contrary to the majority of interpreters, that this section "legitimates and defends the priests' monopoly."[60] Rather than illustrating priestly disobedience,

Nadab and Abihu prove that priestly failure is uncommon. When priests fail, swift divine retribution follows, which suggests that at all other times, the work of priests is legitimate. The story of Nadab and Abihu is "a momentary reversal of the theme of compliance."[61] It may be an unintended consequence of this story that the dangerous and impulsive divine character evident on Mount Sinai in Exodus 32–34 and about to be revealed more fully in Numbers is revealed as still present behind all of this mediated speech. If this is true, then something profound and troubling is happening to the divine character here. Punitive action is presented as overt and deadly, and the lack of overt divine action becomes presumed approval.

The divine character soon retreats once again, speaking only in the tent to Moses and Aaron about a variety of seemingly mundane subjects, such as food, childbirth, skin conditions, and bodily discharges. Miles has argued that Leviticus serves as "a breather in God's story."[62] One might wonder and ask whom this breather is for. In many ways, the building of the tabernacle is like the creation story in Genesis 1, and at the end of the latter, God needs to rest.[63] Miles clarified his own understanding of this, however, in a set of observations about the effect of the book of Leviticus, which "contained the object of their fear in a complex set of rituals designed to guarantee Israel's purity, immunity, and safety." This set of rituals functions as a "symbolic domestication" of God, because "one cannot be bored and terrified at once."[64] It is Israel that needs a rest. Still, the emphasis on purity here seems a veiled reminder of the danger of the deity, which seems accentuated by the preceding story of Aaron's sons.

The most influential voice in the discussion of the laws of Leviticus and the general subject of purity in recent years has been Mary Douglas. Douglas's groundbreaking work, *Purity and Danger: An Analysis of Concepts of Pollution and Taboo*, is primarily anthropological in nature, so it says little directly about the divine character whose voice presents the laws of Leviticus, but it has established the framework for the discussion of these texts and ideas for the last four decades.[65] So, it is in response to Douglas that John Sawyer produced a most helpful line of argument on this subject, which applies to the entirety of the legal material in the book. Whereas the focus of interpreters has often been on these texts as artifacts for the study of the history of Israelite religion, the framework for understanding them in that way has been obscured by their placement within a written text that has an overall narrative quality.[66] Thus, they no longer seem usable as a coherent set of instructions but testify more clearly to the nature of the characters involved in the story, including God.

The divine character reemerges in more direct fashion in Leviticus 16, the description of the Day of Atonement. Warning has presented an elaborate argument concerning the connectedness of this chapter with Leviticus 8–10, in many more ways than simply the recollection of Nadab and Abihu in 16:1. The "repetitive resumption" of "and they died," which connects 16:1 back to 10:2 also leads into the warnings against priestly error in 16:2 and 16:13.[67] Again, it is priests, as mediators, who face the deadly danger of divine wrath in this otherwise placid book. The now familiar scene of animal sacrifice accentuates the puzzling surprise to come as the ritual progresses. No interpreter truly knows what to do with the Azazel figure, who appears only in this text, and some English translations disguise the difficulty by rendering the term as "scapegoat." The critical question in relation to the identity and development of the divine character is whether some of its traits are being relegated to this mysterious figure. It is a good place to admit to the unresolved frustration that sometimes accompanies the search for this elusive divine character, who so often lies outside the edges of our vision. The text does not let us look for long, though, before it beckons us back, through its characteristic mode of divine speech, to more ordinary concerns.

Whether Leviticus 17–26, typically called the Holiness Code, represents an originally separate and distinct source now incorporated into the book of Leviticus, matters little to this study.[68] It is sufficient to observe that the literary features of this section are distinctive enough to make this label and its assumptions viable in the discussion of Leviticus. The divine self-introductory formula, which most characterizes this part of Leviticus, appears first, in its shorter form, "I am YHWH," in 18:5. The longer form, "I am YHWH your God," first appears in 18:29. The phrase appears frequently throughout chapters 17–26 until it finally punctuates the entire legal collection in 26:45. The structure of this long collection of laws is designed to remind the hearer constantly who is speaking. Leviticus 17–26 contains seventeen of the thirty-seven divine speeches that Warning identified in the book.[69] An end is clearly marked in the summative statement in 26:46: "These are the statutes and ordinances and laws that the LORD established *between* himself and the people of Israel on Mount Sinai *through* Moses" (emphasis added). It is difficult to imagine that the effects of the book of Leviticus could be disclosed more clearly than this, yet the probative perfection of this statement also serves to expose the jumbled incoherence of the final chapter of the book.[70] The collapse of coherence in Leviticus 27, however, is a realistic acknowledgment of what must inevitably follow.

In many ways, the divine character of Numbers 1–10 is an extension of the one found in the book of Leviticus. It is difficult for the Israelites to leave Mount Sinai. They will now be carrying a dangerous presence with them, and this will require careful coordination. The God of the mountain, whom they came to worship, will now depart with them and become a God of the wilderness. The orderliness of law will give way to the wild chaos of the desert. The opening chapters of Numbers will attempt to counter this chaos with the careful enumeration and organization of the Israelites through a census, marching orders, and campsite assignments, but this orderliness will often be overwhelmed.

The God of Mount Sinai outside the Torah

The preeminent text about Sinai outside of the Torah is 1 Kings 19, the only time anybody ever attempts to return to YHWH's mountainous abode. The story of Elijah at the mountain, which this text calls "Horeb" (19:8), is brief and enigmatic. It seems that YHWH helps Elijah on the forty-day journey from Israel back to the mountain, but then meets him with the strange question, uttered twice, "What are you doing here, Elijah?" (19:9, 13). At first, Elijah's experience in this place looks and sounds tantalizingly like that of the Israelites in Exodus 19, but the noisy theophany evaporates into silence, and YHWH sends Elijah away. This is no place for even the greatest of prophets.

The ongoing story of Mount Sinai is a subject of mystery. The actual location is long forgotten, but in the biblical tradition it becomes something other than a geographical location. Jon D. Levenson compared this mystery to the other great forgotten locations in Israelite tradition: "In fact, so unavailable is that Mosaic mode of revelation that even the site of the grave of the great prophet is unknown. It is surely no coincidence that the site of Mount Sinai is similarly unknown. The legacy of Mount Sinai, what Jewish tradition calls Torah in the broadest sense, endured. But the mountain itself long ago vanished from the consciousness of Israel."[71] It is easy enough to say, on one level, that Sinai needed to be eliminated as a potential, or ultimate, site for religious pilgrimages, if the temple in Jerusalem was to flourish as such a site, but the effectiveness of the move is stunning. This means we must look for Sinai differently in the ongoing story of God. Mount Sinai appears by name only 4 times outside the Torah, and its Deuteronomic equivalent, Horeb, only 5 additional times. The word *torah*, however, appears 164 times outside of the first five books of the Bible; its synonymous partners, translated by words such as "commandments," "statutes," and "ordinances," add many more appearances to the list, too numerous to catalog here, but a few prominent ones must be addressed.

It may seem counterintuitive to connect the Torah to the book of Psalms, but the word *torah* itself appears far more in the book of Psalms than any other book of the Bible.[72] Our understanding of the process that shaped the book of Psalms is vague, but a general outline has emerged in recent scholarship. One of the apparent stages of this process took a collection of poems shaped by the story of Israel's monarchy in the current Psalms 2–89 and added a different framework. Oddly, this framework, which produced the current Psalms 1–119 sequence, is sometimes characterized as one generated by the wisdom tradition, but much more powerful are the matching expressions about Torah in 1:1-2 and 119:1. Eventually, the addition of the Songs of Ascents sequence, in 120–34, and the Hallelujah Psalms, in 146–50, would further subsume Israel's hymnic tradition to the Second Temple hierarchy, but the retention of the remnants of this Torah framework in the canonical book of Psalms helps to ensure the continuing presence of the God of Sinai in a portion of the biblical tradition where it might seem most foreign.[73] Furthermore, the whole of Psalm 119 stands like Sinai in the book of Psalms, its 176 verses approximately seventeen times the length of the average psalm. It is really a sequence of twenty-two eight-verse psalms, one for each of the twenty-two letters of the Hebrew alphabet, in which the word *torah* and its three closest synonyms appear approximately one hundred times. The divine character in this massive poem is the source of all of these laws, commandments, statutes, and ordinances that promise happiness to those who observe them. The light and sound of the mountain are gone, like the geographical location of the mountain itself, but this is how Israel wanted it all along. The ordered mathematics of acrostic poetry mediates the presence of the divine character, and all trace of fright is gone.

One final, prominent appearance of the God of Sinai outside of the Torah is in the great recital of Nehemiah 9. This text will receive extensive attention in the final chapter of this book, but it requires brief mention here. The recollection of Sinai in Neh. 9:13-14 is brief, but it does at least three important things. First, by opening with "You came down also upon Mount Sinai, and spoke with them from heaven . . . ," it connects this past event with God's present, more removed location. It also recalls the role of Moses, at the same time distinguishing him from Ezra, who now only reads the written law. Finally, it promotes Sabbath, perhaps the most culturally portable law, as the centerpiece of all the laws.

God of the Wilderness

The primary collection of wilderness narratives is in Numbers 10–21. This collection is bounded by the departure from Mount Sinai in Numbers 10 and the strange, detached story of Balaam in Numbers 22–24. Within the narrative of the Torah, Numbers 10–21 forms the bulk of the forty-year wilderness journey of the Israelites and offers an important expansion and reflection of the brief, three-month wilderness episode in Exodus 16–18. This part of Numbers is dominated by a series of complaint stories, listed in table 3-5, which firmly establish the "murmuring tradition."

Table 3-5: Wilderness Complaint Stories in Numbers

11:1-3	General complaining at Taberah
11:4-35	Craving for meat
12:1-16	Aaron and Miriam challenge Moses' leadership
14:1-12	Reaction to the report from the spies
16:12-40	The rebellion of Korah
16:41-50	Complaints about the killing of the Korah group
17:1—18:7	The selection of the Levites
20:1-13	The waters of Meribah
21:1-9	The bronze serpent

The story of the quails in Num. 11:4-35 reveals new facets of the divine character. God's surprise that the Israelites need food and water in the wilderness is a puzzling feature that first arises in Exodus 16–17. There is a small amount of contentiousness in those earlier stories of divine provision in the wilderness, but the anger that erupts in Numbers 11 is of an entirely different magnitude. On the other side of Sinai, this response reflects the divine reaction to the golden calf in Exodus 32. Num. 11:33 reports that YHWH struck the Israelites with a great plague in the wake of the quail episode. The divine character is conflicted here, uncertain whether to provide for or attack the people, and the plague hits them while the meat from the quails is still "between their teeth." It may be in his observation of the wilderness episodes in Numbers that Miles's narrative analysis reaches its most powerful level: "The profound originality of a divine-human pact in which both parties complain endlessly about each other has too rarely been acknowledged as such."[74]

As is noted earlier, the pattern of complaint in the exodus story is established early in Exod. 2:23-25, when the groaning of the Israelites in slavery reminds their forgetful God of promises made long ago. This pattern is advanced in the brief collection of wilderness stories prior to the arrival at Mount Sinai in Exodus. After the intricate and laborious process of extracting the Israelites from the brutal oppression of Pharaoh, there seems to have been no plan for the basic sustenance of these people in the wilderness. After all, their requests are merely for food and water, as they are watching their children die of thirst and hunger. This is true unless the complaining is part of the plan. God needs to hear from the Israelites what they need before providing it. The difficulty with this explanation is that it fails to explain the divine anger, which may be muted enough to pass over in Exodus 16–17 but which overflows all bounds of reason in Numbers 11–20. Within the field of biblical theology, the blame for all of this conflict is often too easily passed off onto the stubborn Israelites alone. Interpreters who take this view are following biblical precedents such as Psalm 106 and Neh. 9:16-22, but they typically fail to ask what the Judahites of the restoration period might have to gain by disparaging the faith of their ancestors. Neither is it difficult to find the accusations against the Israelites even in direct divine speeches to Moses, such as in Num. 14:11-12 or 14:26-27. However, the former of these complaints misses two important points: "And the LORD said to Moses, 'How long will this people despise me? And how long will they refuse to believe in me, in spite of all the signs that I have done among them? I will strike them with pestilence and disinherit them, and I will make of you a nation greater and mightier than they'" (14:11-12). The first problem is the failure of the divine character to acknowledge that all the "signs and wonders" are triggered by the complaints of the Israelites. The second is that Moses, whom God proposes as a progenitor for an entirely new people, has been just as much of a complainer (see Num. 11:10-15, for example). How would a new people sired by him be any different? Again, Miles has recognized the point that so many others have missed:

> God is not a stoic, does not teach stoicism, does not honor or encourage resignation or acceptance, and is, by and large, impossible to please. In each of these regards, Israel is made in his image. Which is not to say that God ever acknowledges Israel as a chip off the old denunciatory block. Nothing of the sort: He complains endlessly about their complaining. And yet, from the outside, a certain symmetry may be seen, never more clearly than in the Book of Numbers, as Israel complains about Moses, Moses complains about Israel, God complains about Israel, Israel complains about God, God complains about Moses, and Moses complains about God.[75]

The divine character needs a complaining Israel with and against whom to develop, and the repetitions of this pattern place tremendous emphasis on this stage of the divine character's development.[76]

The sheer weight of the wilderness stories is difficult to manage. It may be that the writer of the book of Numbers sensed this and offered the strange story of Balaam as a respite. The most striking element of the Numbers 22–24 episode is the sudden absence of Moses from the narrative. This liminal figure, part human and part divine, has been present in every chapter of the Torah since Exodus 2. His disappearance generates three possible explanations for its occurrence in the text. First, because Moses' death was predicted for the first time in Num. 20:12, and this prediction was followed by the death of Aaron, perhaps the writer meant for readers to think that Moses might be dead. Second, and less jolting, is the possibility that the writer is beginning to develop a sense of an ongoing story without Moses in it. Third, the absence of Moses in the story may cause readers to notice with greater clarity that the divine character is still present and active in Numbers 22–24. The divine story may not be dependent on the presence of Moses after all, but it will have to prove this. If this final line of reasoning is true, then the presentation of the divine character in the Balaam narratives trips over its own goal to some extent, because the divine behavior is startlingly uncertain. God first appears in 22:9 after Balaam's initial contact with the emissaries of Balak, the Moabite king. In Numbers 22, God does four things: tells Balaam not to go with the men, tells Balaam to go with the men, gets angry at Balaam for going and tries to block his way, and then tells Balaam to go with them. By contrast, it is Balaam who is the picture of consistency, who does everything God tells him to do and even stands up in the face of human power in 23:26 and 24:12-13, refusing to do anything other than what YHWH has told him to do. Perhaps the most encouraging aspect of this odd story is that it demonstrates YHWH's commitment to blessing Israel, but if this is an indication of where the divine character is going as Moses begins to fade from view, then the value of such a blessing is in question. If the Balaam story is strange and disconcerting, this sense is easily surpassed by the nature of its ongoing life in later Israelite traditions. In biblical texts from Deut. 23:3-4 to Joshua 24:9-10 to 2 Pet. 2:15, the faithful Balaam is transformed into a villain in ways that make sense only as attempts to transfer the uncertainty of the divine character in Numbers 22–24 onto him. The particulars of these interpretations are not a matter of great importance here except as an indicator of how far an extrapolated tradition can wander when the initial direction in which the text points is so odd. This deity is not ready to be without Moses yet.[77]

The remainder of the book of Numbers looks like a disjointed collection of laws and narratives. The most significant divine actions occur in the wild Baal of Peor story, in Numbers 25. In many ways, this narrative reflects the golden-calf episode in Exodus: it is triggered by worship of another deity. The resulting divine anger brings a plague upon the Israelites, and the effects are mitigated by the action of a member of the tribe of Levi, another indication that the story may be moving away from the necessity of Moses. The event is followed by the second census in Numbers 26, just as the golden-calf episode precedes the first census. This second census assures YHWH that everyone from the previous census is dead, except for Joshua and Caleb (24:64–65). In some ways, this episode also continues the wilderness tradition, except that it is not instigated by complaint. The text never says so directly, but it would seem that the lesson the divine character should be learning here is that the forty years of wandering have had no effect; this generation behaves just like the one before it. Perhaps there is a tacit acknowledgment of this in the lack of a parallel punishment. There is no second forty years of wandering imposed. Instead, attention turns almost immediately to the occupation of Canaan, a process that receives divine approval on both ends of the section in God's commands concerning the daughters of Zelophehad, in 27:11 and 36:10. In between these two points of divine approval, the Israelites fight battles, draw boundaries, and elect leaders, often without direct divine guidance.

Deuteronomy is the most difficult book, up to this point, to fit into the narrative flow of Israel's story, but the challenge of placing Deuteronomy within the organization of this chapter says something important about what this book is. The chaos of wilderness cannot have the final say in the Torah, but the Israelites cannot go back to Sinai. Deuteronomy is a book on the verge. It is not really set in the wilderness, but the Israelites have not yet entered the promised land. God is no longer commanding, but the Israelites are still receiving commandments. The exodus and wilderness stories are in the past, but the book opens with a reiteration of those stories. All of these factors serve as a narrative reflection of the development of Israel's legal tradition. Although it is all placed back in the Torah, on the lips of God and Moses, the development of such laws is obviously the process of the complex negotiations of life in a human society. The chicken-and-egg cliché is at work here. The Israelites cannot function as a society without the law, but the law can be formed only through societal interaction.[78]

For the bulk of Deuteronomy, the Israelites do nothing but listen, and an important change takes place here in voice, as the divine character moves further into the shadows and Moses does all of the speaking, until the divine voice directly enters the narrative at 31:14. Earlier parts of Deuteronomy contain what some interpreters refer to as "divine speeches," but it is important to recognize that even these are reported secondhand by Moses, such as at 1:6–8.[79] This does not represent a significant change for the characters inside the narrative, who, ever since that dramatic moment at Sinai in Exod. 20:19-21, have heard the voice of Moses transmitting the words of God, though Patrick D. Miller has claimed that the mode of Moses' speech shifts subtly in Deuteronomy as he teaches or instructs the Israelites in YHWH's law.[80] For the reader, however, the change is significant, as the divine voice goes silent in the book of Deuteronomy until its final few chapters. Readers overhear Moses speaking to the Israelites, rather than YHWH speaking to Moses, as in Leviticus.

The death of Moses looms over the end of Deuteronomy, and the involvement of the divine character becomes more overt as this event approaches, but this divine activity will be addressed further later in this chapter, because there is divine behavior of a mediated sort going on in the beginning and the middle of Deuteronomy. Dennis Olson has produced a compelling argument that the death of Moses is the unifying theme throughout the entire book of Deuteronomy. He has located twelve explicit references to Moses' death dispersed throughout the book and has argued that "Moses was a reminder that the full experience of the Promised Land would always in some ways be beyond their [the Israelites'] grasp. Moses' demise is a metaphor for the necessary and inevitable losses and limits of human life and power before God."[81] It is understandable why everyone involved would be disconcerted by this pending death: the Israelites would have to wonder how they would continue to communicate with God, God would wonder how he could continue to communicate with the Israelites, and the writer would have to wonder how to continue to tell the story without the central character of Moses upon whom to focus.

Moses begins his opening speech in Deuteronomy by recounting the events of the exodus, the wilderness travels, and the visit to Mount Sinai. The power of YHWH lies behind everything Moses says. He is speaking to a new generation that did not witness the power of YHWH in Egypt or at Sinai, so the reiteration of the exodus story, leading up to a reformulation of the Ten Commandments in Deuteronomy 5, is a formative event for this group. It is easy to see how these Israelites would become captivated by Moses, which is one reason that constant reminders of his pending death, such as at 1:37, 3:23-27, 4:21-22, and 5:25-27, may be necessary. Indeed, as is indicated in the first chapter of this study, Jerome Segal has argued that Moses has become a problem for God by this point in the story, but the double mediation of law through Moses has offered a way out. In Segal's words, "[God] is becoming less in need of Moses, less in need of a human intermediary who will protect the Israelites from [God]. What happens is that just as Moses is becoming more problematic for God, he is becoming more dispensable."[82]

In Num. 20:12 and 27:12-14, the first time Moses' death seemed close at hand, his own behavior at Meribah was blamed for this pending event, which sounded like a punishment. The view of Moses' death in Deuteronomy is significantly different. In Deut. 4:21, Moses blames his pending death on the Israelites, who were the cause of YHWH's misdirected anger at Moses. By the end of Deuteronomy, God seems preoccupied with the death of Moses. It is the first thing God speaks of directly in 31:14. Peter Vogt is correct that the primary theme of the book of Deuteronomy is "the supremacy of Yahweh,"[83] but he does not identify Moses as the primary threat to that supremacy. When YHWH returns to the death of Moses just two verses later, in 31:16, it becomes obvious that this is the primary divine concern. At this point, death is forestalled only by two very long poems recited by Moses. The Song of Moses, in 32:1-43, is first, and as soon as Moses is finished, God returns to the subject of Moses' death in 32:48-50. The Blessing of Moses fills Deuteronomy 33 and stalls for time again, but then the climactic moment can be delayed no longer. The final chapter of Deuteronomy is a stunning piece of literature. Readers suddenly find themselves once again on top of a mountain with only YHWH and Moses, and the rest of the story fades away into the distance as our gaze aligns with the gaze of Moses, who sees the Promised Land already divided by tribal boundaries. The visual tour is swift, however, as YHWH kills Moses in 34:5. There is no reference to divine punishment here, and the expressions about Moses are laudatory, but 34:7 makes it clear that he did not die of natural causes.[84]

The process of recollecting that dominates so much of Deuteronomy, along with the withdrawal of direct divine presence, seems to be moving in the same direction in terms of divine characterization, as we observed at the end of Genesis. Even when the divine character appears directly in the story again, he is alone on a mountain with Moses, and Moses stands between the divine character and the view of the reader.

God of the Wilderness outside the Torah

This is a character difficult to find in the remainder of the Old Testament, but it is not surprising that such volatility might be muted in portrayals subsequent to the Torah. There are hints of the complaint stories found in the cyclical narratives of Judges 2–16, but here it might be appropriate to take the language of "mediation," used thus far to describe the development of God's presence in the biblical story, and utilize it to describe the process of punishment. Although the book of Judges, and the remainder of the Deuteronomistic History, understands God to be the ultimate cause of Israel's misfortune, the proximate cause consistently becomes the armies of the surrounding nations. With this mediation of divine punishment comes a sense of expectation, regularity, and inevitability that moves away from the surprising and impetuous deity of the wilderness in the book of Numbers.

The poetry of Psalms finds in the wilderness experience and its divine presence an effective image, particularly in Psalms 78 and 106. Psalm 78 is a long poem centered around the wilderness experience, much of which reviews the traditions found in Exodus and Numbers in significant detail. The singer opens with the admission in verse 2b that "I will utter dark sayings from of old." Dozens of verses go on to accuse the Israelites of faithlessness and rebellion in the wilderness, to justify YHWH's wrath in response, and to extol YHWH's mercy for not utterly destroying these people. Readers may wonder about the purpose of all of this bashing of the ancestors, but elements in the framework of the song reveal it. Those being denounced are named in verse 10 as Ephraimites, and the result of their disobedience is described in verses 67-68:

> He rejected the tent of Joseph,
> he did not choose the tribe of Ephraim;
> But he chose the tribe of Judah,
> Mount Zion, which he loves.

It is more than surprising that one tribe of Israelites could look back on this tradition and place all of the blame on another tribe, that the struggles of the ancestors would become ammunition for internal accusations in later disputes, but this songwriter looks back on the wilderness experience as the beginning point of the divine choice to make Jerusalem the site of the temple.

Psalm 106 contains a stunning catalog of the sins of Israel in the wilderness and the resulting divine responses, but it is very important to notice the framework around this retelling of the tale, too. This is the poem that closes book 4 of the book of Psalms, which began in Psalm 90 with the voice of Moses pleading with YHWH to "turn" and "have compassion on your servants." Psalm 106 begins with a hallelujah like the hymns of praise that dominate the end of the book, but at verse 6 it turns to confession of sin. Although the singer acknowledges that "both we and our ancestors have sinned," the next forty verses describe the sins of the ancestors, including twenty-seven verses describing the wilderness period. The lack of any description of current sins leaves the unmistakable impression that they pale in comparison to the sins of old. The final lines of the story of the ancestors, in verses 44–46, include a remarkable claim:

> Nevertheless he regarded their distress
> when he heard their cry.
> For their sake he remembered his covenant,
> and showed compassion according to the abundance of his
> steadfast love.
> He caused them to be pitied
> by all who held them captive.

There is nothing in the biblical tradition to which this final statement might be connected. Instead, it seems to acknowledge the present reality of the defeated and dispersed Israelites. These lines are followed by a request in verse 47 as the psalm draws to a close:

> Save us, O LORD our God
> and gather us from among the nations,
> That we may give thanks to your holy name
> and glory in your praise.

If this request is to be a reality in the world in which the Israelites who shaped the book of Psalms and the final form of the Hebrew Scriptures lived, then it depends upon subtle divine influence on the mighty empires that shape this world, rather than upon the overt, mighty actions of the God who freed the Israelites from Egypt and led them through the wilderness. This is a request for a kind of divine assistance portrayed in books such as Daniel, Esther, and Ezra-Nehemiah, which will be explored more fully in chapter 6 of this book.

The odd appearances of the wilderness tradition in Hosea 13 and Ezekiel 16 are difficult to reconcile with the wilderness story found in the Torah. It is not uncommon in human experience to look back at a time of struggle through a romantic lens. This phenomenon has been given a name, the "golden-age mentality." The portrayal of the wilderness period in Hosea 13 as a honeymoon between God and God's new bride, Israel, might seem the ultimate example of this way of remembering. Some of this also seems present in Ezekiel 16, which includes the image of Israel as an abandoned baby in the wilderness, rescued by God, who waits for her to grow up and marry her. Ezekiel 20 follows a more traditional path, criticizing the disobedience of the Israelites in the wilderness, but it takes the initial step of linking this rebellion of the past to the ultimate destruction and dispersion of Israel in 20:23. The references to the forty years in the wilderness in Amos 2:10 and 5:25 are fleeting, but they emphasize two factors about the ancient relationship between God and the nascent Israel: God's faithful deliverance and the lack of any demand by God for gifts of sacrifice in return for this deliverance.

The distant recollection of the wilderness is a flexible paradigm, but whether it illustrates deliverance and care or rebellion and punishment, it recalls a time long ago when the relationship between God and Israel was immediate. These remembrances serve the purposes of prophets and poets urging obedience in worlds that are significantly more complex, where the direct hand of Israel's God is not so readily apparent.

The Commanding and Delivering God in Old Testament Theology

The deity acting in these texts is the one who lies at the center of the bulk of Old Testament theology. Within the historical framework of the modern era, the establishment of Israel as the people of YHWH was the central theological datum. Even with a move toward a literary or canonical framework, this was still the case. Cecil B. DeMille's *The Ten Commandments* (1956) was the ultimate God-movie of the modern era, but when moviemaking moved into the post-modern era, it was replaced only by Disney's *The Prince of Egypt* (1998). It was a whole new look, but the same divine character.

In Walther Eichrodt's version of Old Testament theology, the themes of deliverance and command were wrapped up together into the unifying theme of covenant.[85] The fatal flaw of his approach was the need to insist that this concept and the divine reality that accompanied it persisted, relatively unchanged, throughout the entire Old Testament. This insistence created significant tension in Eichrodt's outline because of all he had inherited from the Christian practice of Old Testament theology, particularly in the work of Julius Wellhausen and the many streams that flowed from it. This strand of scholarship saw in Judaism, organized around the Torah, a rigid system of legalism that had drifted away from the vitality of ancient Israelite religion.[86] It becomes clear in retrospect that Eichrodt saw in texts such as Pss. 40:7 and 51:18, Amos 5:21, and Jer. 7:9 a simplistic struggle between the piety of the psalmists and prophets and the ritual legalism of the priesthood, no doubt viewed through the lens of the disputes between Jesus and the Pharisees in the Christian Gospels. A clear path away from these presuppositions and the conclusions to which they lead has been provided by Jon D. Levenson. In *Sinai and Zion: An Entry into the Jewish Bible*, Levenson offered a cogent critique of Christian Old Testament theology and a fresh way of approaching the two traditions around which the Hebrew Scriptures are organized.[87] Perhaps the problem Levenson addressed may be understood as the odd presumption that the unmediated divine character of old could have been retained. Even the mediation that this strand of Old Testament theology loved most, prophecy, was rarely treated as mediation by these Christian theologians, because the focus was so often on the prophets themselves and their divine encounters, rather than on the verbal messages they produced and the effects of these messages on their audiences.[88]

Although Gerhard von Rad did not demand the persistence of a central concept, it was the accrual onto Israel's creedal statements of more divine acts that fit into these categories of deliverance and command that defined a dynamic tradition.[89] Old Testament theologians practicing a dialogical method broke away from such history-dependent models, but promising, delivering, and commanding have still constituted God's primary way of being within this model. As I have demonstrated, some of the more problematic aspects of God's character appear in this part of the story, but for the dialogical model, these are typically treated separately and secondarily, as the divine character's other, occasional side.

In the Torah struggle between order and chaos, represented respectively by wilderness and law, the latter has the final word. The wilderness stories find echoes in Joshua and Judges, but these look significantly different and serve quite different literary purposes there. The unpredictability of the divine character will eventually prove a poor fit for an Israel working to build a home, and the divine deliverer will turn out to be an incomplete warrior. The carefully ordered divine character of the legal traditions in the Pentateuch will prove equally problematic for a people trying to settle into a new land that already has its ways of operating.

Notes

1. Elsa Tamez, *Bible of the Oppressed,* trans. Matthew J. O'Connell (Maryknoll, NY: Orbis, 1982); Jorge V. Pixley, *On Exodus: A Liberation Perspective,* trans. Robert R. Barr (Maryknoll, NY: Orbis, 1987); Robert McAfee Brown, *Unexpected News: Reading the Bible with Third World Eyes* (Philadelphia: Westminster, 1984). On the tendency and inherent dangers of the rejection of such a view of the divine by those who possess adequate power of their own in this world, see Paul D. Hanson, *The Diversity of Scripture* (Philadelphia: Fortress Press, 1984), 101–2.

2. Of course, readers aware of the full biblical story cannot miss the reflection of the exodus story in miniature here.

3. W. Lee Humphreys, *The Character of God in the Book of Genesis* (Louisville: Westminster, 2001), 88–89.

4. Phyllis Trible, *Texts of Terror: Literary-Feminist Readings of Biblical Narratives* (Philadelphia: Fortress Press, 1984), 16–17.

5. Elements within the text make it seem likely that this second story about Hagar has been moved out of its original chronological sequence, which would have had it following closely after the first one. Most notably, Ishmael, who, by the simple arithmetic of 16:16 and 21:5, would have been fourteen to sixteen years old when Isaac was weaned, is carried by Hagar (21:14) and thrown under a bush when she runs out of water (21:15).

6. Trible, *Texts of Terror*, 25. Trible's deliberate and powerful use of the language of Isaiah 53 may distract from the issue somewhat. The primary point here is that Hagar's story is intimately intertwined with the story of Abraham and Sarah, and, more significantly, the story of the development of the character of God in relation to Hagar is tied to the story of the development of God's character in relation to Abraham, Sarah, and Israel.

7. Esther Hamori, *When Gods Were Men: The Embodied God in Biblical and Near Eastern Literature* (Berlin: de Gruyter, 2008), 1–25. This phenomenon is more widespread in other Ancient Near Eastern literature.

8. Jack Miles, *God: A Biography* (New York: Vintage, 1995), 55–56.

9. See, for example, Karl Allen Kuhn, *Having Words with God: The Bible as Conversation* (Minneapolis: Fortress Press, 2008), 11.

10. See the discussion of this problem in Humphreys, *Character of God*, 119–25.

11. Walter Brueggemann, *Theology of the Old Testament: Testimony, Dispute, Advocacy* (Minneapolis: Fortress Press, 1997), 274.

12. Richard Elliott Friedman, *The Disappearance of God: A Divine Mystery* (Boston: Little, Brown, 1995), 35–36.

13. It might be possible to understand some of Abraham's experiences as dreams, especially Gen. 15:12-16, but there is always some sense of uncertainty, and the word *dream* is not used in relation to this experience.

14. Miles, *God*, 69–70.

15. For more on this theme in the life of Jacob, see Mark McEntire, *Struggling with God: An Introduction to the Pentateuch* (Macon, GA: Mercer University Press, 2008), 72–73. This pattern in Jacob's life also establishes the template for the early life of Moses as presented in Exodus, which will be addressed later in this chapter.

16. Humphreys, *Character of God*, 186.

17. For a full accounting of these interpretations and their shortcomings, see Hamori, *When Gods Were Men*, 13–23.

18. Stephen Geller, "The Struggle at the Jabbok: The Uses of Enigma in Biblical Narrative," *Journal of Ancient Near Eastern Studies* 14 (1982): 54.

19. Friedman, *Disappearance of God*, 38.

20. The variation of these designations has been tied to source divisions in Genesis, a practice that is helpful for some interpretive activities, but the object of this study is the narrative presented by the final form of the book of Genesis, regardless of the origins of the independent literary units.

21. Miles, *God*, 79.

22. Humphreys, *Character of God*, 205.

23. Karen Armstrong, *In the Beginning* (New York: Ballantine, 1997), 119.

24. Miles, *God*, 81.

25. It is possible to assume that God is deliberately multiplying the Israelite population, given that this is one of the promises made to Abraham in Genesis, but nothing within the book of Exodus itself overtly supports this assumption.

26. For more on the actions of the midwives and the connections between Moses and Joseph, see Mark McEntire, *The Blood of Abel: The Violent Plot in the Hebrew Bible* (Macon, GA: Mercer University Press, 1999), 42–43.

27. Lyle Eslinger, "Freedom or Knowledge? Perspective and Purpose in the Exodus Narrative," *JSOT* 52 (1991): 55–56.

28. The parallels between Genesis 28–29 and Exodus 2 are more numerous than those listed here. See McEntire, *Struggling with God*, 91–92.

29. Miles, *God*, 99.

30. Friedman, *Disappearance of God*, 42–45.

31. Miles, *God*, 102–3.

32. See the discussion in Dorian G. Coover Cox, "The Hardening of Pharaoh's Heart in Its Literary and Cultural Contexts," *BSac* 163 (2006): 303–4.

33. See more discussion of this phenomenon and its role in the plague narratives in McEntire, *Struggling with God*, 96–100.

34. Cox, "Hardening of Pharaoh's Heart," 311.

35. For further discussion of this view, see David M. Gunn, "The 'Hardening of Pharaoh's Heart': Plot, Character, and Theology in Exodus 1–14," in *Art and Meaning: Rhetoric in Biblical Literature*, ed. David J. A. Clines et al. (Sheffield: JSOT Press, 1985), 73–74.

36. Ibid., 89.

37. Ibid., 83.

38. Eslinger, "Freedom or Knowledge?" 49–50.

39. Perhaps this is most apparent in the work of two of the most prominent Old Testament scholars of the second half of the twentieth century, Frank Moore Cross and David Noel Freedman. For example, see Cross, "The Song of the Sea and Canaanite Myth," in *Canaanite Myth and Hebrew Epic* (Cambridge: Harvard University Press, 1973), 112–44; and Freedman, "The Song of the Sea," in *Pottery, Poetry, and Prophecy* (Winona Lake, IN: Eisenbrauns, 1980), 179–86.

40. For more on this way of reading the book of Psalms, see Nancy L. deClaissé-Walford, *Reading from the Beginning: The Shaping of the Hebrew Psalter* (Macon, GA: Mercer University Press, 1997), 105–18.

41. For a more thorough discussion of the literary features and theological effect of this story in 1 Samuel 4, see McEntire, *Blood of Abel*, 77–88.

42. The idea of a reversed exodus as punishment in the Prophetic literature will be developed further in chapter 5 of this book.

43. Joel S. Burnett, *Where Is God? Divine Absence in the Hebrew Bible* (Minneapolis: Fortress Press, 2010), 51–52.

44. Ibid., 59-68. Burnett identified and described much of the Ancient Near Eastern background of Israel's struggle to put this part of its experience into words. He also incorporated the work of Terence E. Fretheim on divine presence, particularly the idea of "varying intensifications." See Fretheim, *God and World in the Old Testament: A Relational Theology of Creation* (Nashville: Abingdon, 2005), 24–26.

45. Brueggemann, *Theology of the Old Testament*, 569–70.

46. Ibid., 578–99.

47. See the discussion in Ernest W. Nicholson, *Exodus and Sinai in History and Tradition* (Atlanta: John Knox, 1973), 64–67.

48. Brueggemann, *Theology of the Old Testament*, 663–64.

49. This same struggle will emerge more clearly at two much-later points in Israel's story. First, in the early moments of the restoration of Judah in the sixth century BCE, as reported in Ezra, the Jerusalem community will start performing sacrificial ritual quickly (3:3-6) because of one fear, and will halt its rebuilding efforts just as quickly (4:1-5) because of another. This behavior will be examined more extensively in chapter 6 of this book. A second illustration lies in Josephus's account of Herod the Great's renovation of the temple in the first century BCE, during which Herod arranged the project so that the appropriate cultic rituals could continue in the old structure

right up to the day on which they could begin in the new one. This included, for example, the training of priests to do the actual construction work so that unclean personnel would not create impurity in the temple space (*Antiquities of the Jews* 15:11).

50. Howard Schwartz, "Does God Have a Body?" in *Bodies, Embodiment, and Theology of the Hebrew Bible*, ed. S. Tamar Kamionkowski and Wonil Kin (New York: T&T Clark, 2010), 201–5.

51. Ibid., 217–23.

52. This is not only the translation of the NRSV but also its punctuation and poetic structure. In this particular form, it is difficult to miss the breathless quality of the divine utterance.

53. See the section called "Adjectives: Yahweh with Characteristic Markings," in Brueggemann, *Theology of the Old Testament*, 213–28.

54. Ibid., 220–21.

55. Miles, *God*, 126.

56. Stephen K. Sherwood, *Leviticus, Numbers, Deuteronomy* (Collegeville, MN: Liturgical, 2002), 3.

57. Wilfred Warning, *Literary Artistry in Leviticus* (Leiden: Brill, 1995), 40-42. The most controversial portion of Warning's work lies at the center of the book of Leviticus, in the crucial sixteenth chapter. Here the divine speech formula appears twice, in 16:1 and again in 16:2, with no speech content provided for the former. Warning's count of thirty-seven divine speeches, which makes 16:2-34 the central speech in the book, requires counting each of these as divine speeches, despite the lack of content in the first. Warning provides a substantial argument in favor of this approach (43–45).

58. There are numerous places where the traditional chapter divisions and verse enumeration of the Christian Old Testament vary from those of the Hebrew Scriptures. In some cases, these differences may seem trivial, but the end of Leviticus 5 may be an important one. At this point, the Hebrew chapter 5 extends seven more verses, to the end of the sin-offering instructions. Leviticus 6 in Hebrew then begins with what most English versions label as 6:8.

59. James W. Watts, *Ritual and Rhetoric in Leviticus: From Sacrifice to Scripture* (Cambridge: Cambridge University Press, 2007), 55–61.

60. Ibid., 97–98.

61. Ibid., 111.

62. Miles, *God*, 130.

63. Joseph Blenkinsopp has developed the parallels between creation and tabernacle extensively in "The Structure of P," *CBQ* 38 (1976): 275-76. See the analysis of this argument in McEntire, *Struggling with God*, 111–12.

64. Miles, *God*, 129–30.

65. See especially the essay called "The Abominations of Leviticus," in Mary Douglas, *Purity and Danger: An Analysis of Concepts of Pollution and Taboo* (New York: Routledge, 1970), 65–70.

66. John F. A. Sawyer, "The Language of Leviticus," in *Reading Leviticus: A Conversation with Mary Douglas*, ed. John F. A. Sawyer (Sheffield: Sheffield Academic, 1996), 15–20.

67. Warning, *Literary Artistry in Leviticus*, 44–45.

68. A thorough review of the scholarship that led to this identification can be found in John E. Hartley, *Leviticus* (Waco, TX: Word, 1992), 247–60.

69. Warning, *Literary Artistry in Leviticus*, 40–42.

70. McEntire, *Struggling with God*, 145–46.

71. Jon D. Levenson, *Sinai and Zion: An Entry into the Jewish Bible* (San Francisco: Harper & Row, 1985), 90.

72. The idea of connecting Psalms to Torah on a constitutive level has gained recent prominence in works such as Gordon J. Wenham, *Psalms as Torah: Reading Biblical Song Ethically* (Grand Rapids, MI: Baker, 2012); and John S. Vassar, *Recalling a Story Once Told: An Intertextual Reading of the Psalter and the Pentateuch* (Macon, GA: Mercer University Press, 2007).

73. For a more thorough discussion of the development of the canonical book of Psalms, see William L. Holliday, *The Psalms through Three Thousand Years: Prayerbook of a Cloud of Witnesses* (Minneapolis: Fortress Press, 1993), 76–80.

74. Miles, *God*, 133.

75. Ibid.

76. For a discussion of many of the other specific complaint stories, see McEntire, *Struggling with God*, 165–78.

77. For a more complete illustration of the developments of the Balaam tradition, see James L. Kugel, *The Bible as It Was* (Cambridge, MA: Harvard University Press, 1997), 482–97.

78. Within the world of biblical scholarship and the broader study of the Ancient Near East, legal traditions are sometimes categorized as "apodictic" and "casuistic." These categories are somewhat artificial, but they can be a helpful indicator that legal traditions such as those in the Torah are the product of a long accretion based on the adjudication of actual cases. See Albrecht Alt, "The Origins of Israelite Law," in *Essays on Old Testament History and Religion* (Garden City, NY: Doubleday, 1967), 112–25.

79. Casper J. Labuschange has identified ten of these relayed "divine speeches" in Deuteronomy 1–3 and eight in Deuteronomy 4–11, so it is common throughout the book for Moses to quote YHWH directly. See Labuschange, "Divine Speech in Deuteronomy," in *A Song of Power and the Power of a Song: Essays on the Book of Deuteronomy*, ed. Duane L. Christenson (Winona Lake, IN: Eisenbrauns, 1993), 375.

80. Patrick D. Miller, "'Moses My Servant': The Deuteronomic Portrait of Moses," in Christenson, *Song of Power and the Power of a Song*, 302–3.

81. Dennis T. Olson, *Deuteronomy and the Death of Moses: A Theological Reading* (Minneapolis: Fortress Press, 1994), 17.

82. Jerome Segal, *Joseph's Bones: Understanding the Struggle between God and Mankind in the Bible* (New York: Riverhead, 2007), 208.

83. Peter T. Vogt, *Deuteronomic Theology and the Significance of Torah: A Reappraisal* (Winona Lake, IN: Eisenbrauns, 2006), 227. Vogt identified the central struggle as the negotiation of God's presence. This is an important point, and Vogt has given appropriate attention to the repeated emphasis in Deuteronomy on "the place that YHWH will cause his name to dwell" (228). The problem is that as long as Moses is alive, God's presence will always be wherever Moses is.

84. Ibid., 207.

85. Walther Eichrodt, *Theology of the Old Testament*, trans. J. A. Baker (Philadelphia: Westminster, 1961), 1:36-38.

86. Ibid., 168–69, 364–65.

87. Levenson, *Sinai and Zion*, 2–4.

88. This is a tendency that has shifted considerably in the last few decades, particularly as rhetorical and sociological methods have been applied to the Prophetic literature. Much of the impetus for this development has been located in the work of Walter Brueggemann, beginning with his transformative work *The Prophetic Imagination* (Philadelphia: Fortress Press, 1978). For a detailed presentation of the finished prophetic scrolls as sociorhetorical products of exilic and postexilic communities, see Rainer Albertz, *Israel in Exile: The History and Literature of the Sixth Century BCE.* (Atlanta: Society of Biblical Literature, 2003), 203–434. Such approaches have found their way into more accessible surveys of the prophetic material; see Louis Stulman and Hyun Chul Paul Kim, *You Are My People: An Introduction to Prophetic Literature* (Nashville: Abingdon, 2011), 9–27. A more comprehensive treatment of the Prophetic literature and its place in Old Testament theology is in chapter 5 of this book.

89. Gerhard von Rad, *Old Testament Theology*, trans. D. M. G. Stalker (New York: Harper & Row, 1962), 187–90.

4

A Nation-Building God

If Deuteronomy represents a withdrawal of direct divine presence akin to that found in the Joseph narrative that brings Genesis to a close, then the book of Joshua represents a divine reinvigoration resembling that found at the beginning of the book of Exodus. The previous chapter demonstrated significant parallels between the end of Genesis and the end of Deuteronomy; the parallels between the beginning of Exodus and the beginning of Joshua are of similar significance. These will be presented in detail later in this chapter, but for now it is enough to observe that God has become an active speaking character in the narrative again.

The perceived normal state of Ancient Israel is a unified nation, governed by a single monarch residing in the palace in Jerusalem, which was adjacent to an active temple dedicated to the worship of YHWH. Even in the Bible's timeline, however, this state of existence persisted for only a couple of decades. Perhaps this construct was in place for about a century, minus the temple for the first half of that period.[1] This is considerably less than 10 percent of the total time covered in the biblical chronology. It is impossible to say for certain, but there is a case to be made that a broad, surface reading of the biblical story is intended to leave such an impression. The stories of the "united monarchy" fill up the majority of the books of Samuel-Kings and Chronicles. When asked to name the Israelite kings during this period, many competent readers of the Bible will readily list "Saul, David, Solomon." Few are likely to provide the more precise list of Saul, Ishbaal, David, Absalom, David, Adonijah, Solomon. The reading of this story on multiple levels seems such a likely occurrence that it can be the result only of either deliberate literary intent or literary incompetence, and the latter would seem an unfair judgment. On one level, perhaps we are supposed to see the united monarchy as a norm for Israel regardless of its brief duration and the north–south fractures that obviously existed within it. Looking at the divine character in this part of Israel's story also requires that we maintain a sharp awareness of the multiple levels on which the narrative operates.

The texts that lie at the center of the examination of the divine character in this chapter are part of the Old Testament designated in the world of biblical scholarship as the Deuteronomistic History, the books of Joshua through 2 Kings. They cover the period from the death of Moses to the destruction of Jerusalem by the Babylonian army, with the single century of the united monarchy at its center. By any standard, the work accomplished by Israel's deity during this period of approximately one hundred years is impressive, but there is a lot of story on either side of this central element in which the direction of the plot is not nearly as straightforward.[2]

Chronicles and the Multiformity of the Biblical Tradition

What should Old Testament Theology do with the books known as Chronicles? Three factors serve to make this a perplexing question. First, large portions of the books essentially repeat the material found in the books of Samuel and Kings. What is the purpose of such repetition? Of course, the presence of repetition always invites careful attention to variation. Second, the first nine chapters of Chronicles carry the reader from Adam to Saul using little more than genealogies and other types of lists. The Greek title of the book, Paraleipomenon, means something like "Supplements," and this title helps to pose some of the critical questions about the intent of the book. For example, when the writers begin Chronicles with "Adam, Seth, Enosh . . ," do they expect readers to know the related material found in Genesis and to fill in the missing details themselves? Third, no biblical book differs more in its placement in the canons of Judaism and Christianity than Chronicles. The position of Chronicles in the Christian canon, immediately after Kings, invites a parallel reading of these narratives in which Chronicles serves more as a supplement. In the Hebrew canon, however, where Chronicles is placed at the end, it looks more like a retrospective or reconsideration of Israel's story added to end the canonical collection just as Genesis–Kings began it.

The relationship between Chronicles and the Deuteronomistic History has been the subject of intense debate since the groundbreaking work of Martin Noth on these documents in the middle of the twentieth century. Noth's conclusions now look overly simple in retrospect, but they are still extremely useful as a starting point. In isolating the books of Judges–Kings and naming them the Deuteronomistic History, Noth placed the final composition of the work in the late seventh and early sixth centuries BCE. Thus, in its final form, the compilation was exilic. He then identified Chronicles as a later revision of the Deuteronomistic History, produced approximately two centuries later. Thus, they are clearly postexilic.[3] Noth's analysis always included Ezra-Nehemiah in what he considered the Chronicler's history, but a new wave of scholarship in the last quarter of the twentieth century, highlighted by the work of Hugh Williamson and Sara Japhet, successfully detached these works in terms of authorship and compositional development.[4] For the purposes of this study, in tracing the development of the divine character in biblical narrative, it is also essential to separate these two works, and Ezra-Nehemiah will be treated in the final chapter.

A recent influential restatement of the relationship between the Deuteronomistic History and Chronicles has been advanced by Raymond Person, and it is important to recognize how it does and does not alter the basic synthesis in the work of Noth. Person has followed a general trend of developing a more complex compositional history for both works,[5] but this has little or no effect on how they will be used in this study. More significantly, Person has argued that both histories, in their final forms, are products of the Persian period, and that they share a common, older source. They should be understood and read, therefore, as "competing contemporary historiographies."[6] Person still referred to recent work that stays closer to the Noth synthesis as "the consensus model," but his work served, at least, to make the use of that model more cautious. Person argued for "multiformity" in the interplay between written and oral traditions, which resulted in multiple versions of the work known as the Deuteronomistic History, two of which are represented by the Masoretic Text and a presumed LXX *Vorlage*. The work known as Chronicles may then be best understood as one more version of the story of the monarchy produced by this multiformity.[7]

As the period of the monarchy becomes the primary focus of the biblical story, it will be important to keep in mind that the Hebrew Scriptures offer two different views of this part of Israel's story and, therefore, two different presentations of the divine character. The subsequent discussions of this character development will take care not to operate with rigid assumptions about the literary and chronological relationships between these two versions of the story, but will recognize that their coexistence offers a more complex and conflicted portrait of the divine being.

God of War

Measuring the degrees of continuity and discontinuity in the divine character when moving from Deuteronomy into Joshua is a difficult task. Like the characters in the story and the writer of this new text, readers will struggle not to be distracted by the absence of Moses. Perhaps this should be a hint to begin with the examination of the continuity and discontinuity between

God's primary human partners in these two phases of the biblical story. The first five chapters of the book of Joshua go to great lengths to establish Joshua as a new Moses. Joshua makes speeches to the Israelites (1:10-15), sends out spies (2:1-24), parts a body of water so the Israelites can cross it (3:1-17), sets up a stone monument (4:1-9), and removes his sandals during a strange theophanic experience (5:13-15). There is one kind of activity, however, that each of these characters performs that the other does not: Joshua does not produce and pronounce law to the Israelites, and Moses was never a soldier.[8] In a striking inverse pattern, Moses talks a lot about Joshua's pending invasion of Canaan throughout Numbers and Deuteronomy, and God talks to Joshua about Moses' giving laws to the Israelites (1:7). These continuities and discontinuities indicate that Israel and its God are finished dealing with legal matters and are ready for a fight. Throughout the first five chapters of the book of Joshua, YHWH speaks directly to Joshua. One purpose of this speech is revealed in 3:7: "The LORD said to Joshua, 'This day I will begin to exalt you in the sight of all Israel, so that they may know that I will be with you as I was with Moses.'" This way of operating proves effective, as the Israelites consistently do everything Joshua tells them. The events are presented in such fluid fashion that it is difficult when reading the account of the crossing of the Jordan in Joshua 3–4 to separate the divine commands to Joshua, Joshua's commands to the people, and the narrator's description of events, as the three elements work together to tell the complete story.

The holy-war tradition emerges in the book of Deuteronomy and is put into practice in the book of Joshua, and this phenomenon presents one of the greatest challenges for a contemporary biblical theology. The tradition of holy war is complex and inconsistent, and it has been the subject of a number of studies. The first book-length treatment was Gerhard von Rad's *Holy War in Ancient Israel*, first published in German in 1951, in which he carefully isolated the essential texts and synthesized a pattern for Israel's holy-war tradition, which he then attempted to place within Israel's historical development, concluding that holy war was "an eminently cultic undertaking."[9] There have been many treatments of various length since von Rad's, the most definitive of which was Susan Niditch's *War in the Hebrew Bible: A Study in the Ethics of Violence*, in which she rightly criticized von Rad for constructing too harmonious a "typology" of holy war from diverse biblical texts and connecting it too closely to Israel's sacred institutions.[10] Niditch uncovered and named multiple "war ideologies" in the Hebrew Scriptures, at least three of which have already found prominent places within the biblical story to this point. The tradition of total destruction, or "ban," is always the most prominent because of its ferocity.

Niditch found the canonical origins of the ban in Numbers 21 and further development in Deuteronomy 7 and 12, and this ideology plays a prominent role in the book of Joshua.[11]

Once the book of Joshua has adequately established the character named Joshua as the worthy successor to Moses, the last element in this process provides an important transition to the warfare that fills the next seven chapters of the book. Joshua's theophanic experience in 5:13-15 is important to this study in at least two aspects. First, as it has in many such experiences before, the divine presence appears in ambiguity. The ambiguous figure who spoke from the burning bush to Moses was "the Angel of the LORD," and the calling of Moses reflects this divine identity, as he is primarily a messenger or prophet. The divine being in Joshua 5 is "the commander of the army of the LORD," reflecting Joshua's primary identity as a warrior. Second, the role of the divine being in the warfare to follow will be as ambiguous as this character, to whom Joshua must ask the question, "Are you one of us or one of our adversaries?" The response of the divine representative is brutally honest: "Neither." In the next two battles, YHWH will fight once for and once against the Israelites. Divine assistance is highly conditional, and the rules for securing it resist any reasonable explanation.

The warfare section in Joshua 6–12 begins with relatively lengthy, detailed battle accounts and ends with a mere list of thirty-one defeated kings. The story of the battle of Jericho fills all of Joshua 6, and it serves as a case study for one particular expression of holy war and for the role of the divine character in warfare. The story opens with intense divine speech, as YHWH begins to give Joshua very specific instructions about the waging of war against Jericho. The first clue that there is something strange about the divine behavior here, though, is that these instructions fade off into uncertainty. At 6:5, YHWH says, "Charge straight ahead," stops speaking, and never speaks again. Everything that the divine character commands is repeated twice more in the story, once in Joshua's commands to the people and once in the narrator's description of the ensuing events. Thus, the battle is described three times in Joshua 6, and whereas the divine instructions stand alone at the beginning of the text, uninterrupted, the commands of Joshua and the execution of the instructions are carefully interwoven in 6:6-26. Moreover, as the account of the battle is repeated, each time it grows in detail and intensity.[12] Elements that were not explicit in the divine instruction, such as "devoting the city to destruction" (v. 17) and the rescue of Rahab and her family (v. 22), are in Joshua's instructions, and elements not explicit in either set of spoken instructions, such as burning the city (v. 24) and killing all of the people and animals (v. 21), are in the narrator's description. It is only when the reader gets to the final verse of the account that another realization becomes clear: "So, the LORD was with Joshua; and his fame was in all the land" (6:27). It is not just the voice of God that is sequestered at the beginning of the story; as the narrative progresses spatially and temporally, God's presence also diminishes. As the Israelites march around the city for seven days, the voice of God is replaced by the symbolic presence of the ark, God's empty throne, which is carried by the priests. Once the Israelite army begins to charge into the city, even the ark is forgotten. The reemergence of divine presence at the end of the story reveals just how much this presence recedes as the story progresses.[13] It is tempting to make too much of the divine disappearance. In the end, it hardly makes sense to claim that God did not intend the slaughter and destruction. What is apparent is the desire of the writer, who so carefully crafted this story, to back the divine character away from the actual bloodshed, a move that is reminiscent of the sudden appearance of the "destroyer" in the Passover story at Exod. 12:23, who places at least a literary layer between the deity and the killing of children. Such a reticence about getting blood on the divine hands is puzzling. This deity has done plenty of killing and commanded plenty of killing before and will do so again, and ultimately this reluctance cannot be explained but only observed.

On the one hand, the need among some of the Bible's adherents to defend the divine behavior in these texts is powerful, and it infects both ordinary and "professional" readers of the text. On the other hand, this part of the Bible is often the place where many go to challenge the moral character of ancient Israel and its God. Such a wide range of reactions to the divine behavior reveals a lot about it and warrants some exploration. The question of justice with regard to the Canaanites was largely hidden beneath the surface of discussion about Israel's holy-war tradition until the publication of Regina Schwartz's *The Curse of Cain: The Violent Legacy of Monotheism,* in 1997, which identified two important points about the conquest of Canaan by the Israelites, with the help of their deity. First, the biblical tradition very carefully links the conquest to the exodus, thus allowing the latter to serve as a moral justification of the former.[14] Of course, the oppressor in the exodus story was one of the great empires of the ancient world, and the victims of the conquest story, the Canaanites, were a relatively small people-group, one from which the Israelite ancestors had emerged and to whom the invading Israelites were closely related. Further, the sins of the Canaanites are nothing like those of Pharaoh.[15] They were not oppressors of the Israelites but a people so similar that the Israelites would be tempted to blend in with them. Thus, Schwartz could characterize the conquest as a betrayal.[16] Second, historical renderings of this event are necessarily politicized: those from all different angles tend to mute the violence, and, of course, the Israelites did not completely exterminate the Canaanites. History tells us that genocide on this level is impossible, no matter how ruthless and brutal the effort. Biblical texts further along the plotline, particularly in Judges, but even in the book of Joshua itself (13:1-2), admit to this. Failure to execute the command fully does not remove the moral accountability of the command itself, though, nor of the one giving it, especially in a story like this one that has been repeatedly reused for more than two thousand years to reenact the brutal drama.[17]

A counterexample to Schwartz's acknowledgment of morally problematic texts is Paul Copan's recent work *Is God a Moral Monster? Making Sense of the Old Testament God*. It requires very little reading in this book before discovering that the author has determined ahead of time that the answer to the question in the title is negative, and he will go to any length to bend texts around this assumption. A case in point is his explanation of the total destruction of Canaanite cities, such as Jericho and Ai. Copan contends, with no supporting evidence, that "no civilian populations existed at Jericho, Ai, and other cities mentioned in Joshua."[18] Thus, the claim in Josh. 6:21 that "they devoted to destruction by the edge of the sword all in the city, both men and women, young and old" is a mere figure of speech, typical of the exaggerating tendencies of Ancient Near Eastern warriors, indicating that they killed all of the inhabitants of the city, but no women and children were included.[19] Although it would seem logical to assume that many of the commoners of Jericho and Ai may have resided in the land outside the walls, in order to farm the land and graze the livestock, the invasion of a foreign army like the Israelites, coming to lay siege on the city, would have sent these people scurrying inside the walls for protection, which is exactly the purpose for which they were built. Even if Joshua's claim to have killed all the women and children of the place was an exaggeration, to conclude that he killed none of them at all stretches this argument past its breaking point.

The preposterous nature of Copan's claims about "fortress cities" is further exposed by a competing claim in the Bible itself. Although the killing of all the inhabitants of Canaan does not raise legitimate questions about divine morality, because Joshua was merely exaggerating and boasting just as everyone else in the Ancient Near East did,[20] it was the failure to match this rhetoric with actual performance, thus leaving behind Canaanites and their idolatrous religion, that ultimately brought God's punishment onto Israel itself.[21] Even if one were to accept all of Copan's claims, they still require the reader to accept that whereas killing innocent civilians is immoral, making false boasts about having done so is not.

The companion story to the battle of Jericho is the story of Ai in Joshua 7–8. The two stories are linked by the violation of the "ban" rule by Achan (7:1), resulting in an Israelite loss in the first battle of Ai. God speaks directly to Joshua to explain that this violation has resulted in the divine abandonment of the Israelite army. The conclusion of the initial Ai story reports the stoning and burning of Achan and his family and a result reminiscent of Israel's wilderness days: "The LORD turned from his burning anger. Therefore that place to this day is called the Valley of Achor" (7:26). God then speaks to Joshua again in order to initiate a second, successful battle against Ai, but contained within this speech is a hint that Achan's disobedience was not the only problem. Although Joshua took the advice of his spies in 7:3-4 and sent only part of the army to attack Ai, YHWH specifically instructs him to take all of the army, including Joshua himself, to fight against Ai the second time. How can a people attribute victory to divine power and still exert the maximum human effort?

The conclusion to the "conquest" section of the book of Joshua leaves the story in a very odd position, which is revealed in the strange statement that YHWH makes to Joshua in 13:1-7: "Now Joshua was old and advanced in years; and the LORD said to him, 'You are old and advanced in years, and very much of the land still remains to be possessed. This is the land that still remains. . . . I will myself drive them out before the Israelites; only allot the land to Israel for an inheritance, as I have commanded.'" This is an acknowledgment of a massive failure, but is it also a statement of blame? The divine statement is so incongruous with the divine statements in 1:6 and 11:23 that the internal coherence of the book of Joshua threatens to break down. It turns out that the taking of the land that seemed to be moving along at a rapid pace in Joshua 12, which lists thirty-one kings whom Joshua defeated, was too large a project for one human lifetime, and God makes no specific claim about when and how he "will myself drive them out." The problem is that Joshua must divide the land, and he is near death, so he does not have the time to finish conquering it first. The book of Joshua makes a brilliant literary move in the statement at 11:23: "So Joshua took the whole land, according to all that the LORD had spoken to Moses; and Joshua gave it for an inheritance to Israel according to their tribal allotment. And the land had rest from war." This statement is obviously far from reality, but it engages the reader to imagine the land taken, so that it can be allotted. This is one final way in which Joshua is made to resemble Moses, who also envisioned a land complete with future tribal boundaries in Deuteronomy

34. The question left hanging in the air, though, is why it is necessary to use such imagination.

The text tries out various excuses for why this imaginary statement never becomes a reality, and it places some of these in the mouth of God while presenting others as indirect, divine communication. The first is the tacit implication by God at Josh. 13:1 that the Israelites have simply run out of time, because Joshua is too old to be a warrior anymore. The oddity of this statement is revealed again in 23:1-4, after the long and tedious allotment of land, Joshua's equivalent to Moses' production of the tabernacle in the second half of Exodus, when it is reported that

> a long time afterward, when the LORD had given rest to Israel from all their enemies all around, and Joshua was old and well advanced in years, Joshua summoned all Israel, their elders and heads, their judges and officers, and said to them, "I am now old and well advanced in years, and you have seen all that the LORD your God has done to all the nations for your sake, for it is the LORD your God who has fought for you. I have allotted to you as an inheritance for your tribes those nations that remain, along with all the nations that I have already cut off from the Jordan to the Great Sea in the west."

This text is at pains to resolve the tenuous bargain made in the middle of the book of Joshua. Has God delivered on the promise of the land of Canaan or not?

As the story moves into the book known as Judges, other excuses for the failure appear. The book of Judges is an exploration of the reality exposed in Josh. 13:1, and it is the only book of the Old Testament that begins with a question. The reason for this question in Judg. 1:1, "Who shall go up first for us against the Canaanites to fight against them?" is that a significant element at the end of the life of Moses finds no reflection at the end of the life of Joshua, who appoints no successor before his death. The leaderless Israelites first adopt an individual, tribal approach, suggested and approved by YHWH in 1:2, but when this plan collapses in failure, a visit from "the angel of YHWH" marks a new beginning in 2:1. As in previous cases, the angel speaks as YHWH, but the text is too brief for the typical transformation of the angel into a clear theophanic presence. Most significantly, in 2:2-3, the persistence of the Canaanites in the land is posited as YHWH's means of punishing the Israelites for their disobedience.

The notion of indirect divine punishment of Israel through suffering at the hands of their local enemies will become a major element of what is often called the "cycle of the judges" in Judges 3–16.[22] This cycle is described in generic terms in 2:11-23, then played out in six specific stories in chapters 3–16. The well-rehearsed series of events reveals much about the transition in the divine character at this point, so it should be carefully expressed and examined, a process that begins with the list in table 4-1.

Table 4-1: The Cyclical Stories of the Judges

1. The Israelites did what was evil in the sight of YHWH: 2:11, 3:7, 3:12, 4:1, 6:1, 10:6, 13:1.
2. So YHWH gave them into the hand of their enemies: 2:14, 3:8, 3:14, 4:2, 6:1, 10:7, 13:1
3. They were in great distress and/or cried out to YHWH: 2:15, 3:9, 3:15, 4:3, 6:6, 10:9–10
4. YHWH raised up a judge/deliverer who delivered them: 2:16, 3:9, 3:15, (6:34), (11:29), (14:19)
5. And the land had rest from war: 3:11, 3:30, 5:31, 8:28, (12:7), (15:20, 31)

Note: The references in parentheses are statements that have a similar function but exhibit significant variation from the standard pattern.

There are slight variations in the language of each of the elements in table 4-1 from one story to the next, but the book of Judges uses this obvious template repeatedly to demonstrate the failure of the judges to provide adequate leadership. In terms of divine character development, it is important to recognize three important features. First, defeat at the hands of enemies such as the Moabites, the Canaanites, the Midianites, the Ammonites, and the Philistines is presented as divine punishment for Israel's disloyalty to YHWH, usually demonstrated in the form of idol worship. Second, YHWH continues to hear and respond to the Israelites' cries for help, even though this process ends in repeated failure. Every time the cycle ends, it starts back again in the next verse. Finally, the narrator apparently has nothing to report concerning divine activity or any other subject during periods of rest and peace. This is a book about wars, and peace is just the empty space between them.

Because the cyclical pattern is so strong, it is easy to miss the changes that are taking place as the six renditions progress. By the time the book of Judges gets to Samson, the last and best-known "judge," he is no judge at all. Samson never leads a group of Israelites and never engages in any military campaigns against the Israelite enemy of the day, the Philistines. His actions are individual and are those of a vandal or a marauder, and the divine interactions with Samson are enigmatic.[23] Judg. 13:25 says of a young Samson that "the spirit of the LORD began to stir in him," and before his attack on Ashkelon, the text reports in 14:19 that "the spirit of the LORD rushed on him." In this last case, it would seem that the nature of the divine participation matches the rash and reactionary nature of the human character with which it is a partner. These observations about the last judge point to the need to look more carefully at the changes in divine behavior in the full sequence of the judges.

The first rendition of the judge story, the account of Othniel in 3:7-11, is so brief that it offers no perspective on divine behavior other than the characteristic phrasing identified in the cycle in table 4-1. The story of Ehud that follows is considerably longer and, though it offers no additional direct description of divine behavior, the human behavior that God tacitly sanctions here raises some important questions that will persist throughout the book of Judges. The language of Israel's oppression changes slightly: whereas in 3:8, YHWH "sold" the Israelites "into the hand of Cushan-Rishathaim," in 3:12, YHWH "strengthened the hand of King Eglon of Moab against Israel," but this is likely only a stylistic difference. The much more obvious progression is the character of the tale of the assassination of Eglon by Ehud, which is both brutal and comical at the same time. Although there is no presentation in the text of God specifically instructing Ehud about how to be a deliverer, his success is suggested to be a sign of divine favor, and the story establishes a tone that will broaden and expand with the tales of the next four judges. The stomach-turning account of Ehud's assassination of Eglon is outdone only by the assassination of Sisera, the Canaanite general, by a woman named Jael in Judg. 4:18-22. This is the most memorable component of the Deborah story, the graphic details of which are revisited lyrically in the Song of Deborah, in 5:24-30.

The expansion continues in the Gideon section of the book of Judges, which takes several interesting turns while retaining the basic shape of the original narrative template.[24] Unlike the three previous judges, who were simply "raised up" by YHWH as deliverers, Judges 6 contains something like a call narrative of Gideon, divided into two portions. In a move unprecedented in Judges, Gideon receives a theophanic visitation, which, like many such occurrences earlier in the Bible, begins with the appearance of the angel of YHWH in 6:12, but this figure eventually becomes YHWH.[25] The initial, flattering statement of the angel, "The LORD is with you, you mighty warrior," is met with a remarkable set of questions from Gideon about Israel's current suffering at the hands of the Midianites: "But sir, if the LORD is with us, then why has all this happened to us? And where are all his wonderful deeds that our ancestors recounted to us saying, 'Did not the LORD bring us up from Egypt?' But now the LORD has cast us off and given us into the hand of Midian" (6:13). The experience of Gideon's people is not consistent with this promise of divine presence, and it is these questions that prompt the shift from "angel of the LORD" to "the LORD" speaking to Gideon. The divine speech commissions Gideon to lead the Israelite army against the Midianites, but again Gideon asks an appropriate question in 6:15: "But sir, how can I deliver Israel? My clan is the weakest in Manasseh, and I am the least in my family." The language of the question reveals that Gideon is not certain to whom he is talking. Gideon knows that he is not a mighty warrior, so he requests confirmation of the task being assigned him, and he extracts an odd promise from YHWH to stay and wait under the oak at Ophrah while Gideon goes to his house to prepare an offering. When he comes back with the basket of food, the text again describes the "angel of YHWH" sitting under the tree. The sign Gideon requested comes in the form of a flash of fire that consumes the offering he brings, which causes him to realize he is talking to the angel of YHWH, and he suddenly fears for his life in 6:22. Gideon is aware of the danger of direct divine contact, but he is reassured by the angel, and he builds an altar and names it "YHWH *shalom*" (the LORD is peace), a strange designation in a book that is all about warfare.

Gideon's altar-building leads to another request from God, that he tear down his own father's Baal altar. The resulting confrontation with the people of the area leads to the development of Gideon's other name, Jerubbaal, which is explained in 6:32 as meaning "Baal contends against him," though the name could be interpreted in a number of ways.[26] This internal conflict points the way to the expected external conflict when military pressure from the Midianites and Amalekites comes to bear on Israel, and the response in 6:34 is that "the Spirit of the LORD took possession of [literally "clothed"] Gideon." Although the idea of this statement is consistent with the book of Judges and approximates the statement about Othniel in 3:10, the subtle shift in language may be significant in light of the ways that the divine spirit will interact with the two judges who follow Gideon. Surprisingly, Gideon needs more divine confirmation leading into the confrontation with foreign enemies, and, perhaps more surprisingly, YHWH willingly complies. "Putting out the fleece" has gained the status of a widely recognized idiom in the English language, many of the users of which are likely unaware of its origins in the Gideon story. In 6:39, Gideon seems quite aware that this testing, especially on the second night, might arouse the anger of God, but it does not.

This surprising bit of divine behavior may help prepare the reader for something even more strange to follow. In the days of the wilderness, Moses appealed to God's potential loss of reputation to change intended divine behavior (for example, Num. 14:15-16), but a new kind of divine insecurity emerges in Judg. 7:2. Concerned with losing or sharing credit for military victory, YHWH has Gideon reduce the numbers of his troops from thirty-two thousand to ten thousand to three hundred, and the subsequent defeat of the Midianites by this small contingent is presented in miraculous fashion. After this victory, however, the story of Gideon descends into confusion, and the divine character is difficult to find. Gideon commits an act of idolatry in 8:24-27, and in the account of his death in 8:29-35, the text alternates between using the names Gideon and Jerubbaal. This confusing account marks the downward turn of the book of Judges and contains a foreshadowing of what will happen next. Although Gideon refuses the request of the Israelites to become their king in 8:22-23, insisting that YHWH is their king, his son Abimelech does attempt to establish a monarchy. That this son's name means "my father is king" adds even more mystery to the story. In the face of this affront, YHWH reasserts power by sending "an evil spirit between Abimelech and the lords of Shechem" (9:22). The divine character once again recedes into the background as this tangled story develops, but is brought back by the narrator at the end as the arbiter of justice in 9:56-57.

All of this attention to the Gideon story, and the nature of the behavior of the divine character within it, is significant because it marks an important shift in the book of Judges and in the story of God's behavior toward Israel. Niditch has observed that the Gideon character has facets that connect him to Moses and Joshua on one side of this text and to Saul and David on the other side, so it is fitting that the Gideon account is also a pivot point in divine behavior.[27] By the end of the book of Judges, God has abandoned the idea of using figures like the judges, and the beginning of this abandonment lies in the Gideon story, though it is a process that will require two more iterations of the cycle to complete. The downward turn at the end of the life of Gideon/Jerubbaal is magnified in the disturbing story of Jephthah. As table 4-1 demonstrates, the characteristic language about God's behavior breaks down even more, as there is no account of Jephthah being "raised up" by God as a deliverer. Instead, his half brothers, who have made him an outcast because of his illegitimate birth, beg him for assistance because of his military prowess. The preceding story of conflict between Abimelech and his half brothers casts an ominous shadow on this negotiation.[28] YHWH enters the story briefly at 11:10-11 to witness the bargain between Jephthah and his brothers and returns again at 11:29, which reports that "the spirit of the LORD came upon Jephthah." It is the battle with the Ammonites, which this divine act initiates, that leads to the most troubling aspect of the Jephthah story. The vow to YHWH made by Jephthah in 11:30-31 is unprecedented in the book of Judges. It is unclear in the light of the coming of God's spirit why such a vow seems necessary, and there is no divine response to the vow whatsoever. Phyllis Trible has demonstrated the multitude of ways in which Jephthah is an ambiguous character.[29] This ambiguity is reflected onto the divine being whose spirit resides with Jephthah, an ambiguity that reaches theological crisis when Jephthah returns home from his victory and is greeted by his daughter, which leads to his need to murder her in order to fulfill his vow. The parallels between this story and the Akedah story in Genesis 22 highlight the divine absence, and this moves the story of the book of Judges forward with great uncertainty.

The story of Samson (Judges 13–16) begins with important reversals. The period of subjugation to the Philistines is forty years, the standard length of the times of peace in the earliest stages of the judges cycle. As table 4-1 reflects, there is no cry of distress from the Israelites reported in the account. The appearance of the angel of YHWH to the wife of Manoah is unprompted. Whereas Jephthah's vow ended his daughter's life, the Nazirite vow here marks the beginning of Samson's life.[30] If the theophanic experience of Manoah's wife brings a sense of hope that the story is about to take a more positive turn, these expectations are soon muted for careful readers. The typical transformation of the "angel of YHWH" into a more direct divine presence does not happen, and when the woman reports the event to her husband, she refers to this figure only as "a man of God." Moreover, the message of this figure in 13:5 is strikingly limited: "It is he who shall begin to deliver Israel from the hand of the Philistines." Such a statement reflects well the meager accomplishments of Samson in the next three chapters. He is never depicted leading an army, and his individual actions are typically rash, vengeful, and destructive in a vandalistic manner. Even the divine involvement in his behavior in 14:19 fits this pattern and is coupled with what is described as Samson's "hot anger." Samson's story ends with the strange episode of his suicidal destruction of the Philistine crowd in 16:23-31, and although he clearly prays for divine assistance in 16:28, there is no clear statement that he receives it. Rather, this is assumed because he accomplishes the act of vengeance he desires. The cycle of the judges ends with an assessment of Samson that accentuates the failure of this experiment in leadership. There is no period of peace, and the length of time for which Samson "judged Israel" is exactly half of the ideal, twenty years (16:31). At this point, readers of this book can have no certainty as to whether God wishes to be involved in the process, and the remainder of the book of Judges will go to great lengths to confirm that divine ambivalence.

The bewildering nature of the book of Judges, as the cyclical pattern spirals out of control, may make it difficult for the reader to focus ample attention on the divine character. This becomes even more difficult as the book descends into the chaos of chapters 17–21.[31] God appears several times in the first two chapters of this section, most often in the speech of characters who use divine language to speak blessings and express desires. This thin presence vanishes altogether in the horrifying story of the Levite and his concubine in Judges 19. Trible has provided an intricate reading of the story, highlighting its brutal character. She concludes: "Of all the characters in scripture, she is the least. Appearing at the beginning and at the end of a story that rapes her, she is alone in a world of men."[32] Although this statement seems intended to draw attention to the misogyny of the story and the text that tells it—an appropriate goal—it also illustrates the simultaneous divine absence.

The divine character reappears with greater vigor in the final two chapters of the book of Judges, though the behavior is still surprising. The rape, murder, and dismemberment of the unnamed woman in Gibeah leads to the first internal war in Israel, between Benjamin and the other tribes.[33] In 20:18 and 20:20, YHWH commands the Israelites to attack Benjamin, and in 20:35, YHWH is given credit for defeating Benjamin and destroying its army of more than twenty-five thousand men. The victory is not a cause for rejoicing among the other tribes, however, who gather at Bethel, according to 21:2-3, to weep and ask the poignant question, "O LORD, the God of Israel, why has it come to pass that today there should be one tribe lacking in Israel?" In a mystifying development, 21:15 reports that "the people had compassion on Benjamin, for the LORD had made a breach in the tribes of Israel." The text blames God for the division but provides no divine motive for this act. Israel is coming apart, against its own wishes. The only sense of control in this part of Judges is textual. The sentence that ends the book, "In those days there was no king in Israel; all the people did what was right in their own eyes," also appears at the beginning of this section, in 17:6, to form a frame around it, and the first clause is repeated at conspicuous points in 18:1 and 19:1. This framework that shapes the concluding section of the book raises many challenging questions: Is the book of Judges unaware of the Torah? Is this a purely negative statement? Is the purpose of a king to make people do what is right? Given the stories that fill the framework in Judges 17–21, it is difficult to conclude that the statement is anything but negative, and it appears that the book of Judges is making a case for the monarchy as it comes to an end.

Another question that must be posed at some point—and this one may be as good as any—is why a people that so clearly understood its roots to lie in a nomadic, sheep-herding lifestyle suddenly placed so much emphasis on having land in which to make a permanent settlement. This question has to go back all the way to Genesis 12. Why did God promise land to a man who seemed to prosper so greatly without it?[34] Konrad Schmid has observed that the promise of land to the great ancestors, Abraham, Isaac, and Jacob, is an idea that appears throughout the Pentateuch and that is perhaps even a deliberate, unifying element. Significantly, it is a major element of the culminating text in Deuteronomy 34. Strangely, however, this idea then vanishes in the biblical narrative, and it is never repeated in Joshua–2 Kings.[35] Rather, in Joshua 1:3, Canaan becomes the land "I promised to Moses." Switching the promise switches the conditions, of course. On the one hand, the promise of land to the ancestors had no apparent conditions other than their going there and living in it. Calling this the land promised to Moses instead makes all the commandments given at Mount Sinai conditions for its possession, as YHWH declares in Joshua 1:7. On the other hand, this land proved unable to sustain the ancestors, who had to leave it repeatedly because of famines. Detaching the promise from the ancestors and connecting it to Moses also removes the reminder of that previous failed attempt to occupy the land of Canaan. The biblical tradition seems to be struggling with the tension between two realities. Israel clearly understood that its roots and identity were to be found in a nomadic lifestyle. They were the *'brym* (Hebrews), the passers-by.[36] However, the world was not hospitable to such people. Ultimately, the Israelites became settlers, and some even became urbanites. Such a process, so counter to their self-understanding, required divine sanction.

God of War outside of the Books of Joshua and Judges

The divine-warrior image is born in Exodus 15, and it resurfaces from time to time in the wilderness narratives. The concept of holy war appears in Numbers and becomes a major theme in Deuteronomy. These two ideas coalesce in the story of conquest and settlement in the book of Joshua. The notion of a divine warrior will not go away once the monarchy begins, in 1 Samuel, but it will shift significantly once Israel chooses to have a king "to go out before us and fight our battles" (1 Sam. 8:20), so the image of YHWH as the commander of Israel's army is located primarily in the books of Joshua and Judges. The names of the judges themselves appear nowhere else in the Old Testament except for two references in the genealogies that begin the book of Chronicles, which mention Othniel (4:13) and Ehud (8:6). Even the name of Joshua is difficult to find beyond the book of Judges. The son of Nun is mentioned in 1 Kgs. 16: 34 to recall the curse he placed on anyone trying to rebuild Jericho, and Neh. 8:17 describes the returned exiles living in "booths" as the Israelites had done in the days of Joshua. The third and final reference is his inclusion in a genealogy in 1 Chron. 7:27. These ancient heroes are seldom remembered in the canon, but there are texts outside of Joshua and Judges that use the God of war in two primary ways. One of these ways is in recollections of this period in Israel's distant past. Another, often less specific, way is the metaphorical use of a divine-warrior image. One text that combines these two types of usage is the poem in Isaiah 25, which begins by pointing back far into the past:

> O LORD, you are my God;
> I will exalt you, I will praise your name;
> for you have done wonderful things,
> plans formed of old, faithful and sure. (v. 1)

This text is part of what is often identified as the Isaian apocalypse. Apocalyptic thinking, language, and literature elevate the divine-warrior image to a cosmic scale. The connection to the past lies in the references to a destroyed city, specifically in 25:2, a city that "shall never be built," and, in verse 12, a city whose walls have been brought down by YHWH. The images in Isaiah 24–27 that lead to its association with apocalyptic thought, the "laying waste" of the earth (24:3) and the "twisting of its surface" (24:1), are the destruction of Jericho writ large.

Almost all of the violence in the Prophetic literature assumes God as at least its indirect cause. Robert Haak has developed a helpful approach to "mapping violence" in the Prophetic literature, which points to three general kinds of violent experience: violent situations resulting in national victory, situations in which violence is threatened but has not yet occurred, and situations in which the violence and loss have been experienced.[37] These different experiences have characteristic modes of expression and response. Julia O'Brien has produced a careful analysis of the use of the divine warrior as a metaphor in the Prophetic literature, and two of her primary texts deserve some attention here.[38] Isaiah 13 is the first of a section of "oracles against the nations" that fills eleven chapters of this prophetic scroll. After addressing Judah in a predominantly negative tone, the scroll turns its attention to Israel's enemies, Babylon first. That the text does not describe a literal battle allows the imagery to be even more pronounced:

> The LORD of hosts is mustering
> an army for battle.
> They come from a distant land,
> from the end of the heavens,
> the LORD and the weapons of his indignation,
> to destroy the whole earth. (vv. 4c–5)

O'Brien demonstrated that "the march of the divine warrior follows a consistent pattern" in the Prophetic literature: the first step is the observation of injustice, the second is divine anger provoked by the injustice, and the third is divine vengeance.[39] Such a pattern can be observed in classic operation in the little book of Nahum. This "book" is introduced as an oracle against Nineveh, the Assyrian city. The first chapter pulls together a wide variety of traditions from various places in the Bible. The partial quotation of the creedal statement from Exod. 34:6–7 in Nah. 1:3; the mention of Mount Carmel in 1:4; and the description of fire and "rocks breaking in pieces" in 1:6, reflecting the language of 1 Kgs. 19:11–12 all serve to connect this text to two of the most important theophanies in the Old Testament. The divine warrior does not come into clear view until Nah. 1:8:

> He will make a full end of his adversaries
> and will pursue his enemies into darkness.

O'Brien has identified the shift from the cosmic presentation of the divine warrior in Nahum 1 to a soldier fighting with frightening brutality in the streets of Nineveh:[40]

> Horsemen charging,
> flashing sword and glittering spear,
> piles of dead,
> heaps of corpses,
> dead bodies without end –
> they stumble over the bodies! (3:3)

Walter Brueggemann has given significant attention to the Prophetic literature in his discussion of YHWH as warrior, but he has also connected this image to the Psalms.[41] One of the most direct statements of this kind may be Ps. 24:7–8:

Lift up your heads, O gates!
and be lifted up, O ancient doors!
that the King of glory may come in.
Who is the King of glory?
The LORD, strong and mighty,
the LORD, mighty in battle.

The beginning of Psalm 24 recalls creation, and a description of worship in the temple in verses 3-6 lies between the creation imagery and the warrior imagery of verses 7-10, which end the poem. These poetic lines connect the warrior image to ancient times, as it works with creation imagery to form a frame around the contemporary religious experience of the writer of this psalm. The divine warrior appears in other psalm texts, too, particularly in psalms of lament, which complain of enemies and petition YHWH to defeat them, such as in 7:6:

Rise up, O LORD, in your anger;
lift yourself up against the fury of my enemies;
awake, O my God; you have appointed a judgment.

Brueggemann defined such appeals as later, personal expressions of the image born at the crossing of the Red Sea in Exodus 14–15.[42] This points toward a recognition that, for the Israel of the present tense, in such texts the notion of God as a warrior is primarily an analogy, and that any sense of a literal connection to actual warfare is a recollection of the past.

A more pervasive sense of YHWH as a God of war in the Prophetic literature is developed in Edgar Conrad's reading of the book of Isaiah. Conrad has argued that one of the primary features that gives shape to the book of Isaiah is a "military strategy concerning all the earth."[43] This strategy encompasses all of the "oracles against the nations" in Isaiah 13–27 and the so-called Isaian apocalypse in Isaiah 24–27. It is then directed more thoroughly against Babylon in Isaiah 41–47. In those chapters, perhaps the most telling expression is in 41:2:

Who has roused a victor from the east,
summoned him to his service?
He delivers up nations to him,
and tramples kings under foot;
he makes them like dust with his sword,
like driven stubble with his bow.[44]

Conrad pointed beyond a literal reading of a divine military defeat of Babylon. Instead, this text portrays a larger hope for God's symbolic, military victory in the future "as a vision and a hope."[45] The divine-warrior image seems to have become a symbolic vision, woven into worship, rather than a figure who leads Israel in actual battles, as in the stories of the past. This change is exemplified in Zeph. 3:17:

> The LORD, your God, is in your midst,
> a warrior who gives you victory;
> he will rejoice over you with gladness,
> he will renew you in his love;
> he will exult over you with loud singing,
> as on the day of a festival.

A final text that needs attention here is the statement of the story of Israel and God in Nehemiah 9, which has been part of each similar section so far in this book. Neh. 9:24-28 is the only sustained recollection of the period of conquest and settlement of the promised land beyond the books of Joshua and Judges in the Old Testament. These verses are vague in their description of events, making no mention of Joshua or any of the judges by name, and many of the statements, particularly in verses 24-26, are difficult to square with the narrative written in Joshua and Judges:

> So the descendants went in and possessed the land, and you subdued before them the inhabitants of the land, the Canaanites, and gave them into their hands, with their kings and peoples of the land, to do with them as they pleased. And they captured fortress cities and rich land, and took possession of houses filled with all sorts of goods, hewn cisterns, vineyards, olive orchards, and fruit trees in abundance; so they ate, and were filled, and became fat, and delighted themselves in your great goodness. Nevertheless they were disobedient and rebelled against you and cast your law behind their back and killed your prophets, who had warned them in order to turn them back to you, and they committed great blasphemies. Therefore you gave them into the hands of their enemies, who made them suffer. Then in the time of their suffering they cried out to you and you heard them from heaven, and according to your great mercies, you gave them saviors[46] who saved them from the hands of their enemies.

The rather rosy recollection of the initial movement into the Promised Land and its occupation presents a glorified picture of God's performance as a warrior in this part of Israel's past. The full form and function of Nehemiah 9 will be addressed more completely in chapter 6 of this book. Here it is enough to recognize that the character of YHWH as a warrior on behalf of Israel in the distant past is an idealized memory. [47]

God of the Kingdom

The turn from building to destroying in the biblical narrative, which will mark the end of this chapter and the beginning of the next, is not a precise point. I have chosen the division of the kingdoms after the death of Solomon as a distinct point of change. Therefore, this section will treat the story of the monarchy through Solomon, and the remainder of that story, through the Babylonian invasion, will be addressed in chapter 5. There are, of course, signs of division and decline before 2 Kings 12 and 2 Chronicles 10, such as the conflict between David and Ishbaal after the death of Saul, and Absalom's revolt against David after the latter's failure to deal with Amnon's assault of Tamar. Likewise, there are upturns in the story of Judah later in the narrative, most notably the reforms of Hezekiah and Josiah. The biblical story consistently refuses to follow a straight path.

The beginning of the story of the monarchy overlaps with the end of the story of the judges, and this overlap is personified in the figure of Samuel, who has a unique relationship with the God of Israel. The relationship begins with the story of Samuel's birth, which reflects the births of Isaac and Jacob. Though Samuel is described as both judge (1 Sam. 7:15) and prophet (3:20), and sometimes fulfills the role of priest (10:8), at his birth his mother, Hannah, sings of the monarchy (2:10). Samuel does indeed anoint Israel's first two kings and plays many mediating roles between Israel and YHWH.[48] All of these mediating roles flow through Samuel's character and are transformed in the context of the new monarchy, but as they get apportioned into Israel's burgeoning institutions, divine mediation becomes fragmented. A careful look at the character of Samuel will reveal that the attempt to embody all of these facets of divine mediation leads to a crippling uncertainty. As the story moves rapidly to and through the establishment of the monarchy, the uncertain steps of Israel's God are painfully embodied in the figure of Samuel. Some of the fragmentary elements of the books of Samuel can be attributed to the wide variety of sources that have obviously been brought together to compose it, but to give significant attention to this aspect would be an evasion of the central task of this book—the portrayal of God as a narrative character in the final form of the Old Testament—even when the result of this approach is a fragmented theology.[49]

The first divine act in 1 Samuel is "closing the womb" of Hannah (1:5). YHWH is subsequently invoked by the characters numerous times in 1 Samuel 1, but the next divine act reported by the narrator of the book is "remembering" Hannah (1:19). By the end of that first chapter, in an unprecedented move within the Bible, Samuel's parents give him away to YHWH, and the parents are rewarded by YHWH for this gift by the birth of five more children in 2:20-21. Readers of the Bible are in no way prepared up to this point to understand what it might mean for YHWH to possess a child in this way. Even the Nazirite vow proposed to explain this transaction in 1:11 is not understood in this way anywhere else in the Bible.[50] The relationship first manifests itself in the memorable story of YHWH's nighttime visit to the boy Samuel in 3:2-18. The message that Samuel is given by God, and that he subsequently delivers to Eli, simply confirms the message Eli has already received from the unnamed "man of God" in 2:27-36, so its function is not to provide new information but to confirm Samuel as the prophet of YHWH and the successor to Eli.

The passage frequently labeled the "ark narrative" in 1 Samuel 4–7 has qualities that lead many interpreters to understand it as a source of separate origin that has been woven into the narrative of the books of Samuel. Regardless of how one understands this narrative, what this set of stories does in the present form of the book is provide an interlude so that time can pass and Samuel can become an old man who, by the beginning of 1 Samuel 8, resembles Eli. Thus begins the transition to the monarchy and the part of the book in which the divine behavior is most puzzling and disturbing. The recent study by Marti Steussy *Samuel and His God* has examined these two characters and their relationship carefully. The conversation between Samuel and God about the desire of the Israelites to have a king is confusing and has given rise to many different interpretations.[51] As Steussy has observed, YHWH "is sure that kingship will not be good for the people, but the LORD is huffy enough to impose it on them anyway."[52] At the opening of 1 Samuel 8, YHWH and Samuel engage in an unresolved argument about who feels the most rejected by Israel. As the story goes on, it is as though God gives them a king as punishment for asking for one. Steussy commented further on this point: "[The] LORD's touchiness about personal insult overrides whatever concern [the] LORD may have for the welfare of the people."[53]

Saul makes his way into the biblical text at the worst of all times. How does a figure whose existence God has permitted so begrudgingly hope to do well? It is little wonder that so many interpreters wishing to address the subject of tragedy in the Old Testament find their way to the story of Israel's first king. Jack Miles sets the tone for this conversation about these events and the deity's role in them: "There is, strictly speaking, no tragedy in the Bible, no misfortune that comes about inevitably but innocently from human imperfection and from the unintentionally cruel course of events rather than from any angry divine intervention. There is, in other words, nothing in the Bible that 'just happens.' But the story of Saul comes close."[54] Cheryl Exum has noted the many connections between the stories of Samson and Saul.[55] Those who recognize the resemblance can hardly help but expect Saul to fail, so when Saul ends his own life to avoid further humiliation at the hands of the Philistines, it is no surprise. Robert Alter has observed that the little episode in 1 Sam. 9:11-12 is a failed version of the common "betrothal type-scene." Elsewhere in the Bible, when a male character encounters young women at a well, he ends up marrying one of them, but the failure of Saul to do so can be read as a signal early in his life that his story will not end well.[56] In his formative work *The Fate of King Saul*, David Gunn summarized the many failures of Saul and the way they are presented in the text.[57] These failures seem to be what everyone remembers of Saul, and Samuel is always there as YHWH's proxy to observe, magnify, and even manipulate every one of them. Samuel speaks to Saul on YHWH's behalf at two poignant moments in the long and troubled narrative. The first is in 1 Sam. 13:13-14: "Samuel said to Saul, 'You have done foolishly; you have not kept the commandment of the LORD your God, which he commanded you. The LORD would have established your kingdom over Israel forever, but now your kingdom will not continue; the LORD has sought out a man after his own heart; and the LORD has appointed him to be ruler over his people, because you have not kept what the LORD commanded you.'"[58] This painful criticism of Saul comes just after Samuel traps him into offering a sacrifice to YHWH himself rather than waiting for Samuel to do it. The second mediated divine utterance comes in 15:28-29 and repeats many of the same ideas, this time after Saul has defeated the Amalekites but has chosen not to execute their king as instructed: "And Samuel said to him, 'The LORD has torn the kingdom of Israel from you this very day, and has given it to a neighbor of yours, who is better than you. Moreover, the Glory of Israel will not recant or change his mind; for he is not a mortal, that he should change his mind.'" This final, redundant statement is an obvious case of "protesting too much."[59] The passage is leading up to the moment when YHWH will be "sorry that he had made Saul king over Israel," perhaps the biggest divine change of mind in all of the Old Testament, one that demands close examination.

The odd little text in 1 Sam. 15:34—16:1a points back to the initial conversation about monarchy between Samuel and YHWH in 8:6-9. It is unfortunate that the modern chapter division falls in the middle of this shared moment of emotional turmoil. Although the emotions of YHWH and Samuel are powerful in 15:35, they could hardly be more ambiguous: "Then Samuel went to Ramah, and Saul went up to his house in Gibeah of Saul. Samuel did not see Saul again until the day of his death, but Samuel grieved over Saul. And the LORD was sorry that he had made Saul king over Israel. The LORD said to Samuel, 'How long will you grieve over Saul? I have rejected him from being king over Israel.'" The reflexive verb (*'bl*) that describes Samuel's present feelings "toward Saul" is most often translated as "grieved" or "mourned." The relationship between the two men is clearly broken, as they go their separate ways for the remainder of their lives, but what is it that upsets Samuel so deeply? In 16:1, YHWH uses the same verb, followed by a different preposition, and some apparent impatience, to urge Samuel out of this condition, which leaves the reader uncertain about what Samuel grieves. Does he feel bad for Saul, for Israel, or for himself? It could be some of all three, of course, but Samuel's self-centered and manipulative behavior on other occasions points toward a predominant portion of the third concern. Saul will still be king, but the events in 1 Samuel 15 seem to have removed Samuel from even his position of shared power. The two statements of Samuel's grief surround the divine response to the situation. The statement in 15:35 is ambiguous enough on its own. The verb describing YHWH's behavior (*nḥm*) can mean "repented," "regretted," or "was sorry," but is the object of this feeling simply the choice of Saul himself or, more generally, the decision to allow Israel to have a king? The immediate context provided by Samuel's uncertain feelings magnifies the ambiguity of YHWH's emotional response, but the larger context may suggest some clarification. If the sense of *nḥm* includes changing course, then the kingship as a whole seems an unlikely object, because YHWH has already stated through Samuel the intent to replace Saul with a better king, and will immediately send Samuel to find him after this conversation. What is more problematic is that YHWH now seems to share the idea that, even though he thought kingship was a bad idea at the beginning, the blame for its current failure lies entirely with Saul.[60]

The divine abandonment of Saul takes another disturbing turn at 1 Sam. 16:14-23. The "evil spirit from the LORD" that torments Saul in this text is unmatched anywhere else in the biblical text, and it reappears again in 18:10 and 19:9.[61] This is one of several cases where a painting is among the most powerful interpretations of a biblical text. Rembrandt's *David Playing the Harp before Saul* juxtaposes the lightness of the former and heaviness of the latter with such power that the fifteen remaining, tangled chapters of the book of 1 Samuel seem embedded on the canvas. The "evil spirit from the LORD" is all over Saul's face as he dabs at his tears with his robe. It is easy, and tempting, to dismiss such a depiction on at least two different grounds. First, we can recognize that when a text like this was written, the kind of dualistic thinking that would have allowed for this spirit to be assigned to a different source did not exist.[62] Second, from a purely modern perspective, it is possible to replace such language with our language of mental illness. In recent decades, there have been some very productive connections drawn between the Bible and Jungian psychology, and the Samuel–Saul–David triangle of personalities is the place to which most of these efforts seem instinctively drawn.[63] Such evasions, however, are out of place in a narrative evaluation of the text that attempts to stay in its world. Within those parameters, it is difficult to avoid the conclusion of Northrop Frye, who identified in this story "the suggestion of malice within the divine nature, a suggestion that is perhaps essential to all great tragedy." On this basis, Frye identified Saul as "the one great tragic hero of the Bible."[64] Some further comparisons must await a closer look at David first, but there is already enough in the text up to this point to name Saul's one great, irredeemable sin: he is not David.

The story moves on in odd fashion. David has been anointed king by Samuel, but Saul is far from dead, so this situation in which two different men are anointed kings of Israel makes conflict impossible to avoid. During the long contest between the two kings, there is little new in the way of divine behavior, but the narrator and the characters remind readers repeatedly that God is with David and has abandoned Saul. Perhaps the most poignant example of this is Samuel's final appearance in the text, in 1 Sam. 28:3-28. The account of Saul's encounter with Samuel's ghost, through the work of the medium at Endor, is a compelling story.[65] The desperate, flailing king has nowhere to go but to his old antagonist, and he is reminded of his plight once again in 28:17-19:

> The LORD has done to you just as he spoke by me; for the LORD has torn the kingdom out of your hand, and given it to your neighbor, David. Because you did not obey the voice of the LORD, and did not carry out his fierce wrath against Amalek, therefore the LORD has done this thing to you today. Moreover, the LORD will give Israel along with you into the hands of the Philistines; and tomorrow you and your sons will be with me; the LORD will also give the army of Israel into the hands of the Philistines.

With this statement and prediction, the rejection and abandonment are complete. One is left to wonder only why God has let it drag out for so long. One of the great textual problems in all of the Old Testament lies back at 1 Sam. 13:1. Many versions simply leave blanks in the text because of the problems with the numbers providing Saul's age of ascension and the length of his reign. Perhaps the unwillingness, or inability, of the biblical tradition to assign a length to Saul's reign lies in the uncertainty of when it ended. Is it over in 1 Samuel 13, the first time Samuel undermines Saul; or in 1 Samuel 15, when YWHW rejects him; or in 1 Samuel 16, when David is anointed in his stead? Saul's life ends on Mount Gilboah in 1 Samuel 31, in a story that makes no mention of the divine character.

This last observation about YHWH and Saul provides occasion to look at the issue of divine presence in the books of Samuel on a larger scale. Many readers have noticed that God appears irregularly in this long story, and that feeling can be confirmed with numerical data (see table 4-2).

Table 4-2: The Frequency of Divine Designations in Samuel

1 Samuel 1–16	0.699 per verse
1 Samuel 17–31	0.290 per verse
2 Samuel 1–5	0.185 per verse
2 Samuel 6–7	1.173 per verse
2 Samuel 8–21	0.126 per verse
2 Samuel 22–24	0.478 per verse

Note: There are any number of caveats that must go with data like this. The divine designations Elohim and YHWH are not the only way that the divine character can be present in texts. Generally, the frequency of pronouns used for the deity follows similar patterns, but this is not necessarily the case. Spikes in the usage of divine designations appear in texts that are overtly religious, such as 2 Samuel 7 and 22, and these have an effect on broad collections of data. Not all of these occurrences of designations involve divine actions. Many are the result of human characters invoking the deity, but these also indicate a divine presence of sorts. Nevertheless, the stark differences illustrated in this chart, when they align with the intuitive sense of many readers, cannot be ignored.

Perhaps there are many ways to explain this variation. One is to note that the divine character becomes scarce in the text when Samuel, the divine representative, departs after 1 Samuel 16. This scarcity continues until David has his kingdom established and a new divine representative, Nathan, appears. The character most affected by this divine diminishment is David, who, once anointed by Samuel as a boy in 1 Samuel 16, seems largely left to his own devices to make his royal appointment a reality. Even the occasional cluster of divine references, such as in 1 Samuel 26, do not present significant divine activity on David's behalf. Of the sixteen appearances of YHWH in this story of the confrontation between David and Saul in the wilderness of Ziph, fifteen are contained in the speech between these two characters. The only time the narrator describes divine activity is in 26:12, when YHWH causes everyone else there to fall asleep so that the two kings can converse without interruption.

In the book called 2 Samuel, the house of Saul, embodied in his son Ishbaal, provides a surprisingly formidable opponent to YHWH's plan to put David on the throne. After a seven-year struggle, David is finally able to reunite Israel and establish Jerusalem as his capital in 2 Samuel 5. This settled situation prompts a new move by YHWH. The negotiation that will lead to David's famous, eternal covenant with YHWH begins with David's offer to build his God a temple. The offer is temporarily refused, but in response God offers to build David a house in 7:11, and the ensuing verses explain that this "house" entails a family dynasty that will extend "forever" on the throne of Israel. It also includes the approval for David's son to build a temple for Israel's God. The plan for David's son to build YHWH a house is repeated in 1 Chron. 17:12, but Chronicles also adds at a later point an explanation not present in the Deuteronomistic History. The divine speech in 1 Chron. 28:3 is reported secondhand by David: "You shall not build a house for my name, for you are a warrior and have shed blood." In 2 Kgs. 5:3-4, Solomon himself intimates only that conflict with surrounding enemies had kept David too busy for such a project. The writer of Chronicles has made a great effort to clean up the image of David. His bandit years and alliances with the Philistines, in which 1 Samuel seems to revel, are gone, as is any mention of Bathsheba. But David's image as a soldier is too much to erase, so Chronicles uses it to disconnect warfare from worship of YHWH.

At this point, the text allows considerable time to elapse, as indicated in 2 Sam. 8:1 and 10:1, presumably allowing David some time to age considerably. The next episode that the books of Samuel seems eager to tell, for reasons that are difficult to comprehend, requires David to be past his prime as a warrior. Divine appearances in the text become rare again, until the Bathsheba-Uriah incident is finished. Nathan enters the scene again in 2 Samuel 12, and with him God becomes an active narrative character again. The declining side of David's life reveals a divine character of a most troubling nature, nowhere more clearly than in 12:11-15. There is no mincing of words here, as YHWH kills David's infant son as a response to David's actions toward Bathsheba and Uriah. During the remaining years of David's life, the capacity for YHWH to punish others for the sins of David knows no bounds. The pronouncement of judgment by Nathan in 12:11 is a thinly veiled description of Absalom's rebellion, an event triggered by the replay of David's rape of Bathsheba by David's own son, Amnon, who rapes David's own daughter, Tamar, in 2 Samuel 13.[66] The entire nation is thrown into turmoil because of David's inability to take decisive action against Amnon, for to do so would be to judge himself more thoroughly than he is willing.

All of this passivity and deflected punishment is magnified in the final story of the books of Samuel, the last story in which we see David outside of the room in which he will die. The account of David's census in 2 Samuel 24 and 1 Chronicles 21 is perplexing in many ways, not all of which can be addressed here. The conflict in the divine character is paramount, and it is magnified by the partially successful attempt to resolve it in the revision of 1 Chronicles. In 2 Samuel 24, YHWH incites David to take the census, judges this action as a sin, offers David a choice of punishment, executes the one that David chooses, and then repents and halts the punishment when it is only partially completed. For his part, David once again eludes direct punishment, instead choosing a plague that will kill seventy thousand of his people. First Chronicles 21 takes only the first of these actions away from YHWH, by inserting an "adversary" figure.[67] It is easy to see this as a move toward a modified dualism in the Old Testament, but the text offers us too little background to evaluate what it is doing or how well it works. Brueggemann has called 1 Samuel 21–24 an "appendix of deconstruction," and his primary focus in this evaluation is the final chapter of the book: "The deconstruction that operates here is not a deconstruction of everything about David or about kingship, but it is a dismantling of a certain David, a David too certain, a David who believes in, acts on, and is defined by ideological claims that are regarded as alien to the older memory."[68]

The names of David and Solomon go together so easily in the memory that it takes some effort to pull back and notice how strikingly different these two characters are. The difference begins with Solomon's acquisition of the throne, which is so different from his father's long struggle. In 1 Kings 1, there is a struggle for the throne, in which Adonijah seems briefly to gain the upper hand, but the conflict is resolved entirely by others. Solomon's mother convinces David to promote Solomon, while Nathan, Benaiah, and Zadok dispose of Adonijah and his supporters, so that the Solomon who emerges in 1 Kings 3 claiming the innocence of a child and asking YHWH for wisdom is not an altogether unbelievable figure. He must ask for wisdom as a gift, of course, because he has done little of the kind of living by which wisdom is acquired and refined. This gift is part of the initial action of God toward Solomon, and it serves to authorize all that Solomon does, for a while. The incongruous aspect of Solomon's career is that all of these supposedly wise and divinely authorized actions lead rapidly to the division of the kingdom at his death. The central accomplishment of Solomon is the construction of the temple, and, for this study, the most important question it raises is how such a permanent dwelling will change the character of the deity.

It is vital to notice at the outset that when the temple is finished, YHWH agrees to move into it. The decisive event occurs in 1 Kgs. 8:10–12, when the glory (*kbd*) of YHWH fills the temple in the form of a cloud. Thus, just as YHWH chose to come down from Mount Sinai in Exodus 40, to dwell in the tent Moses had constructed, here YHWH signals approval of Solomon's work by visibly occupying the temple. This presence remains mysterious and dangerous in two ways. First, the use of the "glory of YHWH" keeps the divine presence one step removed from human description and containment. That the root word *kbd* has "heaviness" as its most basic meaning points to a sense of greater density that does not preclude divine presence elsewhere.[69] Solomon also uses language reminiscent of the Sinai experience when he speaks of YHWH dwelling in "thick darkness." This presence is not tolerable for humans, as even the priests are chased from the building by the cloud when it first enters in 1 Kgs. 8:10–11.[70]

Solomon's first audience with YHWH, in 1 Kings 3, was in a dream at Gibeon, so there it is presented as an entirely private matter. In the report of his second divine audience, on the other side of the construction of the temple and the palace, there is no description other than "the LORD appeared to Solomon a second time, as he had appeared to him at Gibeon" (1 Kgs. 9:2). The reader is left to assume from this that it is also a private experience. The content of this second encounter is foreboding, as YHWH promises Solomon a dynasty in exchange for obedience but punishment and destruction if he does not keep the commandments. The length and specificity of the divine threat leaves little doubt that this is the way the story will go, and by 11:9, YHWH is already angry with Solomon. The last time we see the wise king alive, he is trying to kill Jeroboam (11:40), who has been told by the prophet Abijah that the northern tribes will be taken away from Solomon and given to him. This conflict will lead to the division of Israel into the divided monarchy, an event that will be the starting point of the next chapter.

The outlines of the account of Solomon in the Deuteronomistic History are repeated in Chronicles, but there are important omissions. The reports of his foreign marriages and accompanying idolatry in 1 Kgs. 11:1-8 are not recounted in 2 Chronicles, and neither are the stories in I Kgs. 11:14-25 about YHWH "raising up adversaries against Solomon." It is easy to combine these omissions with the missing account of David's actions in relation to Bathsheba and Uriah and conclude that Chronicles is simply cleaning up the reputations of its two favorite kings. Another result of this revision of the story, however, is to allow greater acceptance of a king who operates internationally, a concern consistent with the manner in which later parts of the biblical story present foreign kings (such as Cyrus, Darius, Ahasueras, and Artaxerxes) who help Israelites, sometimes as a result of subtle divine direction. This idea will emerge more clearly in chapter 6, but at this point a situation is apparent in which biblical writers have reached back to rethink their own story in a way that allows a more positive perspective of foreign kings by shaping the story of one of their own great kings of the past in their image.

In the end, YHWH's treatment of Solomon seems rather instrumental. If there is any connection between the gift of wisdom in 1 Kings 3 and Solomon's subsequent performance as king, it seems to be his skill as an administrator. The famous story of the two women and the baby in 3:16-28 appears to perform the function of confirming the gift, but it is otherwise a misfit in the text. The very next chapter contains a long list of Solomon's officials, which makes the reader wonder why the king would be adjudicating a child-custody case between two prostitutes. Nevertheless, the biblical account has Solomon manage two massive building projects over two decades, followed by the development of all the personnel and apparatus to operate both temple and palace. According to 1 Chron. 22:8-9, Solomon is an appropriate person to build the temple because he is a "man of peace," unlike his warrior father. This text has YHWH specifically commit to giving Solomon the kind of context free from external threat that would make so much building and administrative development possible. The biblical text does not report directly how Solomon is able to achieve the political and military space for all of this activity, but it does make a list of all of his foreign wives and alliances. Unfortunately for Solomon, these are counted in 1 Kings 11 as the sins that lead to the division of his kingdom after his death. The conclusion is that YHWH gets a house that will stand for more than three centuries and, because the means by which Solomon is able to construct it is evaluated as disobedience, YHWH must give little in return.

God of the Kingdom outside of Samuel, Kings, and Chronicles

This subject first requires a look back in the biblical story. In the midst of the set of laws known as the Deuteronomic code in Deuteronomy 12–26, which Moses spoke to the Israelites in Moab, there is a discussion of Israel's future monarchy. There are hints that this institution will not fare well, and the blame for this is shared in Deut. 17:14 as the people choose to have a king, but YHWH chooses the king. The conclusion is made explicit later in the book, in Deut. 28:36, which says that Israel and its king will be taken captive. The idea of Israel having a king appears one other time before the monarchy actually begins, in Judges 9, when Abimelech presumes to be king of Israel for three years. In 9:22, God "sends an evil spirit" to create conflict between Abimelech and the Shechemites, which ends when Abimelech's head is crushed by a stone (v. 53). These sparse, early indicators that the monarchy will not end well might easily be forgotten in the midst of the successes of David and Solomon, but the eventual collapse of the monarchy recalls them.

In many ways, the entire book of Psalms might be treated under this heading. Even before David's name first appears, in the title of Psalm 3, the great enthronement song called Psalm 2 seems to introduce him anonymously. Two features of the book of Psalms stand in extreme tension to one another. It has long been observed, since interpreters began identifying types of psalms, particularly laments and hymns, that the former are more concentrated in the first half of the book and the latter in the second half. More recent observations about the five-book structure of the book of Psalms tend to identify books 1 and 2 as recollections of the glory days of the monarchy, celebrations of David and Solomon. Of the seventy-two psalms in the first two books, fifty-five have David's name in the title, and of these, ten are connected by these titles to specific events in the life of David. Oddly, most of these are lament poems connected by the titles to David's long period of struggle in the wilderness, awaiting his opportunity to capture the throne from Saul and his family. The two that are not, Psalms 3 and 51, are linked to David's flight from Absalom and the Bathsheba incident. One psalm (72) is connected by name to Solomon in the title, and another (30) by being designated as a song of dedication for the temple. So, the united monarchy and its two great kings are most present in the more negative part of the book, in terms of psalm type. Nevertheless, there is something nostalgic about the presentation of their reigns in books 1 and 2 of Psalms.

Psalm 89 is the pivotal poem in the book of Psalms and may well be regarded as the central text in the story of Israel in the Old Testament. Among the features that cause it to stand out are its size, its reversal of the standard lament pattern, and its position at the end of book 3 of Psalms. The reversed lament, which begins by praising YHWH for the glories of the house of David and its eternal covenant and ends in the depths of despair over broken promises, may serve to resolve some of the tension created by the larger Davidic pattern described in the previous paragraph. The recollection of the Davidic monarchy was a two-edged sword for Israel, prompting both pride and pain. It was the greatest achievement and the greatest loss, which Psalm 89 portrays as powerfully as any text in the Old Testament.

A particular set of psalms, sometimes known as the "YHWH is king" psalms, need brief mention here, though they will be addressed more thoroughly in chapter 6. This phrase or a close equivalent appears in Psalms 93 and 95–99. With the monarchy in ruins, as depicted in Psalm 89, this series of psalms would appear to be an answer to the problem of governance in Israel after the exile.[71] As poetry, they do not have to address questions about how governance actually works in the world, the kind of problem that gave rise to the monarchy in the first place, but these and the surrounding poems plead for YHWH to be a refuge for Israel and to take vengeance on Israel's enemies.

The monarchy, particularly as it is embodied in Solomon, is present in the biblical Wisdom literature as well, but this presence is difficult to evaluate. Solomon's name is never mentioned in Ecclesiastes and appears only three times, in superscriptions, in Proverbs, so, at most, one may assume that Solomon is the dramatic voice proclaiming the words of these books. The content of the wisdom books addresses the daily life of ordinary individuals. Still, the connection of Solomon to the idea of wisdom is substantial enough in 1 Kings and 2 Chronicles that he can credibly play this dramatic role. An idealized king from the distant past may be the best candidate for such a role. The Wisdom literature will be addressed more extensively in chapter 6 of this book, where its role will be examined very differently. At this point, we can see what may be a secondary function of recalling the days of the united monarchy and listening to a voice from Israel's time of greatest national glory.

This book has repeatedly returned to Nehemiah 9 as a critically important text, and it will do so twice more. It is important to observe at the end of this section that the period of the monarchy finds no place in this great recital of Israel's past. "Our kings" are mentioned twice in verses 32-34, but these are both references to the monarchy as something lost because of Israel's disobedience. The monarchy might seem to be one ancient tradition that could be revived in a restored Israel. Whereas the ancient kings such as Saul, David, and Solomon had a kind of direct divine access that was no longer available, later kings, even some good ones such as Josiah and Hezekiah, operated without it, partly because of the growing role of prophets. Some texts connected to the restoration of Judah, such as Ezra 1–6, Haggai, and Zechariah 4, seem to place some hope in Zerubbabel as one who might continue this institution, but such hopes vanish quickly in the biblical story, perhaps replaced by the notion of YHWH as Israel's king, as illustrated in the preceding discussion of Psalms, acting in concert with foreign kings in an international arena.

The Nation-Building God in Old Testament Theology

Among the variegated recollections in the Old Testament, some look back to certain eras fondly, whereas others rebuke such reminiscence. One of the pitfalls of Old Testament theology is the temptation to look backward along with the former group and to fail to listen to the latter. Negative views of the monarchy and suspicion of hierarchical leadership, a layer of which is no doubt found in 1 Samuel, can lead to a longing for the "good old days" of the period of the judges. Such a perspective aligned well with the views of the development of Israel that emerged in the second half of the twentieth century, which characterized Israel's emergence as a result of a gradual infiltration of formerly nomadic peoples and/or a peasant revolt.[72] Developing a more theological perspective from this historical foundation, Paul Hanson could thus describe premonarchic Israelites in glowing, idealistic terms: "Sustained by ongoing communion with the living God, they became strands in a communal fabric that ordered life without excluding, that created harmony without stultifying, that sustained community without extinguishing the challenge to develop and grow."[73] Finding such a community in the act of reading the book of Judges is very difficult.

Von Rad presented both the movement into the land and the development of the state as "crises" in the life of Israel, not so much because their survival was threatened and they had to adapt to survive, but because old ways of thinking and operating had to be resisted and overcome: "On the whole then, the institution of the monarchy was a newcomer in Israel, indeed almost something born out of season. Consequently, it was inevitable that its relationship with central traditions of the faith was strained from the outset and, right down to its end, the monarchy never succeeded in extricating itself from this strain."[74] One of these changes was the unification and sacralization of the monarchy, particularly under David. This was accomplished through the divine covenant with David, presented in 2 Samuel 7, and by David's possession of the ark of the covenant in 2 Samuel 6. A second problem was the establishment of Jerusalem as the capital city. Here is where von Rad found the purpose of the census story in 2 Samuel 24, which ends with the building of the first altar in

Jerusalem, an act that halts the deadly advancing toward the city.[75] At the same time, this story pushes back against the militarization of Israel under the king's leadership by disputing the census, which had a primarily military function.[76] As a final example, von Rad noted the building of the temple as an element of this crisis. The opposition to this project is raised in the text by Nathan but is eventually overcome.[77] Walther Eichrodt also recognized the tension present in the text concerning the institutionalization of Israel, particularly the monarchy. The notion of political power permanently invested in political institutions and handed down through a royal dynasty was in direct conflict with "genuine Mosaic Yahweh religion," in which divine power intervened suddenly through the work of charismatic individuals.[78] The distinction Eichrodt drew, however, between David and Solomon, particularly the differences in the way these two formed the connections between political power and religion, is difficult to see in the text. He saw in Solomon's building of the temple an attempt "to safeguard the monarch's religious position by the one-sided expedient of linking it solidly with the sacramental and cultic wing." In similar fashion, Eichrodt dismissed Solomon's divine encounter at Gibeon as "more a matter of oracle-seeking in accordance with the priestly practice than of a gift of the spirit like the prophets."[79] One sees in such statements both the bias against Judaism identified by Jon Levenson and the means of maintaining a sense of divine constancy by separating and discounting certain parts of the story that the biblical text describes as divine behavior but that do not fit well into a preconceived scheme.

Brueggemann's treatment of the establishment of the nation and the monarchy makes excellent use of his dialogical model. Whereas earlier Old Testament theologians, even though they operated within a historical framework, still dealt with the monarchy primarily in lofty, theological terms, Brueggemann looked through such claims to their material aspects. In his critique of Sigmund Mowinckel's insistence that there was "no conflict between Yahweh's kingly rule and that of his son, the anointed, earthly king,"[80] Brueggemann asserted that "human monarchy in Israel is never simply a matter of theological-theoretical interpretation. Human monarchy in Israel, as anywhere, concerns the distribution of power, goods (land), and access."[81] A dialogical model is capable of asking persistently whom a particular power arrangement like the monarchy serves.

The discussion of the growth of Israel into a nation within Old Testament theology has moved in two characteristic directions. One of these is the harsh judgment of such institutionalization of the people of God by theologians such as Eichrodt and von Rad. The other has been a quick move to "messianism" in order to provide Christian readers background for entering the New

Testament. Werner H. Schmidt, for example, began his discussion of the Israelite monarchy with a carefully developed discussion of kingship in Israel's ancient Near Eastern context but ended it with a lengthy discussion of "the messiah," even though he acknowledged that "the Old Testament does not have this title for the future ruler."[82] Another case in point is the massive work of Brevard S. Childs, *Biblical Theology of the Old and New Testaments*, in which he first attempted to explicate "the discrete witness of the Old Testament."[83] Trying to avoid both the anti-Jewish polemic of attacking the monarchy and a heavy-handed pointing toward the New Testament, Childs produced fewer than two pages of text on David and Solomon combined.[84] It is as though he left himself with almost nothing to say.

The rise of the monarchy is an important part of the development of Israel's God as a narrative character who moves into this arrangement with misgivings. There are extraordinary achievements in this part of Israel's story, but suspicions about this kind of leadership and the deity's wavering relationships to the kings themselves make for a story that is difficult to work with in Israel's recollection. The biblical story and its divine character will eventually move beyond monarchy and push it into the past, but two important aspects will remain in the identity of this people. One is the memory of what Israel could be as an independent political entity, even though that mode of existence lasted for a relatively short time. The other is the monarchy's greatest physical achievement, the building of the temple in Jerusalem, a reality that Israel would reenact and continue to utilize for centuries beyond the monarchy itself.

Notes

1. Fixing this number precisely is challenging for a number of reasons, though the point here is hardly dependent upon such precision. First Sam. 13:1 exhibits some significant textual problems, including its recording of the length of Saul's reign as king of Israel. The bottom of the range reported in the text is produced by taking the literal "two years" of the Masoretic Text and adding it to the forty years of David's reign (1 Kgs. 2:11) and forty years of Solomon's reign (1 Kgs. 11:42). The symbolic nature of these numbers provides an additional problem, of course, along with the forty-year reign later attributed to Saul (Acts 13:21). The three reigns of forty years provide the maximum number.

2. On the general presentation of the deity in the Deuteronomistic History, see Jack Miles, *God: A Biography* (New York: Vintage, 1995), 163. As Miles observed, the divine character comes and goes as a direct actor in the entirety of this material.

3. For a full discussion of this view of the development of these two "histories," see Martin Noth, *The Chronicler's History*, trans. H. G. M. Williamson (Sheffield, UK: Sheffield Academic, 2001), 11–26.

4. See H. G. M. Williamson, *Israel in the Book of Chronicles* (London: Cambridge University Press, 1977), 37–59; and Sara Japhet, "The Supposed Common Authorship of Chronicles and Ezra Investigated Anew," *VT* 18 (1969): 334–70.

5. Raymond F. Person Jr., *The Deuteronomistic History and the Book of Chronicles: Scribal Works in an Oral World* (Atlanta: Society of Biblical Literature, 2010), 16–19.

6. Ibid., 163–69.

7. Ibid., 169–73.

8. The Israelites did fight battles during the period of Moses' leadership, such as the battle against the Amalekites in Exod. 17:8-15 and the battle against the Midianites in Num. 31:1-12, but Moses is kept distant from the fighting.

9. Gerhard von Rad, *Holy War in Ancient Israel*, trans. Marva J. Dawn (Grand Rapids, MI: Eerdmans, 1991), 51.

10. Susan Niditch, *War in the Hebrew Bible: A Study in the Ethics of Violence* (Oxford: Oxford University Press, 1993), 40. See also Niditch's cogent review of biblical scholarship on this subject in the twentieth century (5–13).

11. Ibid., 28–29.

12. For more on this literary development of the story of the battle of Jericho, see Mark McEntire, *The Blood of Abel: The Violent Plot in the Hebrew Bible* (Macon, GA: Mercer University Press, 1999), 64–70.

13. Ibid., 70–73.

14. Regina M. Schwartz, *The Curse of Cain: The Violent Legacy of Monotheism* (Chicago: University of Chicago Press, 1997), 57–58. Like the work of this period by Jack Miles and Richard Elliott Friedman, Schwartz's book was also largely ignored by the field of Old Testament theology.

15. On this point, see Miles, *God*, 154–55. Miles was unusually reticent in his discussion of the books of Joshua and Judges. His treatment of these two books combined is roughly the length of his treatment of the book of Ruth, which is less than 10 percent of their combined length. The reasons for his brevity are not entirely clear, but one of the most compelling aspects of his work is its playfulness, even when the portrayal of God is negative in nature. In his discussion of the conquest tradition, however, Miles seems unwilling to engage in this characteristic playfulness.

16. Schwartz, *Curse of Cain*, 62.

17. Ibid., 60–62.

18. Paul Copan, *Is God a Moral Monster? Making Sense of the Old Testament God* (Grand Rapids, MI: Baker, 2011), 176. It should be noted that many of Copan's attempted arguments are in direct response to the work of Richard Dawkins, a British biologist who has become well known outside biology as an outspoken, self-proclaimed atheist. His best-known book on religion is *The God Delusion* (Boston: Houghton Mifflin, 2006). Anti-Dawkins books have become a veritable industry, some with his name actually in the title. Although he clearly goes beyond the abilities of science to provide evidence for or against the existence of God, the extent of the response against him provides ample evidence of the power of his arguments.

19. Copan, *Is God a Moral Monster?* 175–77.

20. Ibid., 170–7.

21. Ibid., 175–79. In the end, Copan's accumulated claim is that whenever the Bible proposes or supports an idea that might be morally questionable, then this "surface reading" must be wrong. He takes this even as far as trying to relabel Rahab as a "tavern-keeper," rather than a prostitute, in order to evade the question about why the spies whom Joshua sent to Jericho visited a brothel (177).

22. For a fuller description of the narrative shape of the book of Judges, see Mark McEntire, *Dangerous Worlds: Living and Dying in Biblical Texts* (Macon, GA: Smyth & Helwys, 2004), 37–39.

23. On the differences between Samson and the other judges depicted in the book, see Tammi J. Schneider, *Judges* (Collegeville, MN: Liturgical, 2000), 216–17.

24. On the puzzling nature of the Gideon section and its significance in the book of Judges, see E. John Hamlin, *At Risk in the Promised Land: A Commentary on the Book of Judges* (Grand Rapids, MI: Eerdmans, 1990), 90–91.

25. For more on the relationship between this theophany and others in the Bible, see Susan Niditch, *Judges: A Commentary* (Louisville: Westminster, 2008), 90–91.

26. Niditch did not note the ambiguity of the name here but understood it as ironic that "the enemy of Baal bears a Baal-related name." Ibid., 91.

27. Ibid., 88–89.

28. McEntire, *Dangerous Worlds*, 45.

29. Phyllis, Trible, *Texts of Terror: Literary-Feminist Readings of Biblical Narratives* (Minneapolis: Fortress Press, 1984), 93–94.

30. The biblical tradition surrounding the Nazirite vow is difficult to comprehend. The legal description of the vow in Numbers 6 describes a temporary choice made by an adult to separate him- or herself from the community and to change certain behaviors. In the two related narrative accounts, Samson and Samuel, the vow is different from this in many ways, most significantly in that it seems to be a permanent vow made by a parent for a child. See Mark McEntire, *Struggling with God: An Introduction to the Pentateuch* (Macon, GA: Mercer University Press, 2008), 161–62.

31. On the general character of these chapters, particularly the dominating elements of violence and death, see McEntire, *Dangerous Worlds*, 52–54.

32. Trible, *Texts of Terror*, 80.

33. There is no denying that the closing chapters of the book of Judges contain a great deal of anti-Saul polemic. The scene of the crime in chapter 19 is Gibeah, Saul's hometown, and the rebellious tribe in chapter 20 is Benjamin, Saul's tribe. For more on this subject, see Niditch, *Judges*, 208–11. This element will be treated more appropriately in retrospect later in this chapter, in the discussion of the monarchy and Saul's "failures."

34. Miles, *God*, 150–51.

35. Konrad Schmid, "The Late Persian Formation of the Torah: Observations on Deuteronomy 34," in *Judah and the Judeans in the Fourth Century B.C.E.*, ed. Oded Lipschits, Gary N. Knoppers, and Rainer Albertz (Winona Lake, IN: Eisenbrauns, 2007), 6–8.

36. For more on the meaning of this term and the significance of nomadism, see Modupe Oduyoye, *The Sons of God and the Daughters of Men: An Afro-Asiatic Interpretation of Genesis 1–11* (Maryknoll, NY: Orbis, 1984), 63–74.

37. Robert Haak, "Mapping Violence in the Prophets: Zephaniah 2," in *The Aesthetics of Violence in the Prophets*, ed. Julia M. O'Brien and Chris Franke (New York: T&T Clark, 2010), 24.

38. Julia O'Brien, *Challenging Prophetic Metaphor: Theology and Ideology in the Prophets* (Louisville: Westminster, 2011), 101–24.

39. Ibid., 106.

40. Ibid., 111.

41. Walter Brueggemann, *Theology of the Old Testament: Testimony, Dispute, Advocacy* (Minneapolis: Fortress Press, 1997), 241–44. The ubiquity of the divine-warrior image has been demonstrated by H. Wayne Ballard, who located the image in almost all of the poems and presented a thorough analysis of those which it dominates. See Ballard, *The Divine Warrior Motif in the Psalms* (North Richland Hills, TX: Bibal, 1999), 31–82.

42. Brueggemann, *Theology of the Old Testament*, 242–43.

43. Edgar Conrad, *Reading Isaiah* (Minneapolis: Fortress Press, 1991), 52.

44. It should be acknowledged that there are some significant textual problems with this verse. For a discussion of these, see Klaus Baltzer, *Deutero-Isaiah: A Commentary on Isaiah 40–55* (Minneapolis: Fortress Press, 2001), 87–88. It is common for texts that deal with divine warfare to demonstrate such problems in their transmission, e.g. Exod. 15:3 and Hosea 6:5. It may even be theological struggles with the harshness of such imagery that have created divergence within the textual traditions.

45. Conrad, *Reading Isaiah*, 80–81.

46. This is the plural form of the Hebrew word *mwšyh* that is used numerous times in Judges but is translated there by the NRSV as "deliverer."

47. Readers of the Christian Old Testament will notice that we are about to skip over the book of Ruth. There are a number of reasons for doing so. The insertion of Ruth at this point seems entirely artificial. Most significantly, it completely disrupts the movement of the narrative. Just as the book of Judges has convinced readers that the Israelites need a king to enforce moral order and the book of Samuel is about to introduce us to the first, the story of Ruth appears, a story in which all the characters always do what is right, without any authority figure to tell them what to do and compel them to do it. A story like the one in Ruth does not coalesce around the "God of war" image that dominates the book of Judges. For other reasons that will be explained later, the book of Ruth will be discussed in chapter 6.

48. On the variety of roles played by the character named Samuel, see Marti J. Steussy, *Samuel and His God* (Columbia: University of South Carolina Press, 2010), 27–32.

49. For a discussion of the literary shape of the final form of the book of Samuel, see McEntire, *Dangerous Worlds*, 61–64.

50. See the discussion of this tradition in McEntire, *Struggling with God*, 161–62.

51. Steussy describes and evaluates many of these interpretations; see *Samuel and His God*, 60–63.

52. Ibid., 62–63.

53. Ibid., 63.

54. Miles, *God*, 163–64.

55. J. Cheryl Exum, *Tragedy and Biblical Narrative: Arrows of the Almighty* (Cambridge: Cambridge University Press, 1992), 17–18.

56. Robert Alter, *The Art of Biblical Narrative* (New York: Basic Books, 1981), 60–61.

57. David M. Gunn, *The Fate of King Saul: An Interpretation of a Biblical Story* (Sheffield, UK: Sheffield University Press, 1980), 23–56.

58. It is astonishing how commonly people believe that God uttered these words directly about David, calling him "a man after my own heart."

59. It should be noted that the translation "recant" in 15:29 comes from the Greek text and 4QSam[a]. The Masoretic Text has a different word here that means something more like "deceive."

60. For a thorough defense of Saul as one unfairly "scapegoated" for the failures of the nation, see Marty Alan Michelson, *Reconciling Violence and Kingship: A Study of Judges and 1 Samuel* (Eugene, OR: Pickwick, 2011), 133–52.

61. The closest equivalent is the statement in Judg. 9:23 that God "sent an evil spirit between Abimelech and the men of Shechem." The two texts are almost certainly related.

62. The shift in theological language from the Deuteronomistic story of David's census in 2 Samuel 24 to the account of this same event in 1 Chronicles 21 will be discussed later in this chapter. One can surmise that if the writer of Chronicles had reported the events of 1 Samuel 16, then the language would be different, tending more toward dualism, but with no such report from this postexilic writer, such an escape from this difficulty is cut off.

63. See, for example, John A. Sanford, *King Saul: The Tragic Hero* (New York: Paulist, 1985).

64. Northrop Frye, *The Great Code: The Bible and Literature* (New York: Harcourt Brace Jovanovich, 1982), 181.

65. It is important to note that although Chronicles omits almost all of the material about Saul, this is the one "sin" of Saul that it retains (1 Chron. 10:13-14). See the discussion of this text in Scott W. Hahn, *The Kingdom of God as Liturgical Empire: A Theological Commentary on 1–2 Chronicles* (Grand Rapids, MI: Baker Academic, 2012), 45–47.

66. For careful readings of this story that reveal its internal workings and the connections to what happens before and after, see Shimon Bar-Efrat, *Narrative Art in the Bible*, trans. Dorothea Shefer-Vanson (Sheffield, UK: Almond, 1989), 239–82; and J. Cheryl Exum, *Fragmented Women: Feminist (Sub)Versions of Biblical Narratives* (Sheffield, UK: JSOT Press, 1993), 170–201.

67. English translations produced by Christians are all too eager to find the later Satan figure in the Old Testament. Even the minority who avoid the mistake of doing so in texts such as Job 1–2 often do so in 1 Chronicles 21. The references in Job in the Hebrew text all place a definite

article on the word for this figure and are rightly translated as "the adversary." The lack of a definite article in 1 Chron. 21:1 means nothing, because Hebrew has no equivalent of an indefinite article. Therefore, the rendering "an adversary" is preferable to the proper noun Satan, because it is consistent with the use of this word in the rest of the Old Testament. On the emergence of the personified figure properly called by the proper noun "Satan" in Judaism of the second and first centuries BCE, see Elaine Pagels, *The Origin of Satan* (New York: Random House, 1995), 46–60.

68. Walter Brueggemann, "2 Samuel 21–24—An Appendix of Deconstruction?" in *Old Testament Theology: Essays of Structure, Theme, and Text*, ed. Patrick D. Miller (Minneapolis: Fortress Press, 1992), 248.

69. The ideas of "fluidity" and "multiplicity of divine embodiment," developed by Benjamin Sommer and discussed in chapter 1 of this book, also apply here. See Sommer, *The Bodies of God and the World of Ancient Israel* (Cambridge: Cambridge University Press, 2009), 36.

70. See the discussion of "thick darkness" as a mode of divine presence in Samuel Terrien, *The Elusive Presence: Toward a New Biblical Theology* (New York: Harper & Row, 1978), 193–95. Among other issues, Terrien presented this idea as part of Israel's resistance to sun worship in the surrounding cultures.

71. For a discussion of this sequence of psalms and their place within the larger book, see William L. Holladay, *The Psalms through Three Thousand Years: Prayerbook of a Cloud of Witnesses* (Minneapolis: Fortress Press, 1993), 78–79.

72. See George Mendenhall, "The Hebrew Conquest of Palestine," *BA* 25 (1962): 66–87; and Norman K. Gottwald, *The Tribes of Yahweh* (Maryknoll, NY: Orbis, 1979), 191–236.

73. Paul D. Hanson, *The People Called: The Growth of Community in the Bible* (San Francisco: Harper & Row, 1986), 75.

74. Gerhard von Rad, *Old Testament Theology*, trans. D. M. G. Stalker (New York: Harper & Row, 1962), 1:40.

75. Ibid., 45.

76. Ibid., 59.

77. Ibid., 61.

78. Walther Eichrodt, *Theology of the Old Testament*, trans. J. A. Baker (Philadelphia: Westminster, 1961), 1:441.

79. Ibid., 448.

80. Sigmund Mowinckel, *He That Cometh* (Oxford: Blackwell, 1956), 171.

81. Brueggemann, *Theology of the Old Testament*, 604.

82. Werner H. Schmidt, *The Faith of the Old Testament: A History*, trans. John Sturdy (Philadelphia: Westminster, 1983), 198.

83. Brevard S. Childs, *Biblical Theology of the Old and New Testaments: Theological Reflection on the Christian Bible* (Minneapolis: Fortress Press, 1992), 95.

84. Ibid., 153–55. Even in this small amount of discussion of David, Childs did not avoid appeals to messianism entirely, though he used the term only twice, as an uncapitalized adjective in the phrase "messianic hope."

5

A Punishing and Destroying God

It is difficult to say exactly when the story of Israel as a nation begins to take a downward turn, though it is apparent from a fairly early point in the canonical story that this will eventually happen. Deuteronomy is overflowing with awareness of Israel's eventual demise, with Deut. 28:15-68 perhaps functioning as the classic statement of the certainty of divine judgment at the end of the long story. In addition to tracing this primary story line from Genesis to Kings, and its parallel in Chronicles, I have sought to organize the rest of the Old Testament around this story as both a retelling of and a response to it. The Prophetic literature will take a prominent position in the upcoming part of the process. Along with many other interpreters, I understand the Prophetic literature to be a response to crisis,[1] so its presence may serve as an important marker in the downward development of the biblical story. The earliest stages of the Prophetic literature seem to have been generated by figures such as Amos, Hosea, Isaiah, and Micah, who appeared in the late eighth century BCE. The books that bear the names of these characters must be treated with sensitivity and some intentional ambiguity, because they are all literary products of later time periods, which carry the work of these persons forward to new and emerging situations.[2] In the book of Isaiah, for example, YHWH is a character who interacts with Isaiah ben Amoz and King Ahaz in stories about events set in the eighth century, a character who interacts with Cyrus of Persia in the sixth century, and a character who speaks to an implied audience of Israelites during the restoration of Judah in the fifth century.

As I stated in the previous chapter, the division of the kingdoms, as portrayed in 1 Kings 12 and 2 Chronicles 10, is as convenient a turning point as any. The death of Solomon exposes north-south fractures that have always been present in Israel's story. The important question for this study will be how the national schism divides the divine attention, and how the divine character continues to behave toward a people whose organization is not what was intended. This will be difficult to ascertain fully, because our sources for the story are "southern" (1 and 2 Kings) and "more southern" (1 and 2 Chronicles). The Deuteronomistic History reports the story of Israel from a southern perspective, with most of the attention given to Judah, but also keeps the reader apprised of the situation in the northern kingdom, even if through biased lenses. Chronicles, on the other hand, after reporting the division, comes very close to pretending that the northern kingdom does not exist.

Another important shift at about this point in the story is the role of persons called prophets. Through the duration of the united monarchy, these figures appear most often as royal advisers. Even when they criticize the monarch, as Nathan does in 2 Samuel 12, they typically do so within this royal capacity. Ahijah, who appears in 1 Kings 11 to tell Solomon that much of his kingdom will be taken from the Davidic dynasty, is a precursor to prophets such as Elijah, who will engage in open conflict with royal institutions. This makes way for the prophets who have biblical books with their names on them who, other than Isaiah, appear to have no place within the royal court.

This part of the story will end with the destruction of Jerusalem and its temple, the event that is generally considered central to the forces that drove the process of putting Israel's traditions in the final written form that became the Tanak and the Old Testament. A narrative exploration of the canon may seem to be getting ahead of itself by working with an awareness of this ultimate event, but, as is demonstrated in previous chapters, the story itself is aware of this end and shows its hand at many points. The final forms of all of the prophetic books also have this sense of inevitability about them.

God of Decline

The story of the division of the united monarchy into northern (Israel) and southern (Judah) kingdoms in 1 Kings 12 and 2 Chronicles 10 is foretold in 1 Kings 11 only, by Ahijah the prophet, whose presence is partially erased from the story in Chronicles. The story of the revolt led by Jeroboam begins without any explicit divine involvement, though careful readers may think they detect YHWH operating behind the scenes. The way that Jeroboam comes from Egypt and confronts Rehoboam about the enslavement of the northern tribes by the Davidic dynasty resembles Moses' confrontation of Pharaoh.[3] An overt divine presence enters the story only at 1 Kgs. 12:15 (2 Chron. 10:15), in the evaluation of the narrator, who blames the intransigence of Rehoboam on the fulfillment of YHWH's word to Jeroboam through Ahijah. This evaluation is confirmed by a "man of God" named Shemaiah in 1 Kgs. 12:22–24, who utters a standard prophetic oracle, beginning with "Thus says YHWH . . ." The oracle confirms that God is the source of the division of the nations and that, therefore, the people of Judah should not resist it.

At this point, Kings and Chronicles diverge in two important ways.[4] First, Chronicles gives no attention to the development of the northern monarchy after Jeroboam. Second, Chronicles gives somewhat less attention to the emerging role of prophets than does Kings.[5] These two features are related to each other, because the most prominent prophets in Kings, Elijah and Elisha, are primarily northern figures, but Chronicles also diminishes the interactions of King Hezekiah of Judah with Isaiah the prophet. These two factors serve to remove some of the strangeness of the divine character from Chronicles. A case in point is the story of the "man of God from Judah" who visits Jeroboam in Bethel, in 1 Kings 13, to denounce the altar there. The story is so strange as to defy description, and the divine behavior seems to move in fragmented directions.[6] Walter Brueggemann has argued that this text deliberately demonstrates the inscrutability of Israel's God: "The narrative wants to say that in the course of contested theological-political interaction, there is a deep current of meaning and purpose to which human agents have no access, namely, the intention of [YHWH]."[7] The result of such a motive in this case, however, would seem to be a divine character who acts in inscrutable ways just to prove his inscrutability. Jerome T. Walsh, in contrast, argued on linguistic grounds that 1 Kings 13 is characterized by the irony of multiple reversals.[8] Walsh's argument seems more likely in terms of intent, but if it is so, then the writer has overspiced and created an odd-tasting stew. The end result comes back around closer to Brueggemann's sense that the divine character is incomprehensible. This event will serve as a bracket around most of Israel's story observed in this chapter, as it arises again near the end of the Deuteronomistic History in 2 Kgs. 23:17-18, when Josiah fulfills the prophecy against Bethel by tearing down the altar but leaves the grave of this mysterious man of God undisturbed.[9] The contradictory messages and behaviors of the two prophetic figures in this story may serve to prepare the reader both to question the motives and legitimacy of prophets and to accept that their motives and messages may not always be clear and harmonious.

Once the two monarchies are established, the book of Kings settles into a fairly regular pattern. New kings are introduced using the regnal year of the sitting king in the other kingdom, and most of these kings are evaluated as part of their ascension notice, typically using the language of whether they did good or evil "in the eyes of YHWH." Those in the southern kingdom are often compared to David. There is not an explicit correlation between the virtues of these kings and the lengths of their reigns, so the idea of long periods of power connected to divine blessing, which was significant in the book of Judges and in the stories of David and Solomon, appears to have ended. The northern kings are routinely reckoned as evil, and the monarchy there experiences a great deal of violence and disruption after the long initial reign of Jeroboam I, a volatile condition that leads up to the introduction of Elijah in 1 Kings 17.

It is difficult to express all of the ways in which Elijah is an entirely new kind of figure in the biblical story. The foundation for the role of prophet in the Deuteronomic tradition is established in Deut. 18:15-22, but this is a perplexing text. Perhaps the most important question is to whom this text refers, a problem recently addressed by Ernest Nicholson. Although Nicholson acknowledged that none of the preexilic prophets whose "books" appear in the canon are mentioned by name in the Deuteronomistic History, except for Isaiah, he nevertheless argued that prophets such as Amos, Hosea, and Micah must be in view in this statement, along with the likes of Nathan, Elijah, and Elisha, who do appear prominently in the Deuteronomistic narrative.[10] The instructions in Deut. 18:20-22 are thoroughly nonsensical. Although initially claiming that a prophet who declares the word of YHWH falsely will die, the text goes on to claim that the test of prophecy is whether what is prophesied comes true. There is no indication of how long the audience should wait for such a verification. Moreover, in the meantime, the audience is urged not to be frightened by the false prophecy, though the means of determining its lack of truth has fallen apart logically as the instruction has proceeded. It is obvious, in light of our present experience, that the practice of prophecy is a perfect target for abuse, and this must surely have been the case in ancient Israel as well. Though the criteria provided in Deuteronomy 18 make no sense, they do function as a warning to discern the words of prophets carefully. Such texts leave the role and legitimacy of prophets shrouded in mystery; this fits their portrayal in much of Samuel and Kings, as an occasional prophet seems to appear out of nowhere, declare a word of YHWH, and then vanish just as quickly. The appearance of Elijah is abrupt and unexpected, as Brueggemann has emphasized,[11] but his sustained presence in the text as a divine representative may be just as unexpected.

The beginning of Elijah's story in 1 Kgs. 17:1-7 includes not only an introduction to his character but also a conversation between him and YHWH. Previous prophetic figures in the Old Testament have come out of nowhere to perform specific functions and then disappear, but Elijah will be a different sort, as his relationship with YHWH will continue to be an important element of the story. After Elijah announces the drought, he flees the famine-stricken Promised Land like so many of the great characters in this story before him, and he is sustained all the while not by the magnanimity of kings or by massive displays of divine power but by birds and an unnamed widow. Elijah's story looks a little bit like Israel's, and this is a pattern that will continue for some time. In 1 Kings 18, Ahab convenes the prophets of Baal and Asherah for a contest with Elijah and his God, like Pharaoh gathering his magicians. Richard Elliott Friedman has characterized the contest on Mount Carmel as God's last public miracle in the biblical narrative story line. Friedman also drew many connections back to Moses and the exodus event and then labeled this story's position next to Elijah's journey to Horeb as "one of the most remarkable juxtapositions in the Bible."[12] The stories are truly an odd fit. Elijah has just bested all the other prophets, with YHWH's assistance, and has slaughtered them. He has announced the end of the drought, and the rains have poured down, yet suddenly he is running for his life. Elijah's journey to Horeb was discussed earlier, in chapter 3 of this book, because of its connections to the Sinai event, but now it is important to look at it in its own position in the biblical story.

The juxtaposition of Carmel and Horeb is critical, because YHWH's mode of behavior is in a rapid state of flux. Friedman brought together the work of Frank Moore Cross and Samuel Terrien in order to demonstrate the magnitude of this shift. Although his concerns were more historical than literary, Cross had observed two decades earlier that "the abrupt refusal of Yahweh to appear as in the traditional theophany at Sinai marked a beginning of a new era in his mode of self-disclosure."[13] Just a few years later, Samuel Terrien wrote that God's absence within all the phenomena at Horeb "constitutes a repudiation not only of the mode of divine intervention on Mt. Carmel but also of the possibility that the Mosaic theophany on Mt. Horeb could occur again in later history."[14] Friedman used the full context of the Elijah-at-Horeb story to demonstrate God's deliberate, announced intent to stop behaving in this way.[15] When Friedman wrote that the divine speech to Elijah in 1 Kgs. 19:15-16 is the last time that "and YWHW said" appears in the narrative of the Hebrew Bible, thus ending this mode of divine communication, he is not including the Prophetic literature but looking only at the narrative represented primarily by the Deuteronomistic History.[16] Chronicles makes little use of this phrase and stops using it at a similar point. The final occasion is in 2 Chronicles 18, during a story in which a prophet named Micaiah is interacting with King Ahab. This kind of divine speech does not occur in Ezra-Nehemiah. In Elijah, however, God has found a new way of speaking. There have been occasions for prophetic oracles in the Bible before this, but they have been sporadic. Elijah, however, is consistently available to receive and speak the word of YHWH. Another occasion for this is the conflict involving Ahab, Jezebel, and Naboth in

1 Kings 21. The sordid story of royal greed and acquisition ends with the death of Naboth, engineered by Jezebel, and Elijah announces divine judgment on the king in verse 19: "Thus says the LORD: In the place where dogs licked up the blood of Naboth, dogs will also lick up your blood." One other feature of this text is important to observe. In this particular case, the reader is presented with the private reception of the prophetic message by the prophet in verses 17-19, which blend seamlessly into the encounter between the prophet and the king in verse 20. The prophet has taken the place of the "angel of YHWH" as the one who brings the divine presence into a situation and speaks for God. Prophecy is becoming a more standard type of mediation of divine presence, and Elijah is the central figure in this transition. Samuel was something of a precursor of this development, but prophet was only one of his roles, all of which gravitated toward monarchical control when Samuel drifted out of the story. Elijah is the one who wrests this particular type of mediation away from the power of the king and succeeds in turning it against the king, often to his own peril. With Elijah established in this position, the prophets stand ready to navigate the decline and defeat of the nation of Israel.

Elijah outlives Ahab, and the final story of his prophetic activity relates to Ahab's son Ahaziah. It is a strange ending, befitting this strange character. Ahaziah commits an obvious act of idolatry in the wake of his injury, but the divine response is puzzling. When Ahaziah sends messengers to Elijah, twice groups of fifty are consumed by fire called down from heaven, like the offerings on Mount Carmel in Elijah's early days. When the leader of the third group of fifty comes to Elijah, pleading for mercy, the angel of YHWH speaks to Elijah in 2 Kgs. 1:15 with the command, "Go down with him; do not be afraid of him." In light of what has proceeded, it hardly seems that Elijah is the one who should be afraid. Further, when he does go to Ahaziah, he pronounces the king's eminent death.

The famous story in 2 Kings 2 comes out of nowhere. There is nothing else like it in the Old Testament, and it seems to begin in the middle with, "Now when the LORD was about to take Elijah up to heaven by a whirlwind . . ." No reason is given for this divine act, and the plot of Kings is much more concerned with the transfer of prophetic authority to Elisha than it is with what is happening between God and Elijah or why.

Chapter 1 of this book pointed to Friedman's identification of the performance of Elijah on Mount Carmel as the last public miracle in the biblical narrative.[17] This is a debatable point in light of the surprising turn the story takes in 2 Kings by presenting Elisha as the most prolific miracle worker since Moses. In 2 Kings 2–6, Elisha has a hand in as many as ten miraculous acts, so one can only suppose that Friedman classified these as private miracles. The definition of "public" is relative, of course. Nothing Elisha does has the spectacle of Elijah on Carmel, but his purification of the water supply at Jericho in 2:19-22 and his feeding of the crowd at Gilgal in 4:42-44 seem to be performed in front of sizable groups of people, though his raising of a child from the dead in 4:8-37 happens behind closed doors, with no observers. The strange events in 6:15-23 are difficult to classify. Elijah asks twice for YHWH to cause people to see and once to strike people blind. In the first case (vv. 16-17), the servant is caused to see something that is not really there, so this could be understood as a vision, and a miracle in which people are caused to be blind may seem out of place in the biblical tradition. More important, though, is the nature of these miraculous deeds, which range from compassionate to brutal to trivial, thus raising important questions about the purpose of a prophet as a mediator of divine presence and power. When Elisha provides water and food to people, he looks like Moses. When he helps a widow through a famine and raises a child from the dead, he looks like his mentor, Elijah. The profound nature of these acts of compassion causes the bizarre character of two of his other miraculous actions to stand out even more sharply. In 2:23-25, he causes two bears to kill forty-two boys who had been taunting him, and in 6:1-7, he causes the ax head of another prophet, which had fallen into the water, to float so that it can be retrieved. There is a strange surplus of divine power present in Elisha, and this is confirmed in his final miracle, the one he performs after he dies. In 13:20-21, a dead man is raised back to life when he is thrown into Elisha's grave and comes into contact with his bones. Still, even within the story of Elisha, the text seems to be moving away from the wonder-worker role of prophets. Robert Cohn has observed that after the recital of Elisha's miraculous works to the king by the servant Gehazi, in 8:7-15 and 9:1-3, his role changes from wonder-worker to "fomenter of political revolutions."[18] In this role, he sounds more like the prophets to come. Nevertheless, Wesley Bergen has pointed out that much of what might be expected of a prophet is missing from the Elisha narrative. There is no speech from YHWH and no prophetic message from Elisha. He does not denounce Baal worship or make any moral demands on Israel.[19] It seems an overstatement to call this "the end of prophetism," as Bergen does, unless it is prophetism of only a certain kind. The fading of Elisha and the type of prophet he represents make way for the prophet as a person of words. The important question for this study will be the extent to which the divine character goes through an accompanying change, from a God of action to a God of words and their rhetorical influence.

Miracle-working turns out to be a brief diversion for the divine mediation known as prophecy. Only one miracle is assisted by all of the fifteen prophets who have biblical books named after them combined. Friedman was undoubtedly correct when he classified that event, the healing of Hezekiah, in which Isaiah participates, as the last private miracle in the Old Testament.[20] Isaiah is also the only one of the "writing prophets" to figure prominently as a narrative character in the Deuteronomistic History, and most of his activity there involves speaking to the king, Hezekiah. Isaiah helps to conduct two important changes in the work of prophets. First, he moves the primary location of prophecy from the north, the milieu of Elijah and Elisha, to Jerusalem. Second, he shifts the work of the prophet to an almost entirely speaking role. Even the one miracle he performs is understated: while YHWH tells the ailing Hezekiah in 2 Kgs. 20:6 that fifteen years have been added to his life, when Isaiah comes along in the next verse, he merely orders a fig compress to be placed on Hezekiah's boil, causing the reader to wonder if Hezekiah was really as sick as he thought.

In the previous chapter, table 4-2 and the discussion following it examined the frequency of divine designations in the book of Samuel as one possible way of observing the intensity of divine presence in different portions of the narrative. With all of the same caveats, a similar procedure applied to the book of Kings might also yield some useful results. The quantitative data is supplied here in table 5-1.

Table 5-1: The Frequency of Divine Designations in Kings

I Kings 1–3	0.339 per verse
I Kings 4–7	0.156 per verse
I Kings 8	0.758 per verse
I Kings 9–12	0.293 per verse
I Kings 13	1.0 per verse
I Kings 14–16	0.424 per verse
I Kings 17–18	0.743 per verse
I Kings 19—II Kings 12	0.436 per verse
II Kings 13–16	0.286 per verse
II Kings 17	0.829 per verse
II Kings 18–23	0.685 per verse
II Kings 24–25	0.280 per verse

The divisions here are primarily based on the appearance of texts in which the number of appearances of designations for the Israelite deity suddenly increases or decreases. Most of these variations make sense in light of the nature of the content in these chapters. First Kings 8, for example, which exhibits a high degree of divine presence, contains the account of Solomon's dedication of the temple. It follows the report of Solomon setting up his royal administration in 1 Kings 4–7, in which divine designations are predictably low. The intense activity of Elijah, God's prophet, raises the level again in 1 Kings 17–18, and the regular appearances of Elijah and Elijah in 1 Kings 19—2 Kings 12 keep the level of divine designations relatively high until it drops for a few chapters following the death of Elisha. The numbers that may be surprisingly high are those found in 1 Kings 13 and 2 Kings 17. The noticeably high levels of divine presence in these two places point toward a need to examine the contents of these chapters more closely.

First Kings 13 received some treatment already, so it is enough to recall at this point that it records the bizarre story of "a man of God from Judah" who goes to Bethel and denounces the altar Jeroboam has set up there as the northern kingdom's central place of worship. This makes the place a rival of the temple in Jerusalem, and these events lead up to the narrator's pronouncement of judgment against Samaria and the house of Jeroboam. The beginning of the story of the northern state of Israel is connected to the story of its final destruction, which is reported in 2 Kings 17, another text in which the frequency of divine designations signals an intensity of divine presence. The birth and death of the northern kingdom is a challenging set of events for Israel's self-understanding, so it is fitting that reflection on those events becomes intensely theological. The formation of Israel as a people is YHWH's most important act in the Old Testament, and changes in the identity of this people require divine involvement. Changes in the identity of Israel induce changes in the identity of YHWH. The covenant has always demanded undivided allegiance to YHWH from Israel, and worship of other deities has led to harsh punishment, but can YHWH's loyalty be divided? Can this divine character be the patron deity of two nations? Certainly, Israel was never close to the singular entity that much of the Old Testament portrays, and this complexity is reflected in some parts of the story in the book of Kings and in the nature of the composition itself.

Careful reading of the final form of a composite document is a difficult task. Old ideas and even false directions are still embedded in a text that is shaped and edited at a later time. The section near the beginning of chapter 4 called "Chronicles and the Multiformity of the Biblical Tradition" described our present situation, in which we have at least three different versions of the story of the Israelite nation in our extant literature. The "multiforms" exist in the texts we describe as the Masoretic Text of Samuel and Kings; the Greek version of Samuel and Kings, along with its presumed Hebrew source; and the Masoretic Text of Chronicles.[21] The Deuteronomistic History is composed of a mixture of sources, which the text itself confesses many times, some apparently northern, even though the primary point of view of the book is southern.[22] In its final form, the Deuteronomistic History contains pieces that seem out of place. Some of these can be explained to a degree by the recognition that a version of this narrative was composed after the Assyrian conquest of Israel in the late eighth century BCE but before the Babylonian invasion of Judah in the early sixth century. Others might be understood in light of the regional diversity of the sources, along with this temporal complexity. Second Kings 19:35-37 presents what is perhaps the most incongruous divine portrait in all of the Old Testament. The story is repeated in nearly identical form in Isa. 37:36-38. In it, the Assyrian army, led by King Sennacherib, is encamped after its destruction of Samaria, waiting to invade Judah. An angel of YHWH invades the camp one night and kills 180,000 Assyrian soldiers, which causes Sennacherib to abandon his incursion and return home.[23] For centuries before and centuries to come, Israel has been and will be pushed around by the politics and military schemes of the Ancient Near East. In that context, this sudden and dramatic divine intervention makes no sense. Some of the incongruity of the account would be resolved if the story of Israel ended before the Babylonian crisis came along, and there are plenty of reasons to think that in an earlier form it did. The northern kingdom rebelled and became idolatrous, so YHWH allowed the Assyrians to invade and destroy it while intervening to prevent the same force from washing over Judah, Jerusalem, and its temple.

An earlier ending does not resolve all of the difficulty of 2 Kgs. 19:35-37, however. Direct divine intervention on this scale still seems like something from another time, and it would seem that the writer of Chronicles shared that sense of unease about the story, so he edited it significantly. In 2 Chron. 32:20-23, Hezekiah and Isaiah both plead with God specifically to act against this threat to Judah. Rather than reporting 180,000 soldiers dead by morning, the writer of Chronicles reports that "the LORD sent an angel who cut off all the mighty warriors and commanders and officers in the camp of the king of Assyria." Though still direct in nature, the divine intervention is vague enough in its means and scale to reduce the lack of fit significantly in Chronicles.[24]

This exploration of the composition of Kings and Chronicles and the ways in which they present the decline of Judah and its cause points toward a significant challenge for the subject of Old Testament theology. Some recent studies have produced intriguing results on this point, but they are often the product of the application of complex redactional methods. Jeremy Schipper, for example, has noticed that Kings places much of the blame for the destruction of Judah and the end of the Davidic monarchy on Manasseh, whereas the Chronicler spreads the blame for these events more evenly across time and the full population of Judah.[25] Schipper proceeded by asking what the book of Kings would look like if the texts that specifically blame Manasseh (2 Kgs. 21:10–15; 23:26–27; 24:3–4) were removed. His conclusion is that the blame would then fall primarily upon Hezekiah.[26] This is a surprising result, given that Hezekiah is so often understood as one of the great "reformer kings" of Judah and that he seems to be presented, particularly in the book of Isaiah, as the model of a faithful and pious monarch. Schipper used this very idea, however, as the basis on which to build his argument concerning what happened to the book of Kings as it passed through its editorial process. His contention is that forces wishing to deflect blame from Hezekiah, which he associated with both Chronicles and Jeremiah (more significantly, what he calls the "Jeremianic tradition"), inserted the anti-Manasseh texts into Kings.[27]

Such readings present at least two major difficulties for an approach to Old Testament theology such as the one assumed in this book. First, they are working with hypothetically reconstructed versions of the biblical books, rather than the final form of the text. The second problem is that, even if their proposals about the redaction process of books such as Kings and Chronicles are correct, their results are not easily accessible to a relatively straightforward narrative reading of the text. One option is to ignore such treatments and dismiss them as "diachronic" or "hypothetical" or "idiosyncratic," but perhaps there is a better way through this thicket that might be helpful to a study like this one. Regardless of the degree to which Schipper or any of the other scholars working on these texts in such ways are correct, there is every indication that within the Old Testament itself there is an intense debate concerning who is to blame for Judah's eventual demise. The conclusion that blame is being negotiated is accessible to a straightforward but careful narrative approach to the text. Moreover, no matter who takes the bulk of the blame, the offenses are always the same. Judah, its kings, and its general population are denounced, and ultimately condemned, for making alliances with foreign nations, worshiping gods other than YHWH, and not listening to prophets. Reading the whole text, and not just selected parts, reveals this debate and shared sense of blame.

The division in this book between the building of the nation of Israel and the beginning of its decline is not precise, as the end of the previous chapter and beginning of this chapter have explained. Likewise, there is no distinct point at which the decline turns into destruction, so the midpoint of this chapter will also have an arbitrary aspect to it. The reign of Manasseh is a low point for Judah, particularly in the wake of the reforms conducted by his father, Hezekiah, but the story has one more positive turn, in the reign of Josiah. So, the death of Josiah appears to be as good a division as any, and both the Deuteronomistic History and Chronicles treat this as a significant event. Likewise, for Jeremiah, the great prophet of this time, the death of Josiah seems to mark an inevitable end of Judah as a nation. James Linville has argued that the important transformation of the people of Israel takes place in 2 Kings 23, just before the report of the death of Josiah. As part of the reform of Josiah, the people of Judah acknowledge and reaffirm the covenant with YHWH (v. 3), and by doing so they accept the pending punishment. The celebration of the Passover in verses 21-23 represents their "first steps on a new, spiritual journey through the wilderness."[28] The effusive praise of Josiah in verse 25 presents him as perhaps the greatest king in Israel's history: "Before him there was no king like him, who turned to the LORD with all his heart, with all his soul, and with all his might, according to all the law of Moses; nor did any like him arise after him." Any idea, however, that this achievement might halt the decline of Judah is quickly dashed in verses 26-27: "Still the LORD did not turn from the fierceness of his great wrath, by which his anger was kindled against Judah, because of all the provocations with which Manasseh had provoked him. The LORD said, 'I will remove Judah out of my sight, as I have removed Israel; and I will reject this city that I have chosen, Jerusalem, and the house of which I said, My name shall be there.'" Despite Josiah's righteousness, even cast in the precise terms of the Shema, divine anger and vengeance are in control and cannot be stopped.

The writer of Chronicles presents these events in the life of Josiah in significantly different fashion. First, the brutal word of divine judgment is missing. Instead, the words of the prophet Huldah in 2 Chron. 34:22-28, which are very similar to the parallel account in 1 Kgs. 22:14-20, stand as the final divine evaluation. Second, the account of Josiah's Passover is expanded from the terse three verses of 2 Kings into an elaborate account in 2 Chron. 35:1-19, which includes the sacrifice of 41,600 animals in Jerusalem. In 2 Chronicles, this massive sacrificial ritual seems to be part of a collection of such ceremonies that desperately attempt to halt the divine judgment, but at best they only slow it down.[29]

God of Decline outside of Kings and Chronicles

The Prophetic literature of the Old Testament is a daunting collection in both size and character. The appearance of pieces of this collection in all of the previous chapters of this work is a certain indication that the writers of the prophetic books made use of virtually all of the traditions present in ancient Israel's central narrative in order to communicate their messages. At this point, though, I wish to attempt to present the prophetic books in somewhat more holistic fashion. This will require some introduction to my approach to this literature. Two important shifts have taken place in the study of the Prophetic literature over the past three decades. First, as with other biblical literature, a heavily historical paradigm has given way to a more literary-canonical approach.[30] The second, related shift has been away from an emphasis on the prophets themselves as heroic religious figures, toward a focus on the rhetorical nature of their proclamations and the effect of these words on their audiences.

The first of these shifts presents some difficulties in relation to the organization of this book. Because all of the prophetic scrolls exhibit a movement from judgment to deliverance, their opening halves relate to this chapter whereas their closing halves are more closely associated with the discussion in chapter 6. Therefore, careful attention will have to be given to their overall shape, even while dividing them roughly in half for their treatment in other places. Each of the four scrolls is a literary entity unto itself, but parts of various scrolls join together to speak about a particular part of Israel's story and the behavior of the divine character within that part. This may be akin to listening to a harmonic vocal performance in which each of the voices is still individually discernible. As the ensuing discussion attaches the Prophetic literature to the story of Israel, the performance will begin with two voices, that of Isaiah and the Book of the Twelve, both of which address the Assyrian crisis of the eighth century BCE. At a later point, they will be joined by the two other voices, first Jeremiah in the earlier part of the Babylonian crisis, which began in the final decades of the seventh century, and then Ezekiel, whose proclamation to Israel starts in the middle of the Babylonian crisis at the beginning of the sixth century. In the second half of this chapter, which addresses the destruction of Judah, all four voices will still be present, but Isaiah will be barely audible, and the volume coming from both Jeremiah and Ezekiel will make the accompanying parts of the Book of the Twelve difficult to hear. In chapter 6, portions of all four prophetic scrolls will speak to the restoration of Judah and its challenges.

The relationship between the prophetic figures for whom these books are named, and who sometimes appear as narrative characters within them, and the final forms of the prophetic scrolls is difficult to determine and to express. In every case, the "book," or scroll, is much larger than the person whose work generated it. The behavior of YHWH toward Israel, over a long period of time, becomes the primary subject of each of these scrolls. Chapter 4 of this book made reference to the odd conversation between Joshua and the "commander of the army of the LORD" in Josh. 5:13-14. When Joshua asks, "Are you one of us or one of our adversaries?" the mysterious figure responds with, "Neither." Such an enigmatic response would be fitting of the Prophetic literature as well and is reflected in the treatment of the book of Isaiah by Jack Miles, who divided the scroll in half under two headings: "Executioner" and "Holy One." The divine character is sometimes for and sometimes against Israel. Miles's description of the Prophetic literature in general is instructive here and fits my own purposes well: "Prophecy combines preaching, politics, and poetry in a way that tends to baffle theological, historical, and literary commentary alike. Our own approach is literary, but its focus is not on language or literary effect per se but on character. We shall consider prophecy as characterization, the self-characterization of God in nonnarrative form."[31]

The four large scrolls that make up what Judaism calls the Latter Prophets have a great deal in common in macrostructure. All of them begin with their primary focus on the disobedience of Israel and the subsequent threat of YHWH's judgment. Each scroll then moves toward a more positive end, where God's deliverance and restoration of Israel become the more prominent theme, a move that gives each of the prophetic books a polarized form. This observation in literary terms will sometimes lead to divisions of the book in similar places to those that characterized historical approaches, but for different reasons. For example, the book of Isaiah has long been divided by scholars between chapters 39 and 40. It is still undeniable that most of Isaiah 1–39 is associated with the eighth century BCE whereas Isaiah 40–66 relates to the sixth and fifth centuries. It is much more important in this context, however, to recognize that 1–39 has as its focus the decline and fall of Judah and Jerusalem, whereas the salvation and restoration of Israel becomes the primary subject beginning in Isaiah 40.

It is common to think of the Prophetic literature as a product of social crisis, and this is a label I have used often,[32] but naming these crises as Assyrian, Babylonian, and restoration does not get fully to the point. The challenge for this literature is to consider what kind of divine portrait can be produced from the materials of failure, trauma, and death. All four scrolls of the Latter

Prophets focus their early attention on the disobedience of Israel and Judah and declare pending divine judgment if this behavior does not change. The divine character in these parts of the Prophetic literature is, more than anything else, one who threatens humans with punishment. In order to look more completely at the Prophetic literature as a theological enterprise in relation to this study, it is necessary to view it in two different ways simultaneously. Therefore, it is necessary to demonstrate some divisions with the prophetic books, an admittedly problematic task. Table 5-2 begins this process by identifying portions of the Prophetic literature that address the situations in Israel and Judah during the mid- to late eighth century, what is often called the "Assyrian crisis."

Table 5-2: Portions of the Prophetic Literature Addressing the Assyrian Crisis

- Isaiah 1–39 (except for 13:1—14:23, 21, 24–27, and 34–35)[*]
- *The Twelve*
    - Hosea 1–14[†]
    - Amos 1–9[‡]
    - Micah 1–7
    - Nahum 1–3
    - Jonah 1–4[§]

[*]There are many competing arguments concerning the dates of these texts. The section of Isaiah known as the "oracles against the nations" clearly contains some Babylonian material, and even those chapters related to the Assyrian period were likely edited at a later point. For more on this, see Rainer Albertz, *Israel in Exile: The History and Literature of the Sixth Century B. C. E.* (Atlanta: Society of Biblical Literature, 2003), 179-96. The primary criterion here is not the date of composition of prophetic texts but the particular historical situation they seem to be addressing, and the divisions I use are relatively large. Many proposals for the composition of the Prophetic literature include the identification of editorial editions on the verse-by-verse level, but rather than changing the primary event the text is addressing, these kinds of insertions tend to add later perspective on that earlier event.

[†]The four books of Hosea, Amos, Joel, and Micah are accepted by many interpreters as a unit that preceded the final collection of the Book of the Twelve. See James Nogalski, *Literary Precursors to the Book of the Twelve* (Berlin:

de Gruyter, 1993), 278–80. Rainer Albertz accepted this basic idea and proposed a sixth-century BCE "Four Prophets redactor," who made some additions to each book and shaped the collection. See *Israel in Exile*, 204-36.

‡The proposed later additions to the book of Amos have been very small portions of one or two verses. See Hans Walter Wolff, *Joel and Amos* (Philadelphia: Augsburg, 1977), 136-37.

§The book of Jonah is a particularly difficult case. It is included here because it uses the Assyrian Empire and its capital city of Nineveh as a narrative setting. The book itself is undoubtedly from a much later time. Its move of placing an Israelite prophet in a foreign setting connects it to much of the Old Testament literature discussed in chapter 6 of this book, so Jonah will reappear there. This is a good example of a book that participates in a theological discussion like this one on multiple levels.

Hosea

In this literature, Israel's God is most often portrayed as an accuser who is about to bring devastating judgment on Israel. Hosea 4 is a typical text, which begins with the language of a lawsuit:

> Hear the word of the LORD, O people of Israel:
> for the LORD has an indictment against the inhabitants of the land.
> There is no faithfulness or loyalty,
> and no knowledge of God in the land. (v. 1)

Even in a book such as Hosea, which presents its namesake as a narrative character and uses his own personal family situation as an analogy for the relationship between God and Israel, the human prophet seems to recede into the background, and the effect is the nearly direct presentation of the divine voice. Hosea 4 goes on to catalog sins of disobedience, injustice, and idolatry. Contained within this collection of literature is the awareness that northern Israel, where Hosea and Amos conducted their prophetic ministries, was overrun by the Assyrian Empire in its eighth-century BCE expansion, and this is presented unequivocally as God's judgment on a disobedient nation. The Prophetic literature connects itself directly to the book of Kings in the superscriptions found in Hosea 1:1, Amos 1:1, and Mic. 1:1 and in texts such as Amos 9:10-17, which cites the conflict over worship at Bethel (see 1 Kings 13 and 2 Kings 17) as the root cause of the destruction of the northern kingdom and the dispersion of its people. Much of what is found in these parts of the

Prophetic literature is classified as "oracles against the nations" (Isaiah 13–23, Amos 1–2, Nahum 1–3), but this is still a divine voice of destruction. If there is good news for Israel, it seems to be only that their enemies will also be destroyed.

Though the divine voice of anger, accusation, and threat is often overwhelming in these parts of the Prophetic literature, there is an alternative voice that appears occasionally to offer a sense of compassion, hope, or salvation. One of the most notable of these occasions is found in Hosea 11:1-11, an enormously challenging text for two reasons. The first is that issues of textual criticism, syntax, and grammar make this poem so difficult to read that it borders on incoherence. The second is that even when the passage is deciphered in terms of text and language, its meaning remains unclear. Perhaps all of this turmoil is part of the point, however, as is indicated in the most prominent verses:

> How can I give you up Ephraim?
> How can I hand you over, O Israel?
> How can I make you like Admah?
> How can I treat you like Zeboim?
> My heart recoils within me;
> my compassion grows warm and tender.
> I will not execute my fierce anger;
> I will not again destroy Ephraim;
> For I am God and no mortal,
> the Holy One in your midst,
> and I will not come in wrath. (vv. 8–9)[33]

The ambivalence of this text is difficult to manage. It may express an inner sense of divine uncertainty about using destruction to punish, but this is not matched by any outward expression. The northern kingdom, named here as Israel and Ephraim, is completely destroyed and never restored. Although the "again" in verse 9b might seem to hedge the divine promise and allow for an initial destruction, the failure of Ephraim/Israel ever to recover from the first destruction at the hand of the Assyrians never provides any possibility of a second destruction. In the final form of the book of Hosea, the Book of the Twelve, the Prophetic literature, and the canon, the best this can be is an expression of divine regret. Even so, this text does what all prophetic texts focused on destruction do: it blames the victim for actions like "turning away from me" (v. 7) and "refusing to return to me" (v. 6).[34]

Accusations like this in the book of Hosea necessitate careful examination of a widespread phenomenon in the Prophetic literature that has received little attention until the last two decades. One of the most disturbing aspects of the Prophetic literature and the ways in which it identifies disobedience and threatens punishment is the use of the metaphor of marriage between YHWH and Israel. A large number of works addressing this subject have appeared in recent years, the most extensive of which are Yvonne Sherwood's *The Prostitute and the Prophet: Hosea's Marriage in Literary-Theoretical Perspective*, Gerlinde Baumann's *Love and Violence: Marriage as Metaphor for the Relationship between YHWH and Israel in the Prophetic Books*, and Sharon Moughtin-Mumby's *Sexual and Marital Metaphors in Hosea, Jeremiah, Isaiah, and Ezekiel*.[35] As this list of works indicates, concern about this issue has been primarily the domain of female scholars. It is unfortunate that this needed to be so, but until the rise of feminist biblical scholarship, little attention was given to questions and problems generated by the prophets' use of this image. The result of all of this work, however, has been to raise the issue and its attendant challenges to a level of visibility that nobody can ignore.

The issue that has received the most attention from these interpreters is the justification of violence against a spouse who is perceived to be unfaithful. Theories of metaphor often use the words *tenor* and *vehicle* to denote the two parts of this kind of figurative language. In the case of the prophetic marriage metaphor, God is the tenor to whom some or all of the attributes of the vehicle, a human husband, are assigned. The studies mentioned here, which raise challenging questions about this aspect of the Prophetic literature, are often built around the observation that metaphors do not move in only one direction. Put in the most simple and direct terms for the purpose of this particular subject, if a speaker or writer implies often enough that God is in some way like a husband, then eventually the audience will begin to presume, if they do not already, that husbands are like God. This reinforces not only a hierarchical understanding of marriage but one in which violence, even sexual violence, is an acceptable response to fidelity or perceived infidelity.[36] At this point, it is difficult not to think back to the horrifying text in Num. 5:11-31, which described what is often referred to as the "ceremony of the bitter waters," and to understand the ordeal of Israel in the Assyrian crisis as something like that described for the accused woman in that legal text. Perhaps it should not be surprising that when the prophets of Israel began thinking, preaching, and writing about Israel's unfaithfulness to YHWH, in the form of worshiping other deities, this phenomenon seemed analogous to adultery. Given the predominant portrait in Israelite tradition of YHWH as male, the use of this analogy would have required casting Israel as the wife of YHWH. This choice will be carried over into the next section of the prophetic material, that dealing with the Babylonian crisis, and will be magnified far beyond what is found in the book of Hosea, to the point that this understanding of the relationship between YHWH and Israel will become central to the portions of the Prophetic literature that focus on the judgment of Israel.

Jeremiah and Ezekiel

As has been mentioned, when the Prophetic literature as a whole moves into the part of Israel's story known as the Babylonian crisis, two other powerful voices, Jeremiah and Ezekiel, emerge to add to the harmony of judgment, now aimed squarely at Judah, the remaining portion of the Israelite monarchy. The books of Jeremiah and Ezekiel also both have their own unique literary shape, which will also need to be kept in view, but it will be helpful to delineate all of the texts in the Prophetic literature as a whole that address the continuing decline of Israel in this period. Table 5-3 lists the texts from the prophetic books that can be connected to this part of Israel's story.

Table 5-3: Portions of the Prophetic Literature Addressing the Babylonian Crisis

- Isaiah 40–55*
- Jeremiah 1–29, 46–51†
- Ezekiel 1–32
- *The Twelve*
    - Obadiah
    - Habakkuk 1–3
    - Zephaniah 1–3

*This reflects the classic division of the book of Isaiah into three parts, though the complex compositional history of this book makes all attempts at neat division of the text problematic. Some of the material in this section can be understood to relate as closely to the restoration/Persian period as to the Babylonian period, so it will appear again in chapter 6.

†There are two major problems involved in dividing the book of Jeremiah in this way. The first is that, like the other three large prophetic scrolls, it has a complex compositional history, which involves not just later additions but

later editing of earlier portions, down to the level of individual verses. For a thorough and credible account of this process, see Albertz, *Israel in Exile*, 302-44. The unique problem is that two distinct text forms of the book of Jeremiah are extant: the one found in the Masoretic Text, which is used as the basis for all English Bibles, and the Greek version, along with its presumed Hebrew predecessor. This latter version is considerably shorter and has the oracles against the nations near the center of the scroll, rather than at the end, as the Masoretic Text does. For this reason, I have included those chapters, 46–51, here.

In terms of interacting with Israel's story, the book of Jeremiah begins first, chronologically, among the pieces of literature in this group. The book of Jeremiah is like the book of Isaiah in many ways, but it is notably different in at least one, and that is in the much closer relationship between the shape of the book and the prophetic career of the person named Jeremiah. The book begins with what sounds like Jeremiah's initial call experience, and he appears frequently as a narrative character throughout most of the book. The delivery of prophetic messages of judgment and destruction in the first half of the book of Jeremiah does not offer much new in the way of divine characterization, but the book of Jeremiah contains one kind of element found nowhere else in the prophetic literature.[37] Form critics have differed slightly in their delineation of the set of poems that are identified often as the "laments of Jeremiah" but are probably better identified as "Jeremiah's confessions." Woven into Jeremiah 11–20 is a series of five or six poems in which Jeremiah speaks directly to YHWH about the struggles of his prophetic vocation. These intensely personal expressions of pain say a lot about Jeremiah, but they also express some surprising thoughts about the divine character, one of which appears in 15:16-18:

> Your words were found, and I ate them,
> and your words became to me a joy
> and the delight of my heart;
> for I am called by your name,
> O LORD, God of hosts.
> I did not sit in the company of merrymakers
> nor did I rejoice;
> Under the weight of your hand I sat alone,
> for you had filled me with indignation.

> Why is my pain unceasing,
> my wound incurable,
> refusing to be healed?
> Truly, you are to me like a deceitful brook,
> like waters that fail.

Terence Fretheim has emphasized the current nature and function of these poems, which are "no longer (auto)biography—if they ever were—but proclamation in and through which readers hear the voice of God."[38] Jeremiah's accusation of divine deception seems to carry the presumption that faithfulness as a prophet will bring some sense of comfort and blessing to him. YHWH responds in 15:19-21 with a promise to "save and deliver" Jeremiah, but in the text immediately following this conversation commands Jeremiah not to marry and have a family. This central element of God's covenant is not available to Jeremiah. Perhaps a requirement like this should have been made clear at the beginning of Jeremiah's career. The level of his accusations against God is raised again in 20:7:

> O LORD, you have enticed me,
> and I was enticed;
> You have overpowered me,
> and you have prevailed.
> I have become a laughingstock all day long:
> everyone mocks me.

It is apparent in these texts that Jeremiah feels betrayed, both by God and by those to whom he is told to preach. The tension in the relationship between Jeremiah and YHWH and between Jeremiah and Israel is surely intended to say something about the relationship between YHWH and Israel, and there is brokenness all around.[39] As Israel declines throughout the long career of Jeremiah, it is always apparent that destruction is at the end of the process. Jeremiah argues against attempts to avoid it and urges obedience to the process that will make restoration possible.

The book of Ezekiel is also more closely connected to the prophet whose name it bears than is the book of Isaiah, with much of the book presented in a first-person voice. In many ways, Ezekiel is a prophet of extremes. Michelangelo captured this quality brilliantly in his portrait of Ezekiel in the Sistine Chapel. Unlike the pensive Isaiah and the melancholy Jeremiah, the intensity of Ezekiel's gaze and the strain in the powerful muscles of his neck leap out of the fresco. Likewise, the activity of Ezekiel leaps out of the book that has is name on it. Other prophets perform symbolic actions, such as Isaiah walking naked for three years (Isa. 20:1-5) and Jeremiah burying his underwear in a river bank (Jer. 13: 1-7), but the number and detail of Ezekiel's symbolic actions in Ezekiel 4–5 and 12 surpass these. There is little, if any, indication of an audience or a reaction to these actions, so they are transformed for us into literary presentations that give an impression of a prophet whose whole life is taken over by divine power and turned into a divine message. In 4:4-8, Ezekiel must lie on his side, bound by cords, for more than a year. In similar fashion, Ezekiel's visionary experience becomes a dominant feature of the book. Again, other prophets have had visions, but they are relatively simple and briefly described. In Ezekiel, the visions explode in elaborate detail, and Ezekiel himself seems completely absorbed by the experiences. The recent work of Dale Launderville on the book of Ezekiel has highlighted this aspect, the captivating and transformative power of symbol that allows a reordering of reason through the divine spirit, producing a new perception that allows Israel to see its God and itself rightly.[40]

Three of Ezekiel's four visions, which form the framework of the book, are very closely connected. In Ezekiel 1–3, the reader is first introduced to Ezekiel's elaborate description of the "glory" (*kbd*) of God. Ezekiel is in Babylon at this point, having been taken captive there with one of the early group of exiles. The *kbd* does not speak to him but overwhelms him and the reader with visual imagery. Eventually, in the next two chapters, a divine voice does speak to Ezekiel. This vision, which puts the divine presence in Babylon with the captives there makes more sense after the second vision of Ezekiel in chapters 8–10, in which he sees this same entity rise up from the temple in Jerusalem and depart to the east. The divine presence with the exiles has another side to it, however, which is the divine abandonment of Judah. This second vision and the fourth vision (40–48), in which Ezekiel sees the same divine presence return and inhabit a new temple, will receive more attention later. Examined collectively, these three visions present a mystifying visual image of God that strains the limits of human comprehension and language and places the horror of divine rejection at the center of the reader's perception. All of this intense experience might indicate a closer, more direct divine presence, but there is a distinct distancing of the deity in the book of Ezekiel, most clearly expressed in the layered language of 1:28, where Ezekiel claims not to have seen God, as Isaiah did in Isaiah 6:1,[41] but to have seen "the appearance of the likeness of the glory of the LORD." Observation of Israel's God is shielded by three grammatical layers of genitive construction.

Return to the Marriage Metaphor

With this examination of the book of Ezekiel and its focus on divine judgment and rejection, it is necessary to return to the earlier discussion about the use of the marriage metaphor in the Prophetic literature. This imagery, which can be located in Isaiah, Hosea, and Jeremiah, reaches its extremes, not surprisingly, in the book of Ezekiel. Chapters 16 and 23 both contain presentations of the story of Israel and YHWH, fully immersed in the graphic sexual detail of the marriage metaphor. Further, these texts go even beyond Jer. 3:6-14 and Hosea 2:2-13 in threatening Israel as the personified woman with exposure, rape, and murder as punishment for unfaithfulness. It is impossible to know precisely how the original audiences of such texts would have responded to them. As is the case with most of the Old Testament, it is safe to assume that the original audience was primarily male. Indeed, these texts have been used to develop a defense of the use of violent sexual imagery. Along with those who defend these texts simply because Israel's behavior merits any kind of punishment God inflicts,[42] there are those who argue for the shock value of comparing the male audience to an adulterous woman or prostitute.[43] This raises serious questions, however, about the shaming of men by persuading them to identify themselves with female characters. A more productive means of addressing these texts has been proposed by Sharon Moughtin-Mumby, who pointed to the strange and unstable rhetoric of the Prophetic literature itself as a resource for standing up to these texts and their portrayal of God as a perpetrator of sexual violence: "These books have inherent within themselves the ultimate response to their own dreadful language: their astonishing tendency to undermine themselves, unraveling their own assumptions and rhetoric, leaving themselves all but impotent."[44] As we move toward the portrayal of God as a character in the Bible's ultimate story of exposure, destruction, and defeat, and look at the texts that struggle to say something about that experience, it will be important to keep Moughtin-Mumby's notion of "teetering on the brink of meaning and meaninglessness" in mind.[45]

Isaiah

Table 5-3 places Isaiah 40–55 among the prophetic texts that speak of the Babylonian crisis, but this identification is problematic. The book of Isaiah actually contains a massive gap, which is why all interpreters, whether working with a historical or a literary framework, must give attention to the 1–39 and 40–55 (66) division. Texts from 40–55 will play a part in the discussion in the next section and in chapter 6 also. Isaiah 39 ends with the strange story, also contained in 2 Kings 20, of the Babylonian envoys visiting Hezekiah after his recovery and being given a tour of the kingdom. Whereas 2 Kings goes on to chart the decline of Judah over the next century and a half, including the final invasion, in Isaiah, this tour, in which the Babylonians see everything Hezekiah owns, replaces the actual taking of these items. Isaiah's prediction of the future invasion, according to the word of YHWH, provokes an odd response from Hezekiah, "The word of the LORD that you have spoken is good. . . . There will be peace and security in my days," which leads into the long silence. Miles has responded insightfully to this text, proclaiming that "the mix of good news and bad news in Isaiah baffled his contemporaries no less than it does us."[46] The punishment that Isaiah has proclaimed for so long, and has declared is so deserved, goes unspoken as the book averts its eyes.

God of Defeat

To the modern mind, it seems incongruous and unnecessary to ascribe every event to the control of a deity, but this need seems to be present in much of the Old Testament. Although Israel began playing with a sense of dualism at some point, as 1 Chronicles 21 indicates, such a move placed YHWH's power in jeopardy, so it would be a controversial direction.

The destruction of Judah and Jerusalem is dealt with quickly in Kings and Chronicles. Neither account seems to want to dwell on the events. The only place where the biblical text seems to linger in this excruciating moment is in the book of Lamentations, which will be discussed in the next section. The account in 2 Kings 24–25 is largely repeated in the final chapter of Jeremiah. The final years of the monarchy are characterized by a rapid turnover of kings, some of them puppets of the Babylonian Empire. The God of Israel is understood to play a primary causative role in the invasion, and this is stated clearly in 24:2. This sense of causation is also expressed, and perhaps taken further, in 2 Chron. 36:17, where a detailed point of grammar requires some explanation. The first verb in 36:17 has YHWH as the subject and is in the causative (*hipʿil*) stem. Most English translations render the literal "He caused to go up against them . . ." with the smoother "He brought up against them . . ." The difficulty lies in the next verb, which is a straightforward active indicative (*qal*) form of the verb "kill" in the third-person masculine singular but without an explicit subject. Therefore, it has two possible subjects from the first clause, either YHWH or the king of the Chaldeans. The NRSV hides this possibility by inserting a relative pronoun, yielding, "Therefore he brought up against them the king of the Chaldeans, who killed their youths in the house of their sanctuary, and had no compassion on young man or young woman, the aged or the feeble; he gave them all into his hand." It may be that the writer of Chronicles wished to portray the divine character as a more direct actor in this drama of death than most English translations allow.[47]

It is remarkable that both Kings and Chronicles take the reader, albeit briefly, to a point near the formal end of the exile in Israel's story, though they do this in strikingly different ways. The final four verses of Kings take the reader to the middle of the sixth century BCE and move the story geographically to Babylon. The verses accomplish all of this by telling the little story of King Jehoiachin, who had been taken captive two to three decades earlier, being released from prison and given a place to live within the palace in Babylon. Chronicles ignores this story but reports the event a decade or two later that technically frees the exiled Judeans to return to Jerusalem. The report of the "decree of Cyrus" in the last two verses of Chronicles takes the reader even further along the story line and connects with the beginning of Ezra-Nehemiah, which will be addressed in the next chapter. The effect of both of these minimal endings is to skip over most of the exile, which creates an odd situation in the Old Testament. The exile is included in the story, but almost nothing is said directly about it, so it seems to be a hole or gap in the story.

At the same time, scholars such as Daniel Smith-Christopher argue, correctly I think, that the exile is a kind of substratum that runs beneath virtually the entire Old Testament, even if it is often not directly visible. Smith-Christopher has offered a cogent survey of the development of views on the Babylonian exile and its significance for Israel's story in the Old Testament. The accompanying analysis is part of Smith-Christopher's attempt to articulate an adequate "theology of exile" as a response to the primary crisis that generated the Hebrew canon in its final form.[48] This theological argument often gets unnecessarily mired in historical issues Smith-Christopher built his case for the significance of the exile, in part, on historical evidence of its magnitude. A primary proponent of the other side of this argument has been Hans Barstad, who placed much greater emphasis on the remaining community of Judah and argued that the destruction from the Babylonian invasion was not nearly as extensive as many assume.[49] Regardless of the historical extent of the exile, it is apparent that its perspective dominates the biblical literature. An excellent mediating position between these extremes is found in the work of Jill Middlemas, whose coining of the term "the templeless age" allows theological space for all Judeans who survived but suffered through that period, while still placing the reality of destruction at the center of that experience.[50]

God of Defeat outside of Kings and Chronicles

An important feature of the book of Jeremiah presents this aspect of the story well. In the midst of the young prophet's initial experience, YHWH summarizes the message Jeremiah is commissioned to proclaim in 1:10:

> See, today I appoint you over nations and over kingdoms,
> to pluck up and pull down,
> to destroy and to overthrow,
> to build and to plant.

These six abrupt infinitives are repeated in various combinations at many places within the book of Jeremiah. Walter Brueggemann has demonstrated that many of the prose sections of Jeremiah, such as 12:14-17 and 18:1-11, serve as commentary on this and other poetic expressions.[51] The two-thirds negative and one-third positive ratio in this collection of infinitives is a proportion that seems to fit the book of Jeremiah well.

Many interpreters have understood Jeremiah's "temple sermon" in chapter 7 as a central element of his message of destruction. In this condemnation, he takes on the temple establishment and engages the tradition developed in the book of Isaiah (37:33-35), that YHWH would always protect Jerusalem and the temple.[52] It is important here for readers of the book in its present form to observe a common feature of the first half of the book of Jeremiah. The version of the temple sermon we encounter is that imparted by YHWH to Jeremiah. Jeremiah's preaching of the sermon is not reported or described, so it remains part of the private conversation between God and the prophet. The tendency to use this private aspect of prophetic activity is woven together with the confessions of Jeremiah, which were discussed earlier, to make the first half of the book introspective in nature. Mark Biddle has argued that the temple sermon plays at least two other functions. First, "Jer 7:1-8:3 may best be termed a 'divine discourse.' All figures other than YHWH (and the narrator) are only theoretically present; all voices are subordinate to YHWH's voice."[53] The other function of this internal dimension is that it allows the reader to hear YHWH's private instruction to Jeremiah that he is not to pray for Judah. This is a repeated phenomenon that is also interwoven with the laments.[54] The destruction of Judah is inevitable, and it is not Jeremiah's job to stop it. As the poetic verse in 1:10 indicates, the only way toward hope and restoration is through pain and destruction. This is the sound that Jeremiah brings to the harmony of prophetic voices in the Old Testament.

When the book of Jeremiah breaks out of its internal mode, it moves into public conflict. The temple sermon from Jeremiah 7 appears again in chapter 26, and this time the reader hears little of the text of the sermon but sees the public response to it. The prophetic task that has been so privately painful in the first half of the book turns out to be publicly dangerous. Jeremiah is put on trial and threatened with execution for preaching the sermon. Like Elijah, but unlike Isaiah, the divine messenger is now the enemy of royal power, and it is uncertain whether God will protect Jeremiah. In the end, his life is spared, not by divine intervention but by a collection of human individuals who protect both the person of Jeremiah and the prophetic tradition that bears his name.[55] The tendency to see the prophets as solitary heroes is belied by this communal work of prophecy, urging us again to read them in concert.

Isaiah

The first half of this chapter has already given some attention to the way the book of Isaiah evades the decline of Judah and the destruction of Jerusalem and the temple. The opening words of "Second Isaiah" are perhaps most familiar to many readers because of their place in George Frideric Handel's famous oratorio *The Messiah.* The musical work opens with Isa. 40:1-2a, leaving its own conspicuous omission, seemingly unable to utter the horrifying accusation that Jerusalem had "received from the LORD's hand double for all her sins."[56] Although much of Isaiah 40–55 has the restoration of Judah in view, as the reference to Cyrus in 45:1 indicates, there is still a great deal of attention to suffering in this part of the book. The "servant songs" (42:1-6, 49:1-4, 50:4-9, and 52:13—53:12) serve as a cohesive force for this portion of the scroll, now that the character named Isaiah has vanished. The identity of the servant is appropriately uncertain, for to identify a victim too clearly contains suffering within limits too restrictive for Israel's experience. The task of the servant moves from a focus on instruction in the first two poems to the experience of suffering in the third and fourth, with the idea of vicarious suffering emerging finally in 53:4-5, so there is movement in the sequence of poems. Suffering of this kind connects to the portrayal of the Babylonian invasion in 2 Chron. 36:15-17, in which the punishment for Israel's disobedience is delayed until YHWH's compassion is used up, and the full force of YHWH's wrath, embodied in Nebuchadnezzar's army, falls onto one generation, which suffers for all the ones that have come before and that will come after.

Lamentations

Whereas most of the Old Testament hurries past the horror of the Babylonian invasion, or avoids it entirely, the little book of Lamentations corrects for this by sitting in the midst of it and refusing to leave. The siege of Jerusalem in 586 BCE lasted for three years, and it is difficult to imagine what life might have been like inside the city all of that time, but Lamentations takes us inside the walls and shows us in unblinking fashion. Lamentations has been traditionally connected to Jeremiah, prompting its placement in the Christian canon, though there is no evidence that Jeremiah wrote it. This connection is thematically fitting, however, because Jeremiah is the most willing of the prophets to face the consequences of YHWH's judgment on Judah. Amy Kalmanofsky has recognized this characteristic of the book of Jeremiah and has argued that "in Jer 6, the prophet adopts a horror rhetoric that revels in the dangerous aspects of the relationship between God and Israel and communicates to his audience its potential for horror and destruction."[57] This idea also fits the book of Lamentations, which resists the notion of theodicy but simply puts suffering on display. As Adele Berlin has explained, "The burden of Lamentations is not to question why this happened, but to give expression to the fact that it did. . . . The book is not an explanation of suffering but a re-creation and a commemoration of it."[58] Even in the places where Lamentations acknowledges the sin of Jerusalem, it juxtaposes such admissions with descriptions of the consequences, which seem to agree with Isa. 40:2b, that it is simply too much. Lam. 1:20 is an appropriate example:

> See, O LORD, how distressed I am;
> my stomach churns,
> my heart is wrung within me,
> because I have been very rebellious.
> In the street the sword bereaves;
> in the house it is like death.

A few verses later, the writer of Lamentations assigns the action leading to this punishment more directly to Israel's God:

> How the Lord in his anger
> has humiliated Daughter Zion!
> He has thrown down from heaven to earth
> the splendor of Israel;

> He has not remembered his footstool
> in the day of his anger.
> The Lord has destroyed without mercy
> all the dwellings of Jacob;
> in his wrath he has broken down
> the strongholds of daughter Judah;
> he has brought down to the ground in dishonor
> the kingdom and its rulers. (2:1-2)

Psalms

The book of Lamentations has some connections to the psalms of lament found in the book of Psalms, but Berlin has emphasized the differences between the two, particularly the *qinah*, or funeral dirge element, so common in Lamentations but lacking in Psalms: "A *qinah* is an outpouring of grief for a loss that has already occurred, with no expectation of reversing that loss."[59] The lament poems in Psalms not only ask for relief but also tend to be more general complaints about enemies, sickness, or hardship that are not clearly connected to a specific event in Israel's story. There is one powerful exception to both of these differences, and that is where we need to turn next.

Psalm 89 has already arisen in this book at a couple of points. I have argued that it is the center of the book of Psalms, and perhaps a central text in all of the Old Testament. Psalm 89 has many of the elements of a lament poem, but not in the typical order. An expression of anguish that often begins laments, "How long O LORD? Will you hide yourself forever?" appears in verse 46 of this psalm, as it is nearing its conclusion. The shift in mood in the middle of the poem, between verses 37 and 38, is from positive to negative, the opposite of all other lament poems.[60] Most important, however, is the way the second half of the poem specifically addresses the fall of the monarchy and, more specifically, the way Israel's God has treated its king. Verses 38-40 appear to be describing the Babylonian invasion of 586, because they fit no other incident in the story of Israel:

> But now you have spurned and rejected him;
> you are full of wrath against your anointed.
> You have renounced the covenant with your servant;
> you have defiled his crown in the dust.
> You have broken through all his walls;
> you have laid his strongholds in ruins.

The accusation against Israel's God, of abandoning the covenant, is made much more specific later, in verse 49:

> Lord, where is your steadfast love of old,
> which by your faithfulness you swore to David?

The writer of this poem is aware of the covenant between YHWH and David in 2 Samuel 7 and considers the divine behavior in this phase of Israel's story to be a violation of that promise.[61] Not all of the Old Testament literature accepts the assumption that the destruction of Judah and the end of the monarchy are deserved punishment, an observation that leads to the examination of one more text that is not often associated with this part of Israel's story.

Job

In an attempt to do Old Testament theology like this one, it is less important to ask what kind of literature a book or text is, or when it was written, than it is to ask to which part of Israel's story it accrues. Perhaps this is never so important than when reading the book of Job, a book that has only two direct connections to Israel's story. This lack of connection seems to be one of the reasons that Job is customarily placed with the Wisdom literature. Like Proverbs and Ecclesiastes, it makes no mention of the Israelite ancestors, the exodus story, Moses, Sinai, or the entry into the promised land. It is also helpful to use Job to push back against all of the certainty about life that pervades a book like Proverbs. Nevertheless, those narrative connections remain, the most important of which is that Israel's God is a narrative character in the book of Job, and a complex and intriguing one at that. Put this together with the small detail in Job 1:17 that the same enemy that destroys Jerusalem in 2 Kgs. 24:2 and 2 Chron. 36:17, the Chaldeans, also attacks Job's household, and Job's strongest sense of attachment to Israel's story seems to be this crucial point. The story of Job is the story of the destruction of Judah on a personal level. Job becomes an outcast, an exile from his home place, and is forced to live at the city's garbage dump. Such a reading of Job also brings new aspects to the story of the destruction of Judah.[62] God declares Job to be upright and blameless at the beginning of the story (1:8) and to be one who has spoken rightly at the end of the story (42:7). None of Job's misfortune is punishment for disobedience, and God denounces Job's friends who have made such accusations throughout the book (42:8). All that Job and his wife suffer is the result of the heavenly wager, allowed in order to defend divine pride and reputation. If the story of Job is the story of Judah in miniature, then how do these troubling revelations apply on a national level? Gustavo Gutiérrez has argued convincingly for a reading of Job that differs from most others. The book of Job is not, in his view, an attempt to explain suffering but an attempt to assert divine freedom. The common, retributive view of divine justice, that obedience is blessed and disobedience cursed, amounts to a mechanical system that leaves God under the control of human actors. The story of Job is a reassertion of divine freedom.[63] This idea fits the content of the book of Job very well, but it raises a new question that neither the book nor Gutiérrez's reading addresses: If Israel's God does not operate by a predictable, reliable system of justice, then what keeps the divine behavior from becoming entirely capricious?[64]

Job's most powerful statement in the early parts of the book comes at 3:25:

> Truly the thing that I fear comes upon me,
> and what I dread befalls me.

In her powerful musical rendition of the story of Job, "Sire of Sorrows," Joni Mitchell paraphrases this sentiment, putting it into a more poignant second-person expression: "O you tireless watcher, what have I done to you, that you make everything I dread and everything I fear come true." We are told by the narrator and by the divine character directly from the beginning of the story that the thing Job fears is God (1:1, 1:8, 2:3). The divine character may quibble with the adversary in 2:3 over who has attacked Job, but Job, though he has no access to the heavenly contest, knows who has attacked him. Miles has placed proper emphasis on the brute force of God's response to Job in chapters 38–41, as the book struggles toward a conclusion.[65] He correctly concluded that the entire book of Job turns on Job's speech in 42:2-6 and that there are enormous translation problems here, probably due to translators who want the book to end with a particular conclusion.[66] Even the NRSV pushes the reader toward the understanding that Job has sinned in some way and, therefore, must repent to resolve the situation (42:6), but this contradicts the rest of the book entirely and makes the friends correct. Miles moved away from this traditional reading, but his argument that Job laments for all of humanity, an interpretation possible by understanding "dust and ashes" as a metaphor for mortal humans, pushes figurative language beyond the breaking point, given the context of the book of Job.[67] On much firmer ground is the proposal of Dale Patrick, that Job is not "repenting in," but "turning away" from dust and ashes, the state in which he has been sitting for almost the entire book.[68] Job has decided that his mourning is complete, even though not all of his questions are resolved, and it is time to arise and get on with his life. Likewise, eventually, Judah would have to move on past the destruction, and, just as the recovery of Job at the end of the book is nonsensical, so will be the restoration of Judah—but that is a matter for the next chapter.

Excursus: The Order of the Books in the Old Testament Canon

It is difficult to say to what extent the shape of the Christian Old Testament canon helped generate the tendency to dismiss the decline of the monarchy and the restoration, or to what extent this shape was simply the result of that tendency. Too often, even in academic study of the Old Testament, it is assumed that the canonical order of the Christian Bible was inherited from the Septuagint. There is plenty of evidence that Jewish scribes translated the Hebrew Scriptures into Greek during roughly the last two centuries before the Common Era.[69] The work of three Jewish scribes in the second century of the Common Era—Aquila, Symmachus, and Theodotian—indicates the continuing importance of this Greek tradition within Judaism but also demonstrates that it was a significantly fluid tradition. This was, at least in large part, the problem addressed by the massive work called the Hexapla, produced by the Christian scholar Origen in the third century CE. Origen attempted to provide other scholars a tool to compare various versions of the Greek text with the Hebrew text available to him, so he produced all of these texts in six parallel columns. It is important to note that no original manuscripts of any of these works survive. Only a few fragments of what appear to be copies from the Hexapla have been located. Most of what is known of the Hexapla is from quotations of and about it from those who had access to it before it was destroyed, presumably in the seventh century.[70]

This information is enough to demonstrate that a great deal of modern use of the term *Septuagint* is imprecise, at best.[71] It is more precise, to begin with, to speak separately of the "Old Greek" translation of the Hebrew Scriptures into Greek—a Jewish project—while reserving the term *Septuagint* to denote the extant ancient manuscripts of the full Greek Old Testament. The latter is, of course, a Christian project, exemplified primarily by the three great codices of the fourth and fifth century—Sinaiticus, Vaticanus, and Alexandrinus.[72]

There are no manuscripts of the Septuagint earlier than the fourth century CE that are large enough to indicate what their full physical form would have looked like, and this should be kept in mind as we look at a separate, but related, subject that is too often ignored. At some point in first century of the Common Era, scribes in the Mediterranean world began using codices instead of scrolls, but it is difficult to say exactly how widely and quickly the use of the codex spread. It appears that the use of the codex grew far more rapidly in Christianity than in Judaism. This was likely due in part to the ritual and ceremonial value attached to the scroll within Judaism. Even within Christianity, however, the practice of copying the entire Old Testament or the entire Bible into a single codex likely did not happen until the fourth century.[73] This is an important point, because it is not until the entirety of the Hebrew Scriptures / Old Testament, in whatever language, was housed within the covers of a single volume of cut, stacked pages that the precise order of all the books really meant anything. Even when the act of putting all of the Bible together in one physical object occurred, it did not become a common practice. As Robert A. Kraft has observed, the manuscript evidence indicates that partial collections remained more common for another millennium.[74]

All of these developments point to the conclusion that the idea of a long-standing Christian tradition of an Old Testament canon based on a particular order of the books collapses under too many assumptions. There is no mistaking the basic plot of the Old Testament, which moves from Genesis to Kings and finds its parallel in Chronicles and its continuation in Ezra-Nehemiah. Beyond that, the order of the remaining books has an unavoidably arbitrary nature, and the more reasonable and likely way for readers to think about them lies in how they attach to this plotline. The duplications in the Old Testament—2 Samuel 22 / Psalm 18; 2 Kings 18–20 / Isaiah 36–39; and 2 Kings 24–25 / Jeremiah 52—add an additional impulse toward this reading strategy.

The Punishing and Destroying God in Old Testament Theology

The practice of Old Testament theology among Christian interpreters has long made convenient use of a particular way of looking at Israelite tradition. Beginning in the New Testament, it was easy to associate Jesus with Abraham, Moses, and David, those who represented institutional power in the ascending portion of that tradition. When it came to the period of decline, however, most Christian interpretation changed teams and sided entirely with the prophets. Again, this begins in the New Testament, where Jesus can be both "Son of David" and a prophet, like Elijah or Jeremiah. Eventually, the Christian canonical tradition placed the Prophetic literature after the narrative of Israel's decline and destruction, but, as the earlier excursus contends, this may not have been as early and deliberately meaningful a move as is often assumed. Nevertheless, the frequent effect was often to bypass the decline and destruction of Israel, excluding it from the "real" story the Old Testament was telling.

Gerhard von Rad opened the second volume of his *Old Testament Theology* with an assessment of what had happened to the interpretation of the Israelite prophets in the century prior to his writing. He saw most clearly that "the pendulum swung too far" as the conclusions of source criticism were used to separate the prophets as independent, religious geniuses who were unconnected to their national and international contexts.[75] This hyperindependence of the prophets can be seen in the work of Walther Eichrodt, who described the prophets as "freed from all ties of class or professional self-consciousness" and "capable of moving through life in majestic solitude."[76] Von Rad probably did not go far enough for most contemporary theologians in reconnecting the prophets with the other elements of Israel's story. He still saw them as an outside force, distinct from other traditions and institutions: "But the time of the direct intervention of Jahweh which was creative of saving history was clearly over after the beginning of the monarchical period, and within Israel herself the expectation of and readiness for such events had vanished too. This was, of course, the tremendous vacuum into which the great prophets could enter with their message of new actions of Jahweh in history."[77] This does not fit together easily with von Rad's evaluation of the story of Israel's decline and destruction in the narrative portions of the Old Testament. Von Rad found in the Deuteronomistic History a sense of hope that "the judgment of 587 did not mean the end of the people of God." Relying on texts such as Deut. 30:1-10 and 1 Kgs. 8:46-53, he saw the tradition moving into "spiritual" as opposed to "cultic" form.[78] An Old Testament theology built around the recital of the "mighty acts of God" could attempt to survive only by spiritualizing that idea. When the primary mediators of divine presence became speakers, then the primary acts of God became speech. By all accounts, the prophets failed in their efforts to change the course of Israel's decline, which made fitting their literature into a salvation history based on mighty acts difficult.

The struggle to fit all of this together is perhaps a large part of what led to the decline of von Rad's influence in the last quarter of the twentieth century, a story that is succinctly documented by Walter Brueggemann: "In the end, proponents of von Rad's approach were unable to define in any way convincing to modern criticism what was meant by 'act of God.'"[79] It was Brueggemann himself who championed a new and creative way of looking at the story of Israel, particularly its decline, and the work of the prophets in a more holistic manner, giving due credit to von Rad but moving the reading of the Prophetic literature further in a new direction. In Brueggemann's work, the devastation that reached its climax in 587 BCE became a metaphor for loss that the prophetic scrolls addressed with acts of "hopeful imagination."[80] Reading the Prophetic literature, such as Jeremiah, Ezekiel, and Second Isaiah, from the early to mid-sixth century as works of theological imagination, as Brueggemann proposed, reinvigorated this literature, but whether such a move could adequately amplify later prophetic voices is another question.

Dialogical models of Old Testament theology made productive use of prophetic voices that responded to Israel's decline and destruction, but a similar kind of selectivity as that demonstrated in earlier chapters too often prevailed. Isaiah dominated the discussion, with other "eighth-century" prophets such as Amos, Hosea, and Micah speaking loudly as well. An intense focus on Jeremiah during the last two decades of the twentieth century provided some correction, but it was still the case that the further along the Old Testament plotline a particular prophetic tradition attaches, the less attention it tends to receive. The voices of Habakkuk, Zephaniah, Haggai, Zechariah, Malachi, and Isaiah 56–66 have not functioned well in a theological model based upon debate and dialogue. Even when these do appear, they are often part of a move toward a Christian understanding of messianism.[81] The earlier prophets also served as useful tools to comment on contemporary social-justice issues, which is a worthy goal, but this also severed them from the narrative contexts of decline provided to them by the rest of the Old Testament.

As the portion of Israel's story that reported and responded to the decline and destruction progresses, the biblical material becomes less useful for methods of Old Testament theology that have been used up to this point. This pattern of declining attention leads to the nadir that will be examined in the final chapter and to the effort to bring this "end of the story" to the center of the theological discussion.

Notes

1. For a cutting-edge presentation of this idea, see Louis Stulman and Hyun Chul Paul Kim, *You Are My People: An Introduction to Prophetic Literature* (Nashville: Abingdon, 2011), 9–27.

2. I have borrowed the language of "generative" to talk about the relationship between the prophets as persons and the books that have their names on them from David L. Petersen. See his *The Prophetic Literature: An Introduction* (Louisville: Westminster, 2002), 3–4.

3. For more on this resemblance and the literary features that produce it, see Mark McEntire, *The Blood of Abel: The Violent Plot in the Hebrew Bible* (Macon, GA: Mercer University Press, 1999), 92–95.

4. See the section in chapter 4 called "Chronicles and the Multiformity of Biblical Tradition."

5. The role of prophets is still significant in Chronicles, as the recent work of Gary N. Knoppers has demonstrated. Rather than pointing toward an end of prophecy, the writer of Chronicles seems to be transforming it into a different kind of role than that portrayed in the Deuteronomistic History. See Knoppers, "Democratizing Revelation? Prophets, Seers, and Visionaries in Chronicles," in *Prophecy and Prophets in Ancient Israel: Proceedings of the Oxford Old Testament Seminar*, ed. John Day (New York: T&T Clark, 2010), 404–5.

6. On the troubling moral and theological issues raised by this story, see Mordechai Cogan, *I Kings: A New Translation with Introduction and Commentary* (New York: Doubleday, 2001), 374–75.

7. Walter Brueggemann, *1 & 2 Kings* (Macon, GA: Smyth & Helwys, 2000), 175–76.

8. Jerome T. Walsh, *1 Kings* (Collegeville, MN: Liturgical, 1996), 189–90.

9. Ibid., 373–74.

10. Ernest Nicholson, "Deuteronomy 18.19-22, the Prophets and Scripture," in Day, *Prophecy and Prophets in Ancient Israel*, 151–71.

11. Brueggemann, *1 & 2 Kings*, 207.

12. Richard Elliott Friedman, *The Disappearance of God: A Divine Mystery* (Boston: Little, Brown, 1995), 22. On the connections between Elijah and Moses, see also Walsh, *1 Kings*, 287–89.

13. Frank Moore Cross, *Canaanite Myth and Hebrew Epic* (Cambridge, MA: Harvard University Press, 1973), 194.

14. Samuel Terrien, *The Elusive Presence: Toward a New Biblical Theology* (San Francisco: Harper & Row, 1978), 231–32.

15. Friedman, *Disappearance of God*, 23–26.

16. Ibid., 24.

17. Ibid., 84.

18. Robert C. Cohn, *2 Kings* (Collegeville, MN: Liturgical, 2000), 55–61.

19. Wesley Bergen, *Elisha and the End of Prophetism* (Sheffield, UK: Sheffield Academic, 1999), 175–76. Bergen argued further that in Elisha, the role of prophet is being placed back into a position of subservience to royal authority (177–79).

20. Friedman, *Disappearance of God,* 84.

21. The Greek version of Chronicles might be considered a fourth version, but it does not differ so greatly from the Hebrew version.

22. The work of Raymond F. Person was discussed in chapter 4 in the section called "Chronicles and the Multiformity of Biblical Tradition," because it raised important questions about the prevailing view of the relationship between Chronicles and the Deuteronomistic History and some of the simplistic assumptions that go with it. Here it is also instructive to note the work of Graham Auld, who also argued for a different, more complex view. Particularly in 1 Kings 12—2 Kings 24, Auld argued that "we are dealing in Kings and Chronicles with diverging expansions of a shorter common story, a proposal not unlike Person's "multiformity." See Raymond F. Person, *The Deuteronomistic History and the Book of Chronicles: Scribal Works in an Oral World* (Atlanta: Society of Biblical Literature, 2010), 16–19.

23. On the difficulty of this text and the possible development of the account, see Christopher R. Seitz, *Zion's Final Destiny: The Development of the Book of Isaiah* (Minneapolis: Fortress Press, 1991), 95–96. This strange event has even found its way into a prominent work of science fiction, Neal Stephenson's highly acclaimed novel *Snow Crash.* In that story, the sudden death of the entire Assyrian army is used to compare the ancient understanding of a connection between disease and divine power and a futuristic connection between biological disease and technological forces such as computer viruses. See Neal Stephenson, *Snow Crash* (New York: Random House, 1993), 125–26.

24. For other possible motives behind the Chronicler's version of the story, see Graeme Auld, *Kings without Privilege* (New York: Continuum, 1994), 138–39.

25. Jeremy Schipper, "Hezekiah, Manasseh, and Dynastic or Transgenerational Punishment," in *Soundings in Kings: Perspectives and Methods in Contemporary Scholarship*, ed. Mark Leuchter and Klaus-Peter Adam (Minneapolis: Fortress Press, 2010), 81. Schipper summarized and interacted with other writers dealing with the same issue, such as Baruch Halpern, Marvin Sweeney, Francesca Stavrakopoulou, and Ehud Ben Zvi, whose arguments are too lengthy to present here.

26. Ibid., 82–88.

27. Ibid., 89–96.

28. James Richard Linville, *Israel in the Book of Kings: The Past as Project of Social Identity* (Sheffield, UK: Sheffield Academic, 1998), 251–52.

29. See the discussion of these texts and the resulting pattern in Mark McEntire, *The Function of Sacrifice in Chronicles, Ezra, and Nehemiah* (Lewiston, NY: Mellen Biblical Press, 1993), 21–49.

30. For a fuller discussion of this shift and its implications, see Christopher R. Seitz, *Prophecy and Hermeneutics: Toward a New Introduction to the Prophets* (Grand Rapids, MI: Baker Academic, 2007), 93–151.

31. Jack Miles, *God: A Biography* (New York: Vintage, 1995), 195.

32. See the presentation in John H. Tullock and Mark McEntire, *The Old Testament Story*, 9th ed. (Boston: Prentice Hall, 2012), 209–11.

33. For a detailed discussion of the textual and linguistic difficulties of these verses and the full text of Hosea 11:1-11, see Francis I. Anderson and David Noel Freedman, *Hosea: A New Translation with Introduction and Commentary* (Garden City, NY: Doubleday, 1980), 581–90.

34. See the discussion of this text in McEntire, *Blood of Abel*, 129–40.

35. Yvonne Sherwood, *The Prostitute and the Prophet: Hosea's Marriage in Literary-Theoretical Perspective* (Sheffield, UK: Sheffield Academic, 1996); Gerlinde Baumann, *Love and Violence: Marriage as Metaphor for the Relationship between YHWH and Israel in the Prophetic Books* (Collegeville, MN: Liturgical, 2003); and Sharon Moughtin-Mumby, *Sexual and Marital Metaphors in Hosea, Jeremiah, Isaiah, and Ezekiel* (New York: Oxford University Press, 2008.

36. For an example of this kind of argument, see Baumann, *Love and Violence* (Collegeville, MN: Liturgical, 2003), 28–37.

37. One might argue that there are two other places. The remarkable poem in Habakkuk 3 has many of the characteristics of a lament poem, but there is nothing of the personality of Habakkuk himself in the little book. Perhaps closer are two parts of the book of Jonah: the poetic prayer uttered from inside the fish in Jonah 2 and the dialogue between Jonah and YHWH in chapter 4.

38. Terence Fretheim, *Jeremiah: A Commentary* (Macon, GA: Smyth & Helwys, 2002), 189. Fretheim has also provided a helpful survey of differing approaches to this part of the book of Jeremiah (187–89). Whereas the influence of form criticism through much of the twentieth century generated a tendency to isolate the poems, a wave of scholarship near the end of the century sought to put them back in their context in order to ask what they are doing in the book of Jeremiah. See Kathleen O'Connor, *The Confessions of Jeremiah: Their Interpretation and Role in Chapters 1–25* (Atlanta: Scholars Press, 1988); A. R. Diamond, *The Confessions of Jeremiah in Context: Scenes of a Prophetic Drama* (Sheffield, UK: Sheffield Academic, 1987); Walter Baumgartner, *Jeremiah's Poems of Lament* (Sheffield, UK: Almond, 1988); and Mark S. Smith, *The Laments of Jeremiah and Their Contexts* (Atlanta: Scholars Press, 1990). This collection is a powerful illustration of the seismic shift in approaches to the Prophetic literature that was taking place at the time.

39. On this function of the laments within the book of Jeremiah, see Smith, *Laments of Jeremiah and Their Contexts*, 61–62.

40. Dale F. Launderville, *Spirit and Reason: The Embodied Character of Ezekiel's Symbolic Thinking* (Waco, TX: Baylor University Press, 2007), 55–61.

41. Note that this claim of Isaiah's is characterized as blasphemy and used as a cause for his execution at the hands of King Manasseh in the imaginative postbiblical text known as the *Martyrdom of Isaiah*.

42. See, for example, Daniel Block, *The Book of Ezekiel: Chapters 1–24* (Grand Rapids, MI: Eerdmans, 1997), 503.

43. See Moshe Greenberg, *Ezekiel 1–20: A New Translation with Introduction and Commentary* (New York: Doubleday, 1983), 306; and Corrine L. Patton, "'Should Our Sister Be Treated Like a Whore?': A Response to Feminist Critiques of Ezekiel 23," in *The Book of Ezekiel:*

Theological and Anthropological Perspectives, ed. Margaret S. Odell and John T. Strong (Atlanta: Scholars, 2000), 237–38.

44. Moughtin-Mumby, *Sexual and Marital Metaphors*, 275.

45. Ibid.

46. Miles, *God*, 219.

47. See my argument further in McEntire, *Function of Sacrifice*, 44–46.

48. Daniel Smith-Christopher, *A Biblical Theology of Exile* (Minneapolis: Fortress Press, 2002), 30–48.

49. Hans Barstad developed this thesis primarily in *The Myth of the Empty Land: A Study in the History and Archaeology of Judah during the "Exilic" Period* (Oslo: Scandinavian University Press, 1996).

50. Jill Middlemas, *The Templeless Age: An Introduction to the History, Literature, and Theology of the "Exile"* (Louisville: Westminster, 2007), 10–27.

51. Walter Brueggemann, *The Theology of the Book of Jeremiah* (Cambridge: Cambridge University Press, 2007), 37–39.

52. See the discussion of this in Walter Brueggemann, *Jeremiah 1–25: To Pluck Up, to Tear Down* (Grand Rapids, MI: Eerdmans, 1988), 74–75.

53. Mark E. Biddle, *Polyphony and Symphony in Prophetic Literature: Rereading Jeremiah 7–20* (Macon, GA: Mercer University Press, 1996), 71. This polyphonic nature of the Prophetic literature, both within each of the prophetic scrolls and among all of them, cannot be fully explored here and is only beginning to get the attention it requires in biblical studies.

54. Ibid., 64–81.

55. See the detailed narrative analysis of this story in Mark McEntire, "A Prophetic Chorus of Others: Helping Jeremiah Survive in Jeremiah 26," *RevExp* 101 (2004): 301–14.

56. The work of compiling the biblical texts for this oratorio was performed for Handel by Charles Jennens.

57. Amy Kalmanofsky, *Terror All Around: The Rhetoric of Horror in the Book of Jeremiah* (New York: T&T Clark, 2008), 142.

58. Adele Berlin, *Lamentations: A Commentary* (Louisville: Westminster, 2002), 18.

59. Ibid., 24.

60. The unusual form can be explained as the result of a combination of three originally independent poems. See Frank Lothar-Hossfeld and Erich Zenger, *Psalms 2: A Commentary on Psalms 51–100*, trans. Linda M. Maloney (Minneapolis: Fortress Press, 2005), 402.

61. Ibid., 415.

62. Surprisingly few interpreters draw connections between the personal story of Job and the national story of the exile. For one exception, see Samuel E. Balentine, *Job: A Commentary* (Macon, GA: Smyth & Helwys, 2006), 11, 375, 601.

63. Gustavo Gutiérrez, *On Job: God-Talk and the Suffering of the Innocent* (Maryknoll, NY: Orbis, 1987), 67–81.

64. On the problem of a capricious deity, see G. Tom Milazzo, *The Protest and the Silence: Suffering, Death, and Biblical Theology* (Minneapolis: Fortress Press, 1992), 114–16.

65. Miles, *God*, 314–18.

66. Ibid., 317–28.

67. Ibid., 324–25.

68. Dale Patrick, "The Translation of Job XVII, 6," *VT* 26 (1976): 369–71. This reading also plays a major role in the interpretation of Gutiérrez; see *On Job*, 86–87.

69. The most important source of information about this is the so-called "Letter of Aristeas." There is a great deal of dispute about both the contents of this letter and its transmission. Its concern is with the process of translation of the Torah alone from Hebrew into Greek. See the extensive discussion in Sidney Jellico, *The Septuagint and Modern Study* (Oxford: Oxford University Press, 1968), 29–58.

70. D. C. Parker, "The Hexapla of Origen," in *The Anchor Bible Dictionary*, ed. David Noel Freedman, vol. 3 (New York: Doubleday, 1993), 188–89.

71. On this, see Karen H. Jobes and Moisés Silva, *Invitation to the Septuagint* (Grand Rapids, MI: Baker Academic, 2005), 30–33.

72. Emmanuel Tov, *Textual Criticism of the Hebrew Bible* (Minneapolis: Fortress Press, 1992), 134–48.

73. Colin Henderson Roberts and Theodore Cressy Skeat, *The Birth of the Codex* (Oxford: Oxford University Press, 1987), 62–66.

74. Robert A. Kraft, "The Codex and Canon Consciousness," in *The Canon Debate*, ed. Lee Martin McDonald and James A. Sanders (Peabody, MA: Hendrickson, 2002), 229–33.

75. Gerhard von Rad, *Old Testament Theology*, trans. D. M. G. Stalker (New York: Harper & Row, 1965), 2:3–5.

76. Walther Eichrodt, *Theology of the Old Testament*, trans. J. A. Baker (Philadelphia: Westminster, 1961), 1:342.

77. Von Rad, *Old Testament Theology*, 1:69–70.

78. Ibid., 346.

79. Walter Brueggemann, *Theology of the Old Testament: Testimony, Dispute, Advocacy* (Minneapolis: Fortress Press, 1997), 43.

80. Walter Brueggemann, *Hopeful Imagination: Prophetic Voices in Exile* (Philadelphia: Fortress Press, 1986), 2–4.

81. For example, see Brueggemann, *Theology of the Old Testament*, 618, 648.

6

A Restoring God

The first chapter of this book identified a problem and posed a number of questions. These centered on the viability of a theology of the Old Testament that follows the path of the development of the divine character through the narrative of the Old Testament and gives the most prominent position to the place at which this character arrives at "the end of the story." The next four chapters sought to trace this development through its major stages in the narrative of the Old Testament from creation to the end of the nation of Israel and its monarchy. This story holds around it most of the literature of the Old Testament. The end of the monarchy, however, is not the narrative end of the Hebrew Scriptures. The book(s) called Ezra-Nehemiah continue(s) the story of Israel after the end of the Babylonian captivity, and there is a considerable remainder of the literature of the Old Testament that can be organized around this continuation of the story. The divine character in this part of the story is given relatively little attention in the practice of Old Testament theology, for reasons that will become more clear as this chapter proceeds. I have stated my assumption at a number of points in this study that the period described in this part of the story is the period in which the final form of the Hebrew Scriptures was being produced. It is reasonable, then, to presume that the divine character portrayed in this part of the story is the one most consistent with the religious experience of those who shaped this text. This is a safe general assumption that is not dependent upon assigning precise dates to the production of individual pieces of literature. At the same time, we must be careful to remember that the primary community about which the book of Ezra-Nehemiah tells us does not represent all, or even a majority, of Judaism in the sixth and fifth centuries BCE. The elements these communities would have had in common were a decentered religious tradition and a life lived under the political power of foreign empires, whether within those empires or in the Persian province of Yehud.[1]

The first chapter of this book identified and evaluated two basic ways of attending to the wide variety of narrative portraits of God in the Hebrew Bible and described something of an impasse between these two general approaches.[2] The more common of these two involves placing contrasting divine portraits in a situation of dialogue or debate.[3] The other type of approach requires placing texts in some kind of order and tracing a trajectory in the development of the divine character. Within the first approach, the voice of Ezra-Nehemiah has difficulty competing in such a debate or dialogue because of the nature of the divine portrayal in this book. The loud voices of Exodus, Deuteronomy, Joshua, and Psalms too easily overwhelm it. If, instead, we choose a narrative trajectory that presents the story of the divine character from creation to the restoration of Judah, then Ezra-Nehemiah sits in a very important position.[4] The first chapter eventually arrived at the question that I would now put into words something like this: How can we adequately attend to the divine character at the end of the biblical narrative, who resembled, I assume, the religious experience of those who gave final shape to the books of the Hebrew canon, while still keeping earlier biblical portraits of God in view? Chapters 2–5 have already pointed toward some answers to this question, but before I proceed further in that direction, a careful examination of the final part of the biblical narrative and the texts that attend it is necessary.

God of Return

Ezra-Nehemiah is one of the most neglected books in the study of the Hebrew Bible / Old Testament.[5] In the subfields of Old Testament theology or biblical theology, this neglect is perhaps even more acute. It is easy enough to see why this was the case in the past, when historical approaches to biblical theology placed great emphasis on the "mighty acts of God." The God of Ezra-Nehemiah is not a mighty actor. With our field shifting away from historical approaches toward those centered on the literary presentation of the character called God, however, such neglect seems increasingly inappropriate. It will also be necessary to include in this section a discussion of some of the Prophetic literature that relates to this part of the story of Israel and its God. Ezra-Nehemiah has significant points of contact with Haggai, Zechariah, and Malachi, the last three portions of the Book of the Twelve. In addition, a separate section of this chapter will treat a significant collection of parallel biblical literature that relates to the Jewish Diaspora during the restoration/Persian period.

The first task in an examination of the divine character at the end of the biblical story will be to trace the contours of the narrative presented by Ezra-Nehemiah, which is no easy task. Ezra and Nehemiah are, to our modern eyes, obviously composite documents, and we have a strong impulse to take them apart and ask about the origins of the pieces.[6] This is a worthy endeavor, but not the right one for this project. The foremost narrative feature is the dual nature of the work, which gives the portion we call Nehemiah the same basic pattern as that which we label Ezra. This means that many of the events, ideas, and documents have a parallel elsewhere in the book. Both "books" begin in Persia as the major characters, Sheshbazzar in the book of Ezra and Nehemiah in the book of Nehemiah, prepare to return to Jerusalem, and both books end in Judah with the struggle to separate and purify the community by expelling the foreign wives and their children. The first half of both books is dominated by a major building project, the temple in Ezra and the city wall in Nehemiah, both of which are central to the restoration narrative. Both books contain portions of first-person narrative, reported by the characters that give the books their names. These sections are commonly known as the "Ezra memoir" and the "Nehemiah memoir." Both books engage in a significant amount of list making, which serves to establish the identity and the boundaries of the restored community in Judah. In both books there is significant conflict with outside groups deemed to be foreigners. The expulsion of foreign wives and the lists of returnees are, at least in part, responses to these threats.[7] Table 6-1 contains an illustration of what a narrative outline of Ezra-Nehemiah might look like. This type of outline demonstrates an important sense of balance between forward movement and repetition. Getting the Judahites out of Babylon is, in some ways, more complex and difficult a task than getting the Israelites out of Egypt was in Exodus, which was an act of brute force. It is a different kind of process in Ezra-Nehemiah and requires a different sort of divine character. Seeing and understanding this God requires a careful look at divine behavior in Ezra-Nehemiah.

Table 6-1: The Narrative Contours of Ezra-Nehemiah

I. The return of the initial group to Judah (Ezra 1)

II. The list of the members of the Golah group (Ezra 2)

III. The building of the temple amid foreign opposition (Ezra 3–6)

IV. The return of Ezra (Ezra 7–8)

V. Ezra's reforms, including the expulsion of foreign wives and children (Ezra 9–10)

VI. The return of Nehemiah to Jerusalem (Neh. 1:1—2:10)

VII. The building of the wall amid foreign opposition (Neh. 2:11—7:4)

VIII. The list of the members of the Golah group (Neh. 7:5-73)

IX. The reading of the law and renewal of the covenant (Neh. 8–10)

X. Administrative lists (Neh. 11:1-26)

XI. The dedication of the wall and Nehemiah's reforms (Neh. 11:27—13:31)

Note: There are, of course, numerous ways to produce an outline of a unified book of Ezra-Nehemiah. See the attempts and discussion of Tamara Cohn Eskenazi, *In an Age of Prose: A Literary Approach to Ezra-Nehemiah* (Atlanta: Scholars, 1988), 37–42; and Lester Grabbe, *Ezra-Nehemiah* (New York: Routledge, 1998), 94–98. Grabbe also discusses the relationship between the plot of the story and the chronological data supplied by the book. His observations demonstrate that the theological coherence of the story overrules a consistent chronology (98–99). Gordon F. Davies has emphasized a pattern of three movements, which separates Ezra 7–10 as a more independent section that tells of the return of the Ezra group, which "builds up the community" as the Zerubbabel group builds the temple and the Nehemiah group builds the wall. See Davies, *Ezra and Nehemiah* (Collegeville, MN: Liturgical, 1999), xx–xxi.

It is apparent at the outset of Ezra-Nehemiah that divine approval and blessing are sought by the characters in the story but that the nature of divine action will be affected by the acknowledgment of direct sponsorship of their projects by foreign kings. Daniel Smith-Christopher has given special attention to "the culture of permission and the royal correspondence" as an important aspect of the social context of Ezra 1–7.[8] Regardless of whether his conclusion that Ezra-Nehemiah represents a "subversive theology" that acknowledges yet resists Persian authority is entirely correct,[9] this literature and its characters certainly admit that they operate within such a dynamic of power. Ezra-Nehemiah opens with the decree of Cyrus, in which the foreign monarch gets to speak for God and define God's behavior and purpose. A different version of the decree appears at the end of Chronicles, and this has often been considered a deliberate feature that links together these two pieces of literature,[10] but it seems equally likely that the decree at the beginning of Ezra serves to pick up and restart the narrative at the conclusion of Kings, which ends in a foreign royal court. The use of foreign kings as positive implements is indicative of the kind of shift in divine characterization present throughout the book.

The portrayal of the divine character should begin with a thorough examination of this character's actions, an examination that will be based upon the observation of the verbs that appear in the text with God as subject. Because of the nature of the Ezra-Nehemiah narrative, it will be important to divide these verbs into two categories: the present actions of God in the process of the restoration, and the remembered actions of God in Israel's distant past. This is not a simple matter of looking for past-tense and present-tense verbs. Most of the verbs with a divine subject are rendered as past-tense in English translations. The difference is whether these verbs were actions happening within the present of the overall narrative or were past actions being recalled by the narrative.[11] Both of these times are in the past for the writers and readers of the book.

Counting and categorizing these verbs is not as straightforward a task as it might seem. Several difficult decisions are necessary, each of which could affect the count. First, should verbless clauses in Hebrew, which typically require the use of a form of "to be" in English, be counted? In general, I have made an effort to include these, but variations in the identification of verbless clauses may cause counts to differ. Second, should verbs that have parts of God's body as subject, for example the hand or ear of God, be counted? Again, I have attempted to include such occurrences. In contrast, verbs whose subjects are external entities in construct to divine designations, of which "the house of God" is the most common, are not included. Third, constructions that make use of participles can create difficulty, such as in Neh. 1:5, which contains two participles related to God. The first is a *nipʿal* form of *yrʾ*, which could be translated as "the one being feared" but is more often treated by English translations as an adjective, such as "awesome" or "fearsome." The second is a *qal* participle from *šmr*, which is part of the phrase "the one keeping covenant." In this case, I have not counted the former but have counted the latter, because it is more like a verbal construction with a subject and a direct object.

An additional difficulty is created by ways of describing divine action that do not employ either a verb with God as subject or the standard type of verbless clause in Hebrew. A good example of this is in Ezra 9:8, which says something like, "But now, for a short time, grace was from YHWH our God to leave a remnant for us and to give to us a foothold in the place of his sanctuary, to bring light to our eyes, our God, and to give us a little relief in our service." The four infinitives technically have no subject, of course, but they are the result of the grace of Israel's God and are, therefore, expressions of God's action or behavior.

These examples represent precisely the kind of subtle, indirect divine behavior that is so important in this literature, and I have included these as four verbs in the narrative present with God as subject. Indeed, many English translations present them as active indicative verbs.[12]

Given all of these considerations, God is the subject of approximately 103 verbal statements in the book of Ezra-Nehemiah, and 38 of these describe God's actions or potential actions in the narrative present of the story. These occurrences are listed in table 6-2.

Table 6-2: Divine Behavior in the Narrative Present of Ezra-Nehemiah

Ezra 1:1	"YHWH stirred up the spirit of King Cyrus . . ."
Ezra 1:2	According to Cyrus, "YHWH has given me all the kingdoms . . ."
Ezra 1:2	According to Cyrus, "YHWH has charged me . . ."
Ezra 1:3	Statement of blessing by Cyrus: "God be with them . . ." (vc)
Ezra 1:3	Description by Cyrus: "He is the God who is in Jerusalem." (vc)
Ezra 6:12	Decree of Darius: "The God who has caused his name to dwell there . . ."
Ezra 6:22	"YHWH made them joyful . . ."
Ezra 6:22	"He caused the heart of the king to turn . . ."
Ezra 7:9	". . . the hand of God was upon him." (vc)
Ezra 7:27	"YHWH . . . who put such a thing in the heart of the king . . ."
Ezra 8:22	". . . the hand of our God is upon all the ones seeking him." (vc)
Ezra 8:23	". . . and he [God] was supplicated for us."*
Ezra 8:31	"The hand of our God was upon us . . ."
Ezra 8:31	". . . and he delivered [*ncl*] us . . ."
Ezra 9:8	". . . to leave a remnant for us . . ."
Ezra 9:8	". . . to give us a foothold . . ."
Ezra 9:8	". . . to bring light to our eyes . . ."
Ezra 9:8	". . . to give us a little relief from our service."
Ezra 9:9	". . . our God did not forsake us . . ."
Ezra 9:14	". . . would you not be angry with us . . . ?"
Neh. 1:5	". . . the one keeping the covenant . . ."
Neh. 1:11	"[YHWH,] Let your ear be attentive . . ."

Neh. 2:8	". . . the good hand of my God [was] upon me." (vc)
Neh. 2:12	". . . what my God put into my heart . . ."
Neh. 2:18	". . . the hand of my God which [was] good upon me . . ." (vc)
Neh. 2:20	"The God of the heavens will cause success for us . . ."
Neh. 4:15	". . . God frustrated their plot . . ."
Neh. 4:20	"Our God will fight for us."
Neh. 5:13	"May God shake out every one . . ."
Neh. 6:9	"Now, strengthen my hands." (prayer of Nehemiah)
Neh. 6:12	"I recognized, and behold, God did not send him . . ."
Neh. 7:5	"And God put into my heart . . ."
Neh. 9:32	"Now, our God . . . the one keeping covenant . . ."
Neh. 9:32	". . . do not make small before you all the hardship . . ."
Neh. 9:37	". . . the kings whom you have placed over us . . ."
Neh. 13:22	"Remember me, my God . . ."
Neh. 13:22	". . . and be merciful to me . . ."
Neh. 13:31	"Remember me, my God, with goodness."

Note: The phrases in this and subsequent tables are my own somewhat literal translations. The decision to include Hebrew "verbless clauses" is discussed in the text, and they are marked in the list with the abbreviation "vc." The classic discussion of this grammatical phenomenon is Francis I. Anderson, *The Verbless Clause in the Pentateuch* (Nashville: Abingdon, 1970).

*The syntax of this brief clause, which uses a *nip'al* form of *'tr*, is difficult. Many English translations use "answered" and supply a direct object—"our prayer" or "our entreaty." The sense of the text at this point makes the idea that the prayer for protection has been answered look odd. This is not apparent until Ezra 8:31. The NRSV seems to take a middle position with "and he listened to our entreaty," but it is still uncertain how this could be known at this point.

There are two verbal sentences that stand out in this list and require some attention, particularly because they run counter to the general trend in divine characterization that I am trying to illustrate. First, in Ezra 8:31, Ezra states that God "delivered [*nṣl*] us." This is a characteristic verb of the "mighty actor" God present in the earlier parts of the biblical narrative. The root appears approximately 200 times in the Hebrew Bible, but only here and one other time in Ezra-Nehemiah, in Neh. 9:28, part of the recollection of God's actions in the distant past. Second, in Neh. 4:20, Nehemiah claims that "our God will fight for us." This verb is the typical *nip'al* construction of *lḥm*, a verb that appears about 170 times in the Hebrew Bible. This is one of three occurrences in Ezra-Nehemiah, all three in Nehemiah 4, and the only one with God as subject. The notion of God as an active, vigorous character in the narrative present is not lacking entirely, but it is severely diminished, and these two examples could be the result of lingering ways of speaking about God. Both are within the speech of the main characters of the books and do not come directly from the narrator. Furthermore, there are clear examples of direct human actions that represent the effect of these statements, which ultimately turn out to be indirect divine behaviors. With the possible exception of these two verbs, the divine character in the book of Ezra-Nehemiah acts in vague and indirect ways. After the opening sequence of divine actions, which are embedded within the actions and decrees of foreign kings, Cyrus and Darius, the characteristic actions of God take place inside of human beings. Four times God is said to act upon a person's heart by causing it to turn or putting something on it (Ezra 6:26, 7:27, Nehemiah 2:12, 7:5), and five additional times a person's behavior is judged to be a sign that "God's hand was upon him" (Ezra 7:9, 8:22, 8:36, Neh. 2:8, 2:18). God makes people joyful (Ezra 9:8), brings light to their eyes (Ezra 9:8), strengthens their hands (Neh. 6:9), and remembers them (Neh. 13:22, 13:31). Even in instances when God seems to become more active, this activity is limited in quantity, such as "to give us a little relief from our service" (Ezra 9:8); filtered by human perception, as in "I recognized that God did not send him" (Neh. 6:12); or restricted to a vague sense of causation, such as "the God of the heavens will cause success for us" (Neh. 2:20).

Meir Sternberg has distinguished the key difference between Ezra-Nehemiah and other books in the Bible as the differing "models of narrative, the inspirational and the empirical."[13] Sternberg's terminology can be a bit confusing here, so some explanation is warranted. The primary distinction he made was between an omniscient narrator and a limited one. Perhaps his plainest statement of this is, "Nehemiah cannot and does not know more than the next man; nor does he pretend to omnipresence or omnipenetration."[14] Thus, Nehemiah's narration is empirical, which is an appropriate mode in which to describe the way YHWH acts through human beings in Ezra-Nehemiah. Sternberg has correctly addressed the limits of narration and perspective in Ezra-Nehemiah but has not given much attention to how the corresponding limits are present in the divine character who is being narrated.[15] Such narration is not easy and natural, neither to the biblical writer nor later translators. One notable example of this difficulty is the odd clause in Ezra 8:23, which says something like, "and he [God] was supplicated for us."[16] Here in the midst of the Ezra memoir, the narrator seems at pains to describe the divine response to prayer. The KJV retained the awkward passive construction with "he was intreated of us," but later translations changed the statement to make it active, with renderings such as "and he answered our prayer" (NIV), "and he listened to our entreaty" (RSV), and "and he heard our prayer" (NLT). More direct, active ways of talking about divine behavior flow more smoothly in biblical language, and in our own, than do such passive, indirect expressions. One of the ultimate questions that this observation points toward, but that probably cannot be adequately answered, is whether our language about God matches our experience of God. This will be addressed later in this chapter, but for now it is enough to recognize what seems to be a struggle for Ezra-Nehemiah, that is, how to talk about the religious experience of its characters in the shadow of such a strong tradition describing a different kind of experience. The ancestors of Israel portrayed in earlier parts of the Bible experienced an active, engaging God who destroyed cities, sent plagues, parted seas, and made food fall out of the sky. The ensuing discussion will demonstrate that the religious experience of the characters in Ezra-Nehemiah is nothing like this.

The remaining 65 verbal statements with a divine subject are recollections of God's actions in the past, typically in the distant past. These are divided into two separate tables here, because the grand recital of Israel's past by Ezra in Neh. 9:6-37 is such a distinctive part of this collection. The past divine actions described within that recital are in table 6-4, whereas those in the remainder of Ezra-Nehemiah are presented first, in table 6-3.

Table 6-3: Divine Actions in the Narrative Past in Ezra-Nehemiah (outside of Nehemiah 9)

Ezra 7:6	"The law of Moses that YHWH the God of Israel had given . . ."
Ezra 9:10	" . . . you commanded by your servants the prophets . . ."
Ezra 9:13	". . . you, our God, punished us . . ."
Ezra 9:13	". . . and you gave to us a remnant . . ."
Neh. 1:8	" . . . you [God] commanded your servant Moses . . ."
Neh. 8:1	". . . the book of the law of Moses which YHWH had commanded Israel."
Neh. 8:14	". . . the law which YHWH had commanded by the hand of Moses . . ."
Neh. 13:2	". . .but our God turned the curse into a blessing."
Neh. 13:18	". . . and our God brought upon us all of this evil . . ."
Neh. 13:26	". . . and God placed him as king over all Israel . . ."

Most of the recollections of the past in table 6-3 have to do with the giving of laws and commandments. This makes sense as a validation of one of the central elements of the book, Ezra's public reading of the law in Nehemiah 8. Along with connecting this legal tradition to the divine voice in the distant past, it is noticeable that the tradition is also connected to the one who heard that divine voice, Moses, who also restated the law in Deuteronomy.

A large majority of the verbs describing divine behavior in the distant past (55 out of the 65) is found in the creedal statement in Neh. 9:6-37. This text has appeared at several points throughout this study, and it has long been the text in Ezra-Nehemiah that has received the most attention from biblical theologians. One could argue that the writing of this text itself was one of the earliest occasions of doing biblical theology, and it connects this narrative conclusion of the Old Testament to nearly all of the major traditions of Israel's story.

Table 6-4: God's Actions in the Past in the Recital in Neh. 9:6-37

9:6	". . . you made the heavens . . ."
9:6	". . . you enlivened all of them . . ."
9:7	". . . you chose Abram . . ."
9:7	". . . you brought him out from Ur . . ."
9:7	". . . you gave his name, Abraham . . ."
9:8	". . . you found his heart faithful before you . . ."
9:8	". . . you made [inf.] a covenant with him . . ."
9:8	". . . to give [inf.] the land . . ."
9:8	". . . to give [inf.] to his offspring . . ."
9:8	". . . and you established your words . . ."
9:9	". . . you saw the distress of our fathers . . ."
9:9	". . . you heard their cry at the Red Sea."
9:10	"You gave signs and wonders . . ."
9:10	". . . for you knew they [Pharaoh and his servants] acted arrogantly against them [our ancestors]."
9:10	"And you made for yourself a name . . ."
9:11	". . . you divided the sea . . ."
9:12	". . . with a pillar of cloud you led them by day . . ."
9:13	"You came down upon Mount Sinai . . ."
9:13	". . . and spoke [inf.] with them . . ."
9:13	". . . and you gave them ordinances . . ."

9:14	". . . you made your holiness known to them . . ."
9:14	". . . commandments, decrees and law you gave to them . . ."
9:15	". . . you gave them bread . . ."
9:15	". . . and you brought out for them water from the rock . . ."
9:15	". . . you told them to enter . . ."
9:15	". . . you lifted your hand to give to them."
9:17	". . . your wonders which you did among them . . ."
9:17	". . . you [are] a God of forgiveness . . ."
9:17	". . . you did not abandon them."
9:19	". . . you did not abandon them in the desert . . ."
9:20	"You gave your good spirit to teach them . . ."
9:21	" . . . you sustained them in the desert . . ."
9:22	". . . you gave them kingdoms and nations . . ."
9:22	". . . you allotted to them a distant place . . ."
9:23	"You made their offspring numerous . . ."
9:23	". . . and you brought them into the land . . ."
9:23	". . . which you had told unto their ancestors . . ."
9:24	". . . and you subdued before them the ones dwelling in the land . . ."
9:27	". . . you gave them into the hand of their enemies . . ."
9:27	". . . from the heavens you heard them . . ."
9:27	". . . you gave to them deliverers . . ."
9:28	" . . . you abandoned them into the hand of their enemies . . ."
9:28	". . . from heaven you heard them . . ."
9:28	". . . and you delivered them . . ."
9:29	". . . you warned them . . ."
9:30	". . . you had patience on them . . ."
9:30	". . . and you warned them . . ."
9:30	". . . so you gave them into the hand of the peoples of the lands."
9:31	". . . you did not make an end . . ."
9:31	". . . and you did not abandon them . . ."
9:34	". . . or to your warnings that you gave to them."
9:35	". . . and in your great goodness which you gave to them . . ."
9:35	". . . and in the spacious and fertile land you gave to them . . ."
9:36	". . . and in the land you gave to our ancestors . . ."

The lists of verbs and accompanying analysis in Israel's recollection of its distant past, compared to the narrative present in Ezra-Nehemiah, make it apparent that the narrator of Ezra-Nehemiah presumes a very different portrayal of Israel's deity in these two time periods. Perhaps most striking is the contrast between God's work on the hearts of the foreign kings. In the restoration, God causes a king's heart to turn (Ezra 6:27) or places an idea upon his heart (Ezra 7:27). This divine character is hardly recognizable as the same one who, again and again, hardened the heart of Pharaoh just to have an excuse to use brute force to free the Israelites from Egypt. It is difficult, without delving into speculation, to determine precisely why the narrator of Ezra-Nehemiah thought and wrote this way, but a cautious proposal, in the form of a question, seems reasonable at this point: Is the portrayal of God in the narrative present of the restoration closer to the religious experience of the narrator and the narrator's community, and is it possible to imagine that this portrayal is an expression of that experience? If this is the case, then how might we state the difference between the recollection of Israel's God as a narrative character in the past and the religious experience of those responsible for the book of Ezra-Nehemiah, reflected in the portrayal of God in the narrative present of the book?

The notion of covenant has played a central role in Old Testament theology. Covenants are present in Ezra-Nehemiah, but Richard Bautch has identified a very important difference between these covenants and those in the earlier books of the Old Testament: "The covenants depicted in Ezra-Nehemiah are not bilateral pacts between humans and God, as was the Mosaic covenant, but unilateral agreements made by a single community."[17] Human beings have become the initiators of covenant, and God's response is hoped for but not explicitly present. Jack Miles took this observation further in *God: A Biography*, when writing about the book of Ezra-Nehemiah: "The boldness of these Jewish moves is not accompanied, however, by any return to boldness on the part of the Lord God. The very stress in these books on the devotion of the Jewish leaders to the Lord and the eagerness of the people to please him, repenting as soon as their sin is pointed out to them, has a paradoxical effect. It makes the Lord seem less like the Jews' creator, liege, father, or king and more like their enfeebled but cherished ward. His may be the honor, but theirs is the vigor." Here is the point where I would raise a question to Miles about one of his basic presuppositions, that God is the protagonist of the Bible. At the end of the narrative, is it not Israel that is acting more like a protagonist? Miles goes on:

> Human virtue and divine vigor are inversely proportional in the Tanakh. The Lord God never seemed more invincible than when conducting the endlessly complaining, recalcitrant, "stiff-necked" Israelites out of Egypt and through the desert to the land of Canaan. The generation of migrants whom we meet in Ezra and Nehemiah is by contrast the picture of piety. He himself, however, in their company, neither speaks nor acts. It is for this reason that this prelude to their story seems a coda to his. Back then, he seemed to be creating them as his people; now, they seem to be preserving him as their God.[18]

The mighty actor is the object of human memory and storytelling. These memories and the stories they generate are placed within a very different kind of story in the present, one that requires, seeks, and finds a very different divine character. Has the mighty actor God of the past disappeared, been diminished, or matured?

God of Return outside of Ezra-Nehemiah

The previous chapter of this book gave significant attention to the role of Psalm 89 as a reflection on the destruction of Jerusalem and the end of the monarchy, which sets up Psalm 90, at the beginning of book 4 of the book of Psalms, to address the restoration. Psalm 90 is the only psalm that has the name of Moses in the "title." Understandings of these opening lines found on the majority of psalms vary. Many readers take them as statements of authorship, whereas others argue that they are later additions, having more to do with the marking of subcollections within the book of Psalms. One point on which virtually all readers ought to agree, however, is that in the book of Psalms as we have it, these titles suggest the dramatic voice that we should hear reciting this poem. In the case of Psalm 90, it is Moses who declares the exile to be over and calls for the return to Judah like a second exodus.[19] There remains a subtle hint in this poem of the accusation against the divine character made in Psalm 89, when 90:15 makes a request:

> Make us glad as many days as you have afflicted us,
> and as many years as we have seen evil.

There is no reference to punishment here, nor to disobedience. A request such as this one makes little sense if the exile is understood as deserved punishment.

Instead, it gives the impression that YHWH owes Israel blessing and prosperity in return for all of its suffering.

Soon after Psalm 90 comes a set of psalms that proclaim YWHW king of Israel. This statement is overt in Psalms 93 and 95–98 and may be understood as a response to the failure of the returnees to establish another human being, specifically Zerubbabel, as king of Israel. The proximity of these psalms and those in which Moses is prominent, to the psalms that describe YHWH as "refuge" point toward a way of survival for Judah that forgets the Davidic monarchy and looks in other directions.[20] The book of Psalms ends in a grand sweep of restoration. Fifteen consecutive poems, 120–34, carry the title "A Song of Ascents," or literally, "a song for going up." These are pilgrimage songs that urge the reader up to a rebuilt temple in Jerusalem. The last line of the final brief poem in this sequence places YHWH on Zion, ready to bless Israel again.[21] One question this raises is how those who do not have access to Zion might have access to those blessings. The activity of God in relation to Jews in the Diaspora will be the subject of the next section, but for now we should note that the production of the book of Psalms, which was an ongoing process for a long time,[22] may have been one kind of answer to that question, a way of making the experience they produced portable. The book of Psalms is dominated at its end by the "hallelujah Psalms," which bring the collection to a close in a chorus of praise.

Probably all of the books in the Prophetic literature had their final forms shaped to some extent by the restoration, though some are more overtly connected to it than others. The book of Ezekiel ends with a spectacular vision of the new temple that fills nine chapters. This is not the actual rebuilt temple, however, but a wildly imaginative vision befitting the book of Ezekiel, where the "glory of YHWH" that he saw depart Jerusalem and fly away toward Babylon back in chapters 8–10 can return and reside.[23] The closing chapters of Isaiah can also be related to the restoration, though not in a direct or overt manner. Paul Hanson has argued convincingly that the final chapters of Isaiah were born out of conflict among groups in a restored Judah concerning the operation of the temple and the community surrounding it. At the same time, Hanson classified Isaiah 56–66 as an early example of developing apocalyptic literature, a form that seems to resist historical or narrative specificity, perhaps because of its desire to extend hope into the future.[24]

A more concrete connection to the restoration story can be found in the little book of Haggai, which helps to bring the Book of the Twelve into the restoration period. Haggai reports a sequence of events and related prophetic oracles concerning the rebuilding of the temple in Jerusalem. Haggai the prophet is listed in Ezra 5:1 among the early returnees involved in the rebuilding. The book of Haggai carefully crafts its report of the prophet's activity so that it can bring YHWH, the priests, and the people together in a climactic scene in which the divine utterance explains why the efforts of the returnees have been hampered to this point but promises future success.[25] The end of Haggai, however, departs from this sense of reality with a grand pronouncement from YHWH concerning what he will do for Zerubbabel and to the surrounding nations. The language of God here, specifically the statement "I am about to shake the heavens and the earth," moves toward what is commonly identified as apocalyptic language. Like the portions of Isaiah often identified as apocalyptic, this text describes divine behavior, sometimes using ancient images,[26] in a way that seems unconnected to the present reality of Israel's story.

Ezra 5:1 also lists Zechariah son of Iddo as a prophet at work among the early returnees to Jerusalem. The book of Zechariah, which follows Haggai, is attributed to Zechariah son of Berechia son of Iddo, so this second-to-last piece of the Book of the Twelve is also connected to the restoration, but that connection is more abstract. Most interpreters understand the book of Zechariah to fall into two distinct parts, the first of which, Zechariah 1–8, is very close to the book of Haggai and relates to the struggles of rebuilding the temple in the first stage of the restoration. The second half of Zechariah is less concrete and looks more toward the future "Day of YHWH," a concept that continues into the book of Malachi.[27]

There is significant dispute about the origins of apocalyptic thinking and literature, particularly how it is related to the Prophetic literature in the Old Testament. There are those like Hanson, who argue for a strong continuity between these two and often identify the ends of the prophetic corpus as the beginnings of apocalyptic literature.[28] Others, including Tom Milazzo and John Collins, have argued for a different origin for apocalyptic literature but have acknowledged that the two address common issues and themes.[29] This latter observation would seem most important in this context, for among the difficulties that both late Prophetic and early apocalyptic literature address is living in a complex world in which the activity of God is not as apparent as it seems to have been in the past, particularly in the development of a nation and all of its institutions. Such concerns will continue to reverberate in the subsequent discussion of Diaspora literature.

Excursus: On "Literary Histories" of the Old Testament

An examination of the more disparate collection of biblical literature in this chapter, particularly in the next section on dispersion, raises questions about how the processes of production and transmission of each of the pieces are related to each other. Such questions are part of the kind of analysis often called literary history. To a great extent, an approach to Old Testament theology like the one taken in this book sets aside concerns about dating Old Testament materials and describing their development. It is impossible, however, to ignore such issues entirely, and renewed interest in the idea of a "literary history" of the Old Testament in recent years has brought that effort into closer contact with the concerns of biblical theology. Two major projects of this type have been published in just the last year. These are David M. Carr's *The Formation of the Hebrew Bible: A New Reconstruction* and Konrad Schmid's *The Old Testament: A Literary History*. The former "begins with methodological reflections aimed at producing more cautious, less detailed results that may be more useful to colleagues outside a particular school of thought or context."[30] Carr argued, based on comparison to the development of similar bodies of literature in the ancient world, that the writers of the books within the Hebrew Scriptures often relied on oral transmission and memorization of older materials to produce their written works, thus leaving fewer discernible traces of compositional development.[31] Perhaps the most telling feature of Carr's work is that when it begins to trace the literary history of the Hebrew Scriptures, it starts at the end with a chapter entitled "The Hasmonean Period: Finalization of Scripture in an Increasingly Greek World" and moves backward through time. This process leads to other chapters with titles such as "The Babylonian Exile: Trauma, Diaspora, and the Transition to Post-Monarchal Textuality" and "Textuality under Empire: Reflexes of Neo-Assyrian Domination."[32] Such a process reflects a desire to link the literary components of the Hebrew Scriptures to the experiences that shaped the ways Israel thought about its story, rather than a strictly historical concern of assigning them dates and putting them in order. These "orientation points," as Carr calls them,[33] seem, in some cases, to be overtly theological.

Schmid proposed his work as "an attempt to bring together anew the previous sub-disciplines in Old Testament scholarship—not as a substitute for an existing sub-discipline, but as an augmentation of it."[34] This work is more conventional than Carr's, both in its deliberate relation to prior attempts to construct a literary history and in its choice to begin in the tenth century BCE and move forward through time. Schmid is even more overt in expressing his desire to connect this work to biblical theology, even if he is uncertain about how to do that. His brief statement about a literary history's "place within theology" ends on this interesting note: "In the current situation it needs therefore to be asked, what, on the one hand, were the Old Testament texts' own and distinct theological concepts, and how, on the other hand, is their plurality structured within the Old Testament itself."[35] Again, there seems to be an effort to connect texts within the Old Testament to specific events in Israel's experience and the theological perspectives produced by these events. It is when these very different tasks coalesce momentarily and point in the same direction that their relationship is most interesting.

These approaches to literary history have a very interesting and important impact on an understanding of the Wisdom literature, specifically the book of Proverbs. Although Schmid would place the origins of many of the proverbial sayings in this book back in the earliest stages of the development of the biblical literature, in the early monarchy, he proposes that the writing of the book itself, and production of the first nine chapters, which provide the theological perspective of the whole, took place as late as the third century BCE.[36] Such a conclusion would serve to connect the book of Proverbs, the position of which in the canon seems highly arbitrary and which does not have clear connections to any particular point in the narrative of Israel's story, in more direct theological contact with the end of the story. Attempts at developing a literary history, even if problematic in their precise details, may help reveal important connections and questions that will assist a theological exploration of the Diaspora literature.

God of Dispersion

Two features characterize the biblical literature that fits into this section. First, it is international in its perspective, rather than focused inwardly on the land of Israel and its story. Second, its address is toward faithful Israelites living in locations where divine mediation through temple, priesthood, and worship rituals is unavailable. Books such as Daniel and Esther are an obvious fit for this section, but it also includes the book of Ruth and the bulk of the Wisdom literature, though pieces of the latter have been addressed in earlier chapters.

Recent work by Peter Haas points toward a greater theological significance for the book of Daniel than it has been given in the past. Haas began with the problematic assumption that the position of Daniel in the Septuagint, and subsequently in the Christian Old Testament canon, indicates that the book originally had status among the prophets. The book's "demotion" in the Hebrew canon to the Writings may have been an effort to "downplay prophetic or apocalyptic character."[37] The problem with this argument is that the idea that Daniel was placed among the prophets in the Septuagint is based almost entirely on the placement of the book in the fourth- and fifth-century CE codices of the Greek Christian Bible. There is no evidence that mainstream Judaism ever considered the book of Daniel to be among the part of the canon known as the Prophets.[38] One element of Haas's argument that has some merit, however, is that the resistance to the book of Daniel in rabbinic Judaism and the rejection of so many other books like it from the canon are part of a process of "ruling out all claims to private revelations."[39] The result is that "the biblical book of Daniel gives us an important but subtle message of how we are, and are not, to read the Hebrew canon theologically."[40] Haas does not explain this message clearly, but I would argue that the significance of a Diaspora community living faithfully and the divine response to this faithfulness override concerns about the privatizing tendencies of apocalyptic.

The book of Daniel is set entirely outside of the land of Israel. The first half of the book consists primarily of stories about Israelite young men living in the context of the Babylonian and Persian Empires. The resulting absence of the standard institutions of Israelite religion is one of two significant reasons that the book of Daniel does not often appear prominently in the practice of Old Testament theology. The other reason is the nature of the divine character in this book. So, the central question here is, how is God portrayed in the book of Daniel and why? The challenge presented here is that the typical mediating institutions are not available, but the presentation of an unmediated deity seems inappropriate to the situation.

In Daniel 7, the God of Israel is called "the Ancient of Days" three times, a designation this deity receives nowhere else in the biblical text.[41] This designation raises a wide variety of questions about the depictions of deities in the Bible and in other Ancient Near Eastern literature. It has long been considered almost axiomatic that ancient Israelites resisted physical depictions of YHWH and that this prohibition, embedded near the beginning of the Decalogue, extended to the practice of physical description of God in biblical literature. Such descriptions are not completely avoided in the Hebrew Scriptures, however, and there is much debate about how to understand their purpose and role in the text. One of the difficulties created by the Ancient of Days description in Daniel 7 is precisely that it is an image. The visionary Daniel, in 7:9, describes this character using a visual sign of old age: white hair. Biblical texts in which Israel's God has a visual appearance are relatively few. A full discussion of such texts, in which God is fully or partially embodied or appears to a human observer in some visible form, is not possible here, but most have been treated thoroughly in other studies, so a limited review will suffice.

The widespread use of anthropomorphic language referring to God presents some obstacles for the identification of such texts. The problem inherent in understanding this language, specifically the extent to which it is primarily metaphorical, has been the subject of considerable scholarly debate. A focal point for this discussion is James Barr's 1959 article "Theology and Anthropomorphism in the Old Testament." On the one hand, Barr, and others who have followed him, have developed a convincing case that such language is often purely metaphorical and does not constitute true anthropomorphism.[42] On the other hand, there are clear examples of anthropomorphism in the Hebrew Scriptures, and these require some attention. Chapter 3 of this book addressed divine physical appearances in Genesis and Exodus. In Genesis, the two significant examples were 18:1-15 and 32:22-32. These are the only two texts in all of the Old Testament identified by Esther Hamori as examples of an *'ysh* theophany, that is, texts in which God is described using the common Hebrew word for "a man."[43] The most important feature of these stories is that God's body is ordinary. God is not immediately recognized as divine, and he eats with Abraham and wrestles with Jacob, activities requiring a normal human body.[44] There is little indication of the age of this body, except that in the second case, God wrestles a seemingly vigorous Jacob to a draw.[45] The physical appearance of God in Exod. 33:17-23 is quite different. In this case, God is described as having a face, a hand, and a back. In the story, Moses hides in a cleft of the mountainside while God covers him with the hand so that he does not see God's face, but Moses is permitted to see God's back. It is not clear whether this body is complete in the normal human sense, and it is clearly not of ordinary size.[46] Furthermore, there are no apparent signs of age in this depiction.

Closer to Daniel in many ways are the physical descriptions of God in the Prophetic literature, some of which received attention in chapter 5 of this book. In her work that connects Daniel to the theophanic tradition in the Prophetic literature, Amy Merrill Willis has argued that Isa. 6:1-5, Ezek. 1:26-28, and Dan. 7:9-11 stand out as true "anthropomorphic representations of God."[47] She is correct that in each of these cases, the human character sees something that represents God, so these are not examples of purely metaphorical anthropomorphisms. All three of these, however, are presented to us as visions, so it is not clear that there is an embodied deity interacting within the human world as a human being, as in the cases identified in the preceding paragraph from Genesis. In the Isaiah 6 theophany, the divine figure seems at least somewhat human: he sits on a throne and wears some kind of clothing, and he speaks to Isaiah. It is one of the seraphim, though, who interacts physically with Isaiah, touching his mouth with the coal to purify it. The description of the clothing also presents the possibility that the being wearing it is of extraordinary size. Given all of this, it is difficult to confirm that what Isaiah sees is a human body, and he does not describe for us any of its physical characteristics, including age. The Ezekiel 1 passage is problematic for most of the same reasons. The key verse in the midst of this elaborate vision is 1:26. Once again, there is a throne and the figure is seated upon it, but Ezekiel's use of the term *likeness* to refer to both the throne and the human form puts an additional layer of distance between this image and what might be understood as an actual human body, and there is no further description.[48] The Daniel 7 text fits into this tradition, for the most part.[49] The experience is clearly identified as a vision, and Daniel does not have any direct physical interaction with the divine being in it. The critical difference is Daniel's very specific description of the hair on the head of this figure, in 7:9. Thus, this is the clearest indication of divine age in the Hebrew Scriptures, an observation that leads to the question of how this passage fits into the narrative flow of the final form of the book of Daniel.

In the context of examining the development of the divine character in the Old Testament, it is important to ask how God behaves in the book of Daniel and what conclusions this behavior might lead readers to make about the nature of the divine character. Answering this question should begin with a careful examination of God's behavior in the first half of the book of Daniel. This is never an easy task, as is explained in the earlier portion of this chapter concerning Ezra-Nehemiah. Looking for the actions of the divine character is not as easy as simply looking for verbs with God as subject. The biblical Aramaic in this part of Daniel, like biblical Hebrew, makes use of verbless clauses.[50] These will often show up in English translation with forms of the verb "to be" with God as subject, but there is no verb in the Aramaic text. There are also cases in which some extension of God, such as God's "kingdom" (4:34), is the subject of a verb. I will generally include these cases, because they appear to be ways of making indirect statements about God's behavior.

Table 6-5: Divine Actions in Daniel 1–6

1:2	"The Lord gave Jehoiachim into [Nebuchadnezzar's] hand . . ."
	(NRSV) "The Lord let Jehoiakim fall into [Nebuchadnezzar's] power . . ."
1:9	"God gave to Daniel kindness and compassion

	(NRSV) "Now God allowed Daniel to receive favor and compassion . . ."
1:17	". . . and God gave these four boys knowledge and skill . . ."
	". . . you have given me wisdom and power . . ."
	". . . you have revealed to me . . ."
2:23	". . . you have revealed to us . . ."
3:17	". . . our God whom we serve is able to deliver us . . ."
3:28	". . . who has sent his angel and delivered his servants . . ."
4:34	". . . the Most High . . . who lives forever."
4:34	". . . his dominion is an everlasting dominion and his kingdom endures . . ."
4:35	". . . he does according to his will . . ."
5:18	". . . the Most High God gave Neb your father kingship . . ."
5:21	". . . until he knew that the Most High God rules the kingdom of men . . ."
6:16	"May your God whom you serve continually deliver you."
6:22	"My God sent his angel, who shut the mouths of the lions . . ."

Note: Each of these phrases is my own, somewhat literal translation. I have also provided NRSV rendering in cases where this smoother translation contributes significantly to the discussion.

The textual data in table 6-5 establishes Israel's God as a significant narrative character in Daniel 1–6. Comparison to the two other major examples of exilic or postexilic narrative in the Hebrew Bible, Ezra-Nehemiah and Esther, may prove instructive. The latter invites comparison because it also tells the story of a Jewish young person living in a foreign court in Mesopotamia, but the story of Esther is famous for its lack of any direct reference to God. Although most of the narrative action in Ezra-Nehemiah takes place in Judah, there are scenes in which the leaders of the Jewish community interact with foreign leaders in Mesopotamia. Furthermore, God is actively present in the narrative, so this is another appropriate place for comparison. Perhaps most significantly, the book of Daniel shares with Ezra-Nehemiah the tendency to allow foreign kings to make statements about the behavior and character of God (for example, Dan. 6:17). It is difficult to know how to take such evaluations, because of their source, but in general they seem to be presented by the narrator as trustworthy statements.

The divine character portrayed in Daniel 1–6 fits a trend I have demonstrated elsewhere: this is not the God who does "mighty acts" for Israel but one who works subtly, influencing human beings and, in one case, nonhuman animals. When God "delivers" Daniel and his companions from danger, it is in negative fashion. Flames do not burn them and lions do not eat them. Still, these acts of deliverance are acknowledged in the story, especially by the foreign kings involved.

In addition to this broad survey of divine behavior, we might also look more closely at individual texts to understand how the divine character is behaving. Space does not permit a close reading of all of Daniel 1–6, but a closer examination of the first and last stories in this collection, 1:3-21 and 6:1-27, may prove most useful. The story in Dan. 1:3-21 is controlled by the passage of time. Three key scenes take place within the narrative, the first two separated by ten days and the second and third by three years. As the plot proceeds, the reader discovers that the plans and goals of the foreign king, Nebuchadnezzar of Babylon, coincide perfectly with those of Israel's God: the king wants young men with wisdom, knowledge, and insight (1:4), and these are precisely the traits that God wishes to give to the four young men (1:17). The text gives significant attention to the names of the young men, and the way they are listed emphasizes the subtle struggle that is happening within the story. They are introduced by their Hebrew names in 1:6, and although the meaning of two of these names is uncertain, the other two declare that "The LORD is gracious" and "the LORD helps."[51] The Babylonian court seeks to gain control over the young men by renaming them in 1:7, but in the remaining two times the four are listed, 1:11 and 1:19, their Hebrew names are reasserted. Their refusal to eat and drink like Babylonians is reflected in the narrator's refusal of Babylonian names, which helps to confirm for the reader that the achievement of superior wisdom and understanding by these young men in 1:20 is not the result of Babylonian preparation, even though they remain captive within that system. The direct source of Daniel's knowledge and wisdom is difficult to see at first, but his decision to resist the Babylonian diet is based on a desire not to "defile himself." Although Daniel's God is ultimately the source of his knowledge and wisdom, it is obedience to Torah that guides him directly.

As in the initial story in Daniel 1:3-21, Israel's God first enters the story in 6:1-27 indirectly, in the form of Torah. The men who attempt to undermine Daniel know in 6:5 that his obedience to "the law of his God" is his apparent weak point. Daniel's obedience to his understanding of the law and its requirements for prayer and exclusive worship of YHWH establishes the initial conflict of the story.[52] The story commonly known as "Daniel in the Lions'

Den" is dominated by royal decrees issued by the Persian king, Darius. The plot becomes an interplay between strength and weakness. The irrevocable decree issued by Darius in 6:9 is concocted by members of his court. We are given no reason why Darius himself would wish to issue such a decree, sentencing anyone who worships anything other than himself to death, but it smacks of insecurity. The plot works by making the decree itself stronger than the emperor who signs it (6:15). Thus, the king's only way out of the puzzle is to acknowledge dependence on Daniel's God (6:16, 20). Even with Daniel safe, the king does not stop making declarations. First, he orders all of those who had plotted against Daniel, along with their families, to be thrown to the lions, and then the story ends with his stunning decree about the power of Daniel's God. This last element is surprising, at least in part, because it is so out of proportion to what has happened in the story. The deity described in 6:26-27 is the great and powerful God of ancient Israel, who "works signs and wonders in heaven and on earth," though the reality is that this God has merely sent an angel to keep closed the mouths of some lions. Yet, in this story, it is just such subtle divine behavior that constitutes strength.

One difference between the God of Daniel and the deity who performed mighty acts for Israel in the distant past is that the characters in Daniel neither ask for nor expect God to deliver them from captivity in Babylon. What they want, and what God facilitates, is success within the system of the Babylonian court. The God of Daniel is not a warrior or a commander but a giver of knowledge and skill. Miles made a similar point: "Yet for Daniel, history has become more a theater for viewing the action than for taking part in it, and this sometimes seems to go for Daniel's God as well. . . . It is the miracle of prediction—fortune-telling on the international level—rather than any battlefield miracle that is expected to humble the gentiles and bring them to the worship of the true God."[53] This God does not come down to do mighty acts, but humans go to him to make requests of a much less obvious nature. Even the two examples of "delivering" are qualified in important ways. God still allows the three young men to be thrown into the furnace in Daniel 3, and their striking statement of faith allows for the possibility of divine absence or failure. Nowhere else in the Hebrew Bible does a human character make a statement like theirs in 3:17-18. The deliverance of Daniel himself in Daniel 6 is accomplished by an angel, who does not get him out of the lion's den but merely "closes the mouths of the lions."

The aged God of Daniel 7 creates two important theological possibilities. First, it makes God's behavior in Daniel 1–6 sensible. As a source of knowledge, wisdom, and advice, this deity is not just fatherly but grandfatherly. Perhaps just as important, however, is that this possibility retains the idea that this deity could have acted differently in Israel's earlier days, because those were also God's earlier days. Jason Bembry is almost certainly correct when he claims that the use of husband and father imagery for YHWH, even if intended as metaphor, connected Israel's deity to the human life cycle and created the possibility, even if inadvertently, that this deity might age.[54] But why does the image of God in Daniel 7 look old? Bembry has argued that descriptions of God as fatherly, such as the one found in Deut. 32:6, had been diminished in order to enhance the appeal of the image of YHWH as the divine warrior. Israel's God was depicted as young and vigorous, like Baal. Apocalypticism brought back even earlier, cosmic imagery, which included "refracted portrayals" of God, including aged ones.[55]

It is impossible to determine with any certainty the origins of the material in the book of Daniel. The distinctively different halves of the book have been understood to work together in a variety of ways. It is certainly easier to assume that the composer of the book most wanted to present the visions of Daniel, in the second half of the book, and that the first six chapters work in service to this effort by establishing Daniel as a faithful Israelite living amid foreign oppression who is also an authoritative interpreter of dreams. André Lacocque, for example, has argued that the purpose of the author "was to galvanize the spiritual resistance of the Pious against the persecution of Antiochus IV and the Hellenists." Lacocque understood Daniel 7–12 to be "the more original work" of the final author of the book, who used an adapted set of stories in chapters 1–6 to provide examples of this kind of resistance.[56] John Collins takes a similar view, that the tales in the first half of the book, in some form, are earlier than the visions in the latter half.[57] In the final form of the book, they serve to establish the appropriate Diaspora setting for the book as a whole.[58] Gregory Mobley has argued that the stories are earlier than the visions but that the two genres work together, the tales "sketching daytime coping strategies for living in the Diaspora" whereas the visions "offer nighttime cosmic revelations about heavenly struggles taking place that will result in their vindication."[59]

Miles has identified a critical difference between literature such as Daniel and earlier biblical narrative. In Daniel, and later literature such as 1 and 2 Maccabees, Israelites are persecuted by foreigners because of their faithfulness. This stands in stark contrast to earlier stories, much of which are identified with the "Deuteronomic" tradition, in which YHWH used foreign powers to punish Israel for a lack of faithfulness.[60] This shift must have caused an enormous reevaluation of God's character and ways of interacting with the world. The age of the "Ancient of Days" image in Daniel 7 allows for the claim that all of Israel's long story, down to the struggles of the writer and audience of the book, is encompassed by Israel's God. It is also an image that fits divine actions such as giving Torah and sending angels to guide and protect faithful worshipers in strange and distant settings. This international appeal provides an appropriate point of departure for a discussion of the Wisdom literature, which has occasionally been linked to Daniel within Old Testament theology.[61]

Esther

The discussion of the court tales in Daniel 1–6 leads to the book of Esther, which tells a story with many similarities. Once again, a Jewish young person living in a foreign empire, Persia in the case of Esther, rises to a position of influence because of beauty, intelligence, and courage. The major difference in this story is that the book of Esther is famous for making no overt mention of Israel's God.[62] Of course, this may be exactly the theological point that the book is making. One often-unnoticed aspect of the story is that the Persian king, Ahasueras, does not act to save the Jewish people in the Persian Empire from the plot to destroy them. In Esther 8:1-14, he merely permits Mordecai to write letters giving the Jews permission to defend themselves. If we can carry from literature such as Ezra-Nehemiah and Daniel the idea that Israel's God is operating through the beneficial behaviors of foreign kings, then this makes an indirect statement about what this God is doing for the Jewish people. He no longer fights for them, but allows them permission to fight to defend their own interests. Perhaps it remains to be seen whether this constitutes a sense of divine abandonment, but it is important to note that in the book of Esther, under these circumstances, the Jewish people fight so successfully that the celebration of their achievements generates the regular celebration of the fest of Purim (9:18-32). This is a mode of theological storytelling quite different from that produced by the heavy hands of the past, which insisted that the reader understand the divine involvement in a particular way; here, it leaves such evaluation open to the reader. Of course, the additions to the Greek book of Esther may demonstrate that not everyone found this type of theological move satisfactory.

Proverbs

Roland Murphy has stated that the book of Proverbs had no place in biblical theology as it was practiced through the end of the twentieth century and into the first few years of the twenty-first.[63] Although this may be something of an overstatement, Murphy was right that the place of the book in the field is problematic and has not been the subject of major attention. Within this study, a small portion of Proverbs (chapter 8) found a place as one of many recollections of the energetic God of creation, but the bulk of the book of Proverbs awaits inclusion. It may be one of the foremost literary features of Proverbs that makes it so difficult to use as theological data. Brueggemann has recognized Wisdom itself, or more precisely "the sage," as a mediation of God's presence, and has noted that such an inclusion was a departure from most other previous attempts to develop mediation as a theological category.[64] But the book of Proverbs has also been given a monarchical framework in 1:1, 10:1, 25:1, and 31:1, so it is doubly mediated. Moreover, this second layer of mediation is not well integrated into the book. Murphy was right when he proclaimed that "the theological thrust of the Book of Proverbs comes from its obvious intent to shape the character of a human being, to provide moral formation of a worshiper of the Lord."[65] It must be asked, however, to what extent this is a royal concern. Moreover, attempts to place this literary effort at character development within the traditions and geography of Israel have been unsuccessful. Thus, the book of Proverbs would seem more at home in the context of the Judaism of the Diaspora. Leo Perdue's attempt to match each of the wisdom books in the biblical tradition with a specific imperial era is somewhat artificial. He matched Proverbs with the kingdoms of Israel and Judah, and the rest of the Wisdom literature with different foreign empires, so it is difficult to see Proverbs within the same sequence as all of the others.[66] The beginning of the book of Proverbs places the book in the court of Solomon, with references to Israel's infamously wise king at 1:1 and 10:1, but the end of the book of Proverbs is located in foreign territory. The two persons mentioned in the superscriptions in 30:1 and 31:1 cannot be located in Israelite tradition, and the identification of Lemuel as a king puts the book of Proverbs in a foreign court, the kind of setting in which we find characters such as Daniel and Esther. The famous poem at the end of the book may or may not be a continuation of the advice given to King Lemuel by his mother, but it is surely intended to be heard by the young man who has been addressed throughout the book. Whereas that young man is admonished at the beginning of Proverbs that "the fear of YHWH is the beginning of wisdom" (1:7), the description of an ideal mate at the end of the book contains nothing overtly religious, much less a description of faithfulness to Israel's covenant tradition. Nevertheless, the woman described in 31:10-31 would seem to fulfill the spirit of the Torah, even if by accident. Such a reading of Proverbs is consistent with Smith-Christopher's proposal of reading it "from below." Smith-Christopher identified texts in Proverbs, such as 20:2, 23:3, and 25:5-7, that seem to be directed, like the book of Daniel, to persons "outside the sphere of political power and influence."[67] The book of Ecclesiastes also operates in this complex milieu, in which fear of God and obedience to divine commands (12:13) are encouraged as components of a wise way of living, but they are not connected to any of the institutions of Israelite religion or the promises of its covenant. Although it is possible to list wisdom or "wise men" among the institutions of Israel or mediators of divine presence, this is not an easy fit.[68] Even James Crenshaw, the most ardent searcher for some sense of formal education in ancient Israel, admits to a "deadening silence" in the Old Testament on this matter.[69] Instead of pushing back into the realm of speculation for some kind of origin for biblical wisdom, asking where it came from, it seems more important to ask where it is supposed to be taken. In this case, perhaps, we can say with a good deal more certainty that this material and the way of life it proposes is designed to be taken anywhere, by the likes of Daniel, Esther, and Tobias.

Ruth

It seems that the canon fights over the book of Ruth. The Christian Old Testament seizes upon the reference to "the judges" in the first verse of the book and the name of David in the last verse to use the book as a transition between the books of Judges and Samuel. The Jewish canon, however, seems bound by the use of Ruth as one of the "festival scrolls" to place it at the beginning of the collection of Megilloth as part of Ketuvim. Although the book of Ruth tells a story set in the period of the judges, according to the first verse and the Davidic genealogy, nothing in the story itself is specific to any time period. The narration indicates plainly that it comes from a much later period, when old customs must be explained (4:7). In many other ways, however, the book of Ruth has an affinity with the literature of the Diaspora, and it functions as a counterbalance to the ethnic confinement at the end of Ezra-Nehemiah. Like Daniel and Esther, the book of Ruth presents a main character who is a young person trying to make her way in a foreign land. The situation is the inverse of these other examples, however, because Ruth is a foreigner trying to get along in Israel. Unlike Esther, there are overt mentions of God in the book of Ruth, but these are subtle and almost entirely expressed in the speech of the characters. One exception is Ruth 1:6, which attributes the end of the famine in Judah to YHWH, but the book does not attribute the beginning of the famine to either divine power or lack of it. Like the characters in the book of Esther, those in the book of Ruth seem left alone to fend for themselves, and they do so quite admirably.

Job

A discussion of the bulk of the book of Job was placed in the previous chapter under "God of Defeat," but the final eight verses fit better here. If the majority of the book of Job attaches to the destruction of Judah and the exile, then these closing verses, 42:10–17, are most easily connected to the restoration, but we must acknowledge an unavoidable strangeness about this ending. It does not fit the rest of the book at all. Perhaps nowhere in the Old Testament is so much nonsense and incongruity packed into such a small space. How should readers feel about Job's siblings, who come only now to "show him sympathy and comfort"? Job's friends may have said all the wrong things, but at least they were there at the right time. Can the restoring of Job's fortune, even doubling it, be understood as anything other than divine reward for his faithfulness? This would seem to confirm exactly the point made by the adversary at the beginning of the book. Job serves God because God pays him well for the task, even if the payment is sometimes delayed. Of course, the adversary, so prominent in the opening frame of the book, is missing from the end. Is his task with Job finished, so that he has moved on to his next defendant, or has he won the argument so convincingly by revealing God's inability to resist rewarding God's favorites that his being is absorbed into YHWH's?[70] The other missing character at the conclusion of the story is Job's wife. She was not named at the beginning of the book, nor was her own suffering ever acknowledged, and now she is treated with the disregard of total silence. It hardly seems possible that, having raised and lost ten adult children, she would now be in the position to bear ten more, so perhaps we are to assume another wife bears these. If the reader misses all of this, then there is the bizarre genealogy, which names Job's daughters but not his sons. Is this telling us that restoration is gratuitous, that in the end Israel's God cannot help but do it, or that restoration is nonsense? Even if it happens, then, it will not happen in the ways that it should. The plot of the Old Testament is coming to an end, but it is a frayed end with many strands, a few of which might carry hopes for continuation.

Return to Daniel

The court tales in the first half of the book of Daniel received significant attention earlier, followed by a discussion of other Diaspora texts that have strong connections to it. The examination of Daniel cannot be fully complete, however, without some attempt to address the apocalyptic literature that makes up its closing chapters. The preceding discussion was concerned only with the image of God as an old man presented in Daniel 7. This image actually leads to a long series of visions in the remainder of the book. The first half of this chapter dealt with apocalyptic literature briefly, primarily because of its connection to Prophetic literature. As was demonstrated, there are both continuities and discontinuities between prophetic and apocalyptic writings. Too often, the dispute concerning the origins of apocalyptic literature has been treated as an either/or sort of question, but the implications of such discrete answers make little sense. It seems very unlikely that those who produced apocalyptic literature were a unified group carefully drawing upon only one of Israel's theological traditions. What seems more likely is a process of convergence, one in which many different streams of tradition moved in a similar direction because they were dealing with similar concerns.[71]

It is difficult and problematic to move too far with an exploration of apocalyptic literature in the context of an Old Testament theology, particularly one grounded in the canonical tradition of the Protestant Old Testament and thus, indirectly, the Hebrew Scriptures. As this canon reaches its narrative conclusion, it is just beginning to examine the possibilities of apocalyptic. The full flowering of that literature comes later. Daniel 7–12 is the clearest example of apocalyptic literature in this collection, and it is a set of texts that takes a fascinating turn in presenting the behavior of Israel's God. Israel's story has moved away from a portrayal of a deity acting visibly and boldly in the world; apocalyptic literature may be offering the idea of a God who is active in another realm of existence, one that requires a great deal of imagination and that will be revealed only at some date in the distant future. Within the context of an Old Testament theology such as this one, this is too fresh a move to be evaluated but awaits an attempt to follow the continuing story of Israel and its God beyond the bounds of this text.

Along with pulling in some disparate texts and pointing toward a surprising image of God, this section has demonstrated that the divine character of Israel's story of restoration must display a complexity that earlier portraits of Israel's God did not. At the end of the story in the Old Testament, Israel is in a lot of places and moving in many different directions. A God who not only makes a way for Ezra and Nehemiah to return and rebuild Jerusalem but also stays to look after Daniel and Esther in Persia is a different kind of being than the one who talks to Moses on Sinai or helps David build a nation. Placing this God at the center of Old Testament theology is a task to which we will return.

The Restoring God in Old Testament Theology

Contemporary attention to Nehemiah 9 can be traced back to the role it played in Gerhard von Rad's argument in "The Form-Critical Problem of the Hexateuch." Von Rad identified Neh. 9:6-38 as a creedal statement standing at the end of a trajectory of such statements that began with the "little creed" in Deut. 26:5-9. Von Rad's tradition-critical project placed Nehemiah 9 in this position because it is the most complete of the creedal statements he identified, including all of the following elements of Israelite tradition:

- creation
- Israelite ancestors
- Egyptian bondage
- plagues
- exodus
- wilderness
- Sinai
- conquest
- judges[72]

Regardless of one's conclusions about the validity of von Rad's approach, it is clear that Neh. 9:6-37 plays some part in a well-developed tradition of reciting God's actions with, for, and against Israel in the past. One of the distinctive features of this particular portrayal is that it sits in a much later narrative context, one that puts all of these actions in a distant past, far removed from the narrative present in which it is recited. One result of this placement is that it highlights the differences between the ways that the divine character is portrayed in the distant past and the portrayal of God in the narrative present of the book of Ezra-Nehemiah.

Given the preceding analysis, it is not difficult to see why theologians of the Hebrew Scriptures spend most of their time in books such as Genesis, Exodus, Samuel, Isaiah, Jeremiah, and Psalms. Our field may have escaped the historical framework that dominated much of the twentieth century, but the captivation with the "mighty acts of God" has, for the most part, simply changed residences; it is still the focus of most theologians working within a literary or canonical framework. There is not space here to catalog the neglect of Ezra-Nehemiah within the field of theology of the Hebrew Scriptures, but a few examples will illustrate the point. Perhaps the most significant, comprehensive theology of the Old Testament of the last two decades, Walter Brueggemann's *Theology of the Old Testament: Testimony, Dispute, Advocacy*, contains three references to Ezra and eleven to Nehemiah. The combined total of these two is outnumbered by the fifteen references to Psalm 89 alone. The situation is even more stark in James Barr's *The Concept of Biblical Theology*, which functioned as an evaluation of the field at the end of the twentieth century: it contains no references to Ezra or Nehemiah.[73] A somewhat different kind of work in both scope and focus, Terence Fretheim's *God and World in the Old Testament: A Relational Theology of Creation*, contains one reference to Ezra and one to Nehemiah.[74]

John Rogerson's recent contribution to the field, *A Theology of the Old Testament: Cultural Memory, Communication, and Being Human,* does no better on this score, with four references to Nehemiah and none to Ezra, but his proposal that we approach the Old Testament as "cultural memory"[75] may provide some space for greater inclusion of that memory's final narrative destination. Rogerson made extensive use of Claude Lévi-Strauss's categories of "hot" and "cold" societies, applying them to cultural memory to describe "hot" and "cold" histories. He used Chronicles as a primary example of a cold history and the Deuteronomistic History as a hot history. The key distinction seems to be that the former stresses "continuity" and "stability."[76] Again drawing on Lévi-Strauss, Rogerson described a hot history as "one that internalizes the historical process in order to make it the moving power of its development."[77] The application of these categories to Old Testament texts is reminiscent of Brueggemann's powerful distinction between the forces of "structure legitimation" and "the embrace of pain."[78] There is real tension in the Old Testament, but it is not so much the result of multiple contemporaneous perspectives as it is the result of an end of the story that is very different from its beginning, particularly in the way it portrays the divine character.

Once again, von Rad may have pointed us in a good direction, whether he meant to or not, on the final page of his essay "The Form-Critical Problem of the Hexateuch": "The Hexateuch will be rightly understood, therefore, not by those who read it superficially, but only by those who study it with a knowledge of its profundities, recognizing that its pages speak of the revelations and religious experiences of many different periods. None of the stages in the age-long development has been wholly superseded; something has been preserved of each phase, and its influence has persisted right down to the final form of the Hexateuch."[79] If we take this idea further and apply it to the entire canon of the Hebrew Scriptures, it would be difficult to disagree with the first sentence, except that we would likely have less confidence than von Rad that the layers created by all of those different periods could be unraveled and separated. What we could say, with greater confidence, is that the narrator of Ezra-Nehemiah gets to tell the end of the story, and this portrait of God is the final one we see, if we read along that trajectory.

Richard Elliott Friedman has described this literary phenomenon in terms of "disappearance."[80] Long before Friedman's work, von Rad himself pointed toward this same observation in his article that was placed at the end of his two-volume *Old Testament Theology* as a postscript:[81] "Does he [God] not, in the course of his self-revelation, conceal himself more and more deeply from his people?"[82] But the idea of disappearance, or even concealment, may operate with an assumption that needs to be questioned. This assumption is that overt and robust activity is a characteristic mode of presence, and that the lack of such activity denotes absence, hiddenness, or elusiveness.[83] In Brueggemann's forensic model, these phenomena play the role of "counter-testimony."[84] But it is only when presence is defined as activity that lack of activity becomes absence. Is it possible that Ezra-Nehemiah offers us a different kind of presence, one not characterized by actions? Inside the narrative, we might talk instead about the maturation of the character. Outside the narrative, it may be the maturation of the audience, based upon a set of religious experiences that no longer matched earlier divine portraits.

Bringing the End to the Center

When we reach the end of the long story of God and God's people recorded in the Old Testament, how do we respond? The story has an open and troubling end. Is it possible to let that end flow back through the entire story, to become the center around which the conversation about the theology of Old Testament is organized? In the earlier chapters of this book, I observed that earlier elements of the story were often recollected in later texts, and that the presumptions about the divine character were different in the narrative present than in the past. In this chapter, that observation has been advanced further by comparing the way the book of Ezra-Nehemiah talks about divine action in its present compared to its past. An examination of other literature that gathers itself around the parallel stories of restoration life in Judah and Diaspora life in the surrounding empires reveals similar moves in the continuing search to find ways to talk about the behavior of God.

Addressing this kind of shift in speaking of divine action has been especially difficult for Old Testament theology, partly because it is so often presumed that the task is to point forward to the New Testament. This observation raises important questions about how different a Christian theology of the Old Testament and a Jewish theology of the Tanak must be. In his most recent work, Marvin Sweeney has provided a helpful review of Christian Old Testament theology from a Jewish perspective. In this survey, Sweeney gives credit to a number of recent Old Testament theologians who have been more sensitive to Jewish concerns than in the past, particularly in response to the Shoah and what it revealed about Christian attitudes toward Judaism. Although Sweeney thinks it is not possible for Jewish and Christian theologies of these shared texts to become congruent, he does believe that constructive dialogue between the two is possible.[85] Developing a theology of these shared sacred texts has occupied Christians much more than Jews, but Sweeney demonstrated that there have been active attempts to develop a Jewish theology of the Tanak for the past century. His survey of the work of Jewish scholars such as Franz Rosenzweig, Martin Buber, and Yehezkel Kaufmann, among others, developed a stream of Jewish theological work with the text that may not always have been recognized as such because it did not easily fit the mold of the dominant Christian ways of doing Old Testament theology. In more recent years, the work of Jewish scholars such as Michael Fishbane and Jon Levenson has brought this body of scholarship to a level of maturity that even scholars working from a Christian perspective cannot afford to ignore.[86]

From this survey flows Sweeney's description of "the task of Jewish biblical theology." Two facets of this task are most important for this study and provide a means by which we might do the kind of turning back I have described, which allows the end of the story to be at the center of the discussion and to determine its shape. First, Sweeney's assertion that "the term biblical theology denotes properly a concern with the construction of G-d as presented in the Bible" is in harmony with the path this book has followed.[87] Second, Sweeney reasserts the dialogical character of the Jewish Scriptures. Although I have moved away from a dialogical approach in favor of a narrative one up to this point, in order to establish the end of the story as the place where it has been moving and to give it the appropriate place in the discussion, "dialogue" is now possible in a new way. Sweeney uses this dialogical character to point toward an understanding of intertextuality that functions on multiple levels. Although a Christian theology of the Old Testament can participate in a Christian biblical theology that moves to the New Testament, it is my conviction that this should take place only after a Christian Old Testament theology has become a complete statement in and of itself, and this requires not just reaching the end of the story but allowing that end to flow back through the entire narrative, producing a complete reconsideration in its light.[88] This points toward one major point on which I disagree with Sweeney, and this is his assertion that "whereas Christian Old Testament theology can be selective in its treatment of the Old Testament, Jewish biblical theology must take into account the entirety of the Tanak and the Hebrew or Aramaic text which stands as its basis."[89] Obviously, many, if not most, Christian Old Testament theologies have done this, so Sweeney's statement that they "can" is true on its face, but he seems to be acknowledging that such a procedure is appropriate, and with that I disagree. One aspect that should distinguish Old Testament theology from other areas of

Old Testament studies is its determination to engage the entire text. In either case, we need to ask what "take into account" means. On practical terms, it cannot mean a careful interpretation of every text in the Hebrew Scriptures. It should at least mean, however, that every book is given serious consideration and that there is space provided within the framework for an interpretation of every text.

The Tanak and the Protestant Old Testament are the same in content and different in order, of course, but the approach in this treatment, which follows the narrative contours of the text and allows other texts to accrue appropriately around that storyline, minimizes these differences. Two important observations about the relationship of Christianity to the Tanak must be made here.[90] First, the church existed as a Jewish sectarian movement for at least a few decades before any of the New Testament was written, and for considerably longer before any of it came to be considered Scripture. So, the church began with the Hebrew Scriptures as its sacred text. Second, although some of the books of the Tanak, Genesis–Kings for example, fall into a necessary order because of a continuous plot, the order of most of the other books is somewhat arbitrary. Indeed, until sometime in the second century of the Common Era, when the codex began to gain popularity, the Tanak existed as a group of scrolls, for which there would have been no complete, fixed order of books. Evidence suggests that the order of some books remained somewhat fluid in Judaism and Christianity for some time. Even when a fixed order was reached, we have no idea why some books were placed as they are. There is no logical place in any canon, for example, for the book of Daniel. So, some aspects of the canon, in terms of the order of the books, is artificial, made necessary by the particular technology for producing the canon as a physical artifact, beginning about nineteen centuries ago, just as its contents became fully and finally determined. I think it is worth recognizing that whereas the second major technological shift in Bible production, the fifteenth-century move from handwriting to mechanized printing, had no effect on the notion of order of books, because the codex was still the physical form, the technological shift in which we currently find ourselves does have an impact on this. The move toward a digital Bible, coming from "the cloud" onto a handheld electronic device, does not erase all traces of an order of books in the canon, but does make it less visible.

When the way of thinking about and describing the character of God as reflected in the literature that forms and accrues to the end of the biblical story is taken to be the norm, and previous ways of characterizing God are gazed at from afar, a number of responses are possible, even likely. One of these is the assumption that those earlier portrayals of God in the Bible are "primitive," which may even lead to their dismissal. Another response is the insistence that such a change in the way God is portrayed within the Bible has not really happened but that we readers are just not perceiving God's behavior correctly, which leads some to cling to the old way of talking about divine behavior regardless of whether it seems to fit contemporary experience. As the Old Testament arrives at its end, it struggles to walk a line between these options, refusing to forget the past or to deny the realities of the present. The texts that represent this end, such as Nehemiah 9, Psalm 44, Daniel, Esther, Ruth, and Job 42, offer the possibilities of memory, imagination, protest, puzzlement, and defiance as ways of framing the past and moving forward in a very different world. They also make significant progress toward developing a divine character who can accompany the human narrative characters and potential readers in that movement, a God who is as complex as the world has become at that story's end.

Some Concluding Implications

One of the lasting effects of the so-called biblical theology movement of the mid-twentieth century is the preoccupation with a divine being who performs great deeds on Israel's behalf. This preoccupation with mighty acts was part of a historicist framework that attempted to explain the origin of the remarkable entity called Israel as something quite distinct from its environment in the ancient Near East. Only a mighty deity could have established and sustained such an "unmighty" nation. It is probably no accident that this movement found its most comfortable home in the post–World War II United States, a nation in the early days of an unlikely emergence as the world's superpower. The growth and development of the United States in the hundred years from the mid-nineteenth to the mid-twentieth century, despite struggles such as the Civil War and the Great Depression, seemed providential. In such a context, the natural move of biblical theology would be toward the rapid growth and expansion of the first half of the biblical plot and its mighty deity.

As the attention of Old Testament studies has moved toward a literary presentation read in a more multicultural context, however, endings should receive as much attention as origins, or perhaps even more. The world of the twenty-first century is more complex in every way than it was fifty years ago, and our experience is no longer one of seemingly miraculous growth and expansion. We have begun to see that the physical world we occupy has some limits, and that the vastly different experiences of people around the globe produce disparate ways of viewing the biblical text and the world.

There is no way to make the stories and characters, human and divine, in books such as Ezra-Nehemiah as exciting as those in Genesis, Exodus, or Samuel. It will always be tempting to focus our attention on those thrilling earlier portrayals. But a text we now recognize as a story beckoning us inside of it, which we now read in a world demanding a more nuanced sense of vision and understanding, must be allowed to carry us to its conclusion. The biblical story is not about going back to prior moments. The entrance to Eden is blocked, and YHWH tells Elijah to get away from Horeb. Even the so-called restoration of Judah fails to be such when Israel is not reestablished as a nation with a king and most of its people living within its border. Bringing the mature God found at the conclusion of this long narrative journey to the center of the theological discussion, against the grain formed by the nature of the literature found there, may instead require more mature reading.

Notes

1. See the description of the formation of these communities in Jill Middlemas, *The Templeless Age: An Introduction to the History, Literature, and Theology of the "Exile"* (Louisville: Westminster John Knox, 2007), 9–27.

2. Mark McEntire, "The God at the End of the Story: Are Biblical Theology and Narrative Character Development Compatible?" *HBT* 33 (2011): 171–89.

3. Examples of this approach include Walter Brueggemann, *Theology of the Old Testament: Testimony, Dispute, Advocacy* (Minneapolis: Fortress Press, 1997); Karl Allen Kuhn, *Having Words with God: The Bible as Conversation* (Minneapolis: Fortress Press, 2008); and Benjamin D. Sommer, "Dialectical Biblical Theology: A Jewish Approach to Reading Scripture Theologically," the first chapter in *Biblical Theology: Introducing the Conversation,* ed. Leo G. Perdue, Robert Morgan, and Benjamin D. Sommer (Nashville: Abingdon, 2009).

4. Treatments of the divine character that use a trajectory and observe narrative development are not typically given significant attention in the field of biblical theology. The two most notable examples of this are Richard Elliott Friedman, *The Disappearance of God: A Divine Mystery* (Boston: Little, Brown, 1995); and Jack Miles, *God: A Biography* (New York: Vintage, 1995). For a more thorough examination of this phenomenon, see McEntire "God at the End of the Story," 14–16.

5. Much of the discussion of Ezra-Nehemiah in this section is developed from an earlier article. See Mark McEntire, "Portraits of a Mature God: What Would a Theology of the Hebrew Scriptures Look Like if Ezra-Nehemiah Was at the Center of the Discussion?" *PRSt* 39 (2012): 113–24.

6. The decline of historical-critical approaches to the biblical text is sometimes overstated. Attempts to reconstruct the context and process of the production of the text are alive and well. For two recent examples of this, see Lisbeth S. Fried, "Who Wrote Ezra-Nehemiah—and Why Did They?" in *Unity and Disunity in Ezra-Nehemiah: Redaction, Rhetoric, and Reader*, ed. Mark J. Boda and Paul L. Redditt (Sheffield, UK: Sheffield Phoenix, 2008), 75–97; and Margaret Cohen, "Leave Nehemiah Alone: Nehemiah's 'Tales' and Fifth-Century BCE Historiography," in Boda and Redditt, *Unity and Disunity in Ezra-Nehemiah*, 55–74. Each of these articles illustrates both the fruit and pitfalls of such attempts. They are filled with keen observations about the text of Ezra-

Nehemiah but rely on strained reasoning to arrive at deductive conclusions about the production of it.

7. Lester Grabbe has provided a more thorough accounting of these literary parallels in *Ezra-Nehemiah* (New York: Routledge, 1998), 94–99. See also the treatment in Mark McEntire *Dangerous Worlds: Living and Dying in Biblical Texts* (Macon, GA: Smyth & Helwys, 2004), 89–91.

8. Daniel Smith-Christopher, *A Biblical Theology of Exile* (Minneapolis: Fortress Press, 2002), 38–45.

9. Ibid., 45.

10. On the relationship of Chronicles and Ezra-Nehemiah, see Joseph Blenkinsopp, *Ezra-Nehemiah: A Commentary* (Louisville: Westminster, 1988), 44.

11. Of course, it is likely that the final form of Ezra-Nehemiah was completed one to two centuries after the restoration events of the late sixth to mid-fifth centuries BCE. Thus, the description here refers to the narrative present of the literature itself.

12. See H. G. M. Williamson, *Ezra-Nehemiah* (Waco, TX: Word, 1985), 125–27.

13. Meir Sternberg, *The Poetics of Biblical Narrative: Ideological Literature and the Drama of Reading* (Bloomington: Indiana University Press, 1988), 87.

14. Ibid., 86.

15. See my discussion of this in McEntire, "God at the End of the Story," 16–18.

16. See the note that is included in table 6-2.

17. Richard J. Bautch, "The Function of Covenant across Ezra-Nehemiah," in Boda and Redditt, *Unity and Disunity in Ezra-Nehemiah*, 8. Similar observations have been made in Delbert R. Hillers, *Covenant: The History of a Biblical Idea* (Baltimore: Johns Hopkins University Press, 1969), 148–49. Dennis J. McCarthy emphasized the focus on a unified community, not just a leader, in the portrayals of covenant in Ezra-Nehemiah. See McCarthy, "Covenant and Law in Chronicles-Nehemiah," *CBQ* 44 (1982): 34–35.

18. Miles, *God*, 373.

19. For more on the placement and function of Psalm 90 within the entire Psalter, see Nancy deClaissé-Walford, *Reading from the Beginning: The Shaping of the Hebrew Psalter* (Macon, GA: Mercer University Press, 1997), 82–88.

20. See William L. Holladay, *The Psalms through Three Thousand Years: Prayerbook of a Cloud of Witnesses* (Minneapolis: Fortress Press, 1993), 78–79.

21. On this sequence and the way Psalm 134 summarizes its purpose, see Konrad Schaefer, *Psalms* (Collegeville, MN: Liturgical, 2001), 316–17.

22. The evidence from the Dead Sea Scrolls indicates intense activity in copying the psalms and a continuing fluidity in choosing and arranging them into collections for different purposes. See the discussion of this evidence in Holladay, *Psalms through Three Thousand Years*, 98–108.

23. Dale F. Launderville appropriately labels this vision "Eden-like" and "utopian." See Launderville, *Spirit and Reason: The Embodied Character of Ezekiel's Symbolic Thinking* (Waco, TX: Baylor University Press, 2007), 383.

24. Paul D. Hanson, *The Dawn of Apocalyptic: The Historical and Sociological Roots of Jewish Apocalyptic Eschatology* (Philadelphia: Fortress Press, 1979), 79–100. The precise details of Hanson's argument are less convincing than the broader picture.

25. For a detailed explanation of how the literary structure of Haggai operates to accomplish this, see Mark McEntire, "Haggai—Bringing God into the Picture," *RevExp* 97 (2000): 69–78.

26. See, for example, the echoes of Sinai in Isa. 64:4 ("you came down, the mountains quaked at your presence") and the Red Sea event in Hag. 2:22 ("I am about to destroy the strength of the kingdoms of the nations, and overthrow the chariots and their riders").

27. The use of the heading "An Oracle" at Zech. 9:1 and 12:1 and at Mal. 1:1 creates the possibility that these texts were once part of a unified collection.

28. Hanson, *Dawn of Apocalyptic*, 12–16.

29. See G. Tom Milazzo, *The Protest and the Silence: Suffering, Death, and Biblical Theology* (Minneapolis: Fortress Press, 1992), 73–82; and John J. Collins, *The Apocalyptic Imagination: An Introduction to the Jewish Matrix of Christianity* (New York: Crossroad, 1984), 9–30.

30. David M. Carr, *The Formation of the Hebrew Bible: A New Reconstruction* (Oxford: Oxford University Press, 2011), 4.

31. Ibid., 4–7. Carr developed this comparative approach in his previous work, *Writing on the Tablet of the Heart: Origins of Scripture and Literature* (Oxford: Oxford University Press, 2009), 3–16.

32. Carr, *Formation of the Hebrew Bible,* xi–xii.

33. Ibid., 3.

34. Konrad Schmid, *The Old Testament: A Literary History* (Minneapolis: Fortress Press, 2012), 2.

35. Ibid., 14–15.

36. Ibid., 186–88. Carr argues for a much earlier date for the production of the book of Proverbs, specifically for Proverbs 1–9. See *Formation of the Hebrew Bible*, 409–14.

37. Peter J. Haas, "The Book of Daniel: The Strange End of Biblical Theology," in *Jewish Bible Theology: Perspectives and Case Studies*, ed. Isaac Kalimi (Winona Lake, IN: Eisenbrauns, 2012), 258–59.

38. The one small piece of evidence, which Haas does not cite, is the reference to "the book of Daniel the prophet" in the Qumran text known as the *Florilegium* (4Q174). See the discussion of this text and its implications in Martin Abegg Jr., Peter Flint, and Eugene Ulrich, trans., *The Dead Sea Scrolls Bible: The Oldest Known Bible* (San Francisco: HarperOne, 1999), 483–85. The writers of the Christian gospels of Matthew and Mark, both widely considered to be first-century Jews, both have Jesus quote Dan. 7:13 in the midst of his trial (Matt. 26:64 and Mark 14:62). These writers both tend to attribute quotations from biblical prophets either to a specific prophet or "prophets" in general, but there is no designation of the source of this saying in either of these Gospels. Matt. 24:15 does cite Daniel by name and refers to him as "the prophet," but the saying of Jesus here is a summation of Dan. 8:9-27, and it is not cited as are the many "fulfillment citations" in Matthew. Furthermore, there is no evidence that the book of Daniel was ever any part of the Book of the Twelve, which seems to have been a fixed collection by the time Daniel was written. See the discussion in Louis Francis Hartman and Alexander A. Di Lella, *The Book of Daniel* (Garden City, NY: Doubleday, 1978), 24–26.

39. Haas, "Book of Daniel," 260.

40. Ibid., 262.

41. Much of the discussion of Daniel here is developed from a recent article of mine. See Mark McEntire, "The Graying of God in Daniel 1–7," *RevExp*, forthcoming.

42. James Barr, "Theology and Anthropomorphism in the Old Testament," in *Congress Volume: Oxford, 1959* (Leiden: Brill, 1960), 31–38.

43. Esther Hamori, *When Gods Were Men: The Embodied God in Biblical and Near Eastern Literature* (Berlin: de Gruyter, 2008), 1–4. See the previous discussion of this in chapter 3.

44. Ibid., 153–54.

45. Ibid., 25.

46. For more on this text, see Howard Schwartz, "Does God Have a Body?" in *Bodies, Embodiment, and Theology of the Hebrew Bible*, ed. S. Tamar Kamionkowski and Wonil Kin (New York: T&T Clark, 2010), 201–5.

47. Amy C. Merrill Willis, "Heavenly Bodies: God and the Body in the Visions of Daniel," in Kamionkowski and Kin, *Bodies, Embodiment, and Theology of the Hebrew Bible*, 15–16. Whether Jeremiah 1 should be included in this discussion is difficult to determine. There is physical interaction between God and Jeremiah, when God's hand touches Jeremiah's mouth in 1:9, but the description is so minimal that it adds little or nothing to this discussion.

48. In all of his visionary experiences, Ezekiel uses the phrase "The hand of God was upon me. . . ." This is often understood as a signal that the prophet is entering an altered state of some

kind, such as a trance, or even a seizure. An additional possibility is that it connects Ezekiel to the tradition of Moses in Exodus 33.

49. John J. Collins connected Dan. 7:9-10 to the "throne visions" of Isaiah 6 and Ezekiel 1, and saw it as a forerunner of the later throne vision in 1 Enoch 14. See *Daniel: A Commentary on the Book of Daniel* (Minneapolis: Fortress Press, 1993), 299–300. The locations of these visions are never entirely clear. Kathryn M. Lopez has argued that the "judgment scene" in Daniel 7 occurs on earth, rather than in heaven, because God's throne must be set up (7:9) and the Ancient of Days must "come to" the location (7:21-22). See Lopez, "Standing before the Throne of God: Critical Spatiality in Apocalyptic Scenes of Judgment," in *Constructions of Space II: The Biblical City and Other Imagined Spaces*, ed. Jon L. Berquist and Claudia V. Camp (New York: T&T Clark, 2008), 147–48.

50. The bilingual nature of Daniel presents, at most, minor difficulties for this study. The book switches from Hebrew to Aramaic at 2:4 and back to Hebrew at 8:1. The two languages are similar enough in grammatical structure that this narrative analysis can proceed without interruption. Perhaps the greatest challenge is the comparison of vocabulary. For example, there are several occurrences of the Aramaic verb *šyzb* in Daniel (3:17, 28; 6:15, 17, 21, 28), a word that is commonly translated as "delivered." When God is the subject of this verb, how can this divine behavior be compared to the common language of deliverance in Biblical Hebrew, for example, *ncl*?

51. On the meaning of the names, see Collins, *Daniel*, 140.

52. For Daniel to have worshiped Darius would have been a violation of the laws that open the Decalogue. The origin of the specific practice of praying three times daily is difficult to determine. See the extended discussion of this issue by Collins (ibid., 268–69).

53. Miles, *God*, 365.

54. Jason Bembry, *Yahweh's Coming of Age* (Winona Lake, IN: Eisenbrauns, 2011), 148–50.

55. Ibid., 148–49.

56. André Lacocque, *The Book of Daniel*, trans. David Pellauer (Atlanta: John Knox, 1979), 9–10.

57. Collins, *Daniel*, 35–37.

58. Ibid., 51.

59. Gregory Mobley, *The Return of the Chaos Monsters and Other Backstories of the Bible* (Grand Rapids, MI: Eerdmans, 2012), 136–37.

60. Miles, *God*, 366–77.

61. A notable example is Gerhard von Rad, *Wisdom in Israel* (Nashville: Abingdon, 1970), 277–81.

62. The additions made to the Greek book of Esther are a rather obvious attempt to remedy this situation. For a summary of these additions and their impact on the book, see George W. E. Nickelsburg, *Jewish Literature between the Bible and the Mishnah*, 2nd ed. (Minneapolis: Fortress Press, 2005), 202–5.

63. Roland Murphy, "Can the Book of Proverbs Be a Player in 'Biblical Theology'?" *Bulletin of Biblical Theology* 31 (2005): 4.

64. Brueggemann, *Theology of the Old Testament*, 680–82.

65. Murphy, "Can the Book of Proverbs," 5.

66. Leo G. Perdue, *The Sword and the Stylus: An Introduction to Wisdom in the Age of Empires* (Grand Rapids, MI: Eerdmans, 2008), 85.

67. Smith-Christopher, *Biblical Theology of Exile*, 173–75.

68. See, for example, Brueggemann, *Theology of the Old Testament*, 680–85. Even Brueggemann confessed here, however, that "we are largely in an area of speculation, because firm evidence is very thin" (681). A good example of this kind of speculation that seeks to push the wisdom material back into a more primitive setting is found in the work of Erhard S. Gerstenberger, who contended that because Proverbs is "about the minor matters of everyday life," it therefore presupposes the family and clan structure of society. See Gerstenberger, *Theologies in*

the Old Testament, trans. John Bowden (Minneapolis: Fortress Press, 2002), 64. The book of Proverbs hardly thinks of the issues it addresses as "minor," and it is difficult to find any sense in the book that its teaching is restricted to a particular social setting. On the contrary, it seems to break out of all such bounds.

69. James L. Crenshaw, *Education in Ancient Israel: Across the Deadening Silence* (New York: Doubleday, 1998), 90–99.

70. Miles understood a divine loss in this contest as well but perceived Job to be the winner, who in the process saves God from all of God's own worst inclinations. See Miles, *God*, 326–28.

71. I judge this view to be, at least, not inconsistent with that expressed by John J. Collins, who has portrayed a complex and disparate milieu for the development of apocalyptic literature. See Collins, *Apocalyptic Imagination*, 19–28.

72. An earlier creed such as Josh. 24:2-28, for example, contains no reference to creation or Sinai law, which von Rad considered the latest parts of the tradition. See Gerhard von Rad, "The Form-Critical Problem of the Hexateuch," in *The Problem of the Hexateuch and Other Essays* (New York: McGraw-Hill, 1966), 12–13.

73. James Barr, *The Concept of Biblical Theology: An Old Testament Perspective* (Minneapolis: Fortress Press, 1999).

74. Terence E. Fretheim, *God and World in the Old Testament: A Relational Theology of Creation* (Nashville: Abingdon, 2005).

75. John W. Rogerson, *A Theology of the Old Testament: Cultural Memory, Communication, and Being Human* (Minneapolis: Fortress Press, 2010), 19.

76. Ibid., 29–34. The primary work that Rogerson draws upon here is Claude Lévi-Strauss, *The Savage Mind* (London: Weidenfeld & Nicolson, 1966).

77. Rogerson, *Theology of the Old Testament*, 29.

78. Walter Brueggemann, "A Shape for Old Testament Theology I: Structure Legitimation," *CBQ* 47 (1985): 28–33.

79. Von Rad, "Form-Critical Problem of the Hexateuch," 77–78.

80. Friedman, *Disappearance of God*. Friedman argued that this is a long and gradual process in the Hebrew canon that ends with the absence of God in Esther (82–84).

81. This essay was originally published as "Offene Fragen im Umk einer Theologi des Alten Testaments," *TLZ* 88 (1963): 401–16.

82. Gerhard von Rad, *Old Testament Theology*, trans. D. M. G. Stalker (New York: Harper & Row, 1965), 2:415. The full significance of this essay for understanding the direction of von Rad's theology at the end of his career was highlighted by Magne Saebo in his 2000 article "Yahweh as *Deus absconditus*: Some Remarks on a Dictum by Gerhard von Rad," in *Shall Not the Judge of All the Earth Do What Is Right? Studies on the Nature of God in Tribute to James L. Crenshaw*, ed. David Penchansky and Paul L. Redditt (Winona Lake, IN: Eisenbrauns, 2000), 44. Saebo identified the significance of differing English translations of this important sentence in von Rad's essay: "Ist es Nicht ein Jahwe, der siche von Mal zu Mal in seinen Selbstoffenbarungen vor seinen Volk tiefer und tiefer verbirgt." Saebo's own translation, "Is he not a Yahweh who from time to time in his self-revelation is hiding himself more and more deeply from his people?" may provide a bit more of the sense that this hiddenness progresses over time than does the translation by Stalker quoted in the text.

83. *Elusive* is the characteristic term of the important work of Samuel Terrien.

84. Brueggemann, *Theology of the Old Testament*, 316–19.

85. Marvin Sweeney, *Tanak: A Theological and Critical Introduction to the Jewish Bible* (Minneapolis: Fortress Press, 2011), 10–11.

86. Ibid., 11–20.

87. Ibid., 26.

88. At least one disclaimer is necessary at this point. A Christian religious experience will shape the reading of the Old Testament, so this requires very careful attention. Holding off an

inclusion of the New Testament in the process is an act of careful and deliberate intellectual discipline and is part of the process developed and practiced by Miles in *God*.

89. Sweeney, *Tanak,* 28.

90. These are addressed in greater detail in the excursus "The Order of the Books in the Old Testament Canon," in chapter 5.

Bibliography

Abegg, Martin, Jr., Peter Flint, and Eugene Ulrich, trans. *The Dead Sea Scrolls Bible: The Oldest Known Bible.* San Francisco: HarperOne, 1999.

Albertz, Rainer. *Israel in Exile: The History and Literature of the Sixth Century B. C. E.* Atlanta: Society of Biblical Literature, 2003.

Alt, Albrecht. "The Origins of Israelite Law." In *Essays on Old Testament History and Religion.* Garden City, NY: Doubleday, 1967.

Alter, Robert. *The Art of Biblical Narrative.* New York: Basic Books, 1981.

Anderson, Bernhard W. *Creation versus Chaos.* Philadelphia: Fortress Press, 1987.

Anderson, Francis I. *The Verbless Clause in the Pentateuch.* Nashville: Abingdon, 1970.

Anderson, Francis I., and Dean A. Forbes. *The Vocabulary of the Old Testament.* Chicago: Loyola Press, 1993.

Anderson, Francis I., and David Noel Freedman. *Hosea: A New Translation with Introduction and Commentary.* Garden City, NY: Doubleday, 1980.

Andersonn, Greger. *Untamable Texts: Literary Studies and Narrative Theory in the Books of Samuel.* New York: T&T Clark, 2009.

Armstrong, Karen. *In the Beginning.* New York: Ballantine, 1997.

Auerbach, Erich. *Mimesis: The Representation of Reality in Western Literature.* Princeton: Princeton University Press, 1953.

Auld, Graeme. *Kings without Privilege.* New York: Continuum, 1994.

Balentine, Samuel. *The Hidden God: The Hiding of the Face of God in the Old Testament.* New York: Oxford University Press, 1983.

———. *Job: A Commentary.* Macon, GA: Smyth & Helwys, 2006.

Ballard, H. Wayne. *The Divine Warrior Motif in the Psalms.* North Richland Hills, TX: Bibal, 1999.

Baltzer, Klaus. *Deutero-Isaiah: A Commentary on Isaiah 40–55.* Minneapolis: Fortress Press, 2001.

Bar-Efrat, Shimon. *Narrative Art in the Bible.* Translated by Dorothea Shefer-Vanson. Sheffield, UK: Almond, 1989.

Barr, James. *The Concept of Biblical Theology: An Old Testament Perspective.* Minneapolis: Fortress Press, 1999.

———. "Theology and Anthropomorphism in the Old Testament." In *Congress Volume: Oxford, 1959*, 31–38. Leiden: Brill, 1960.

Barstad, Hans. *The Myth of the Empty Land: A Study in the History and Archaeology of Judah during the "Exilic" Period*. Oslo: Scandinavian University Press, 1996.

Barton, John. "The Dark Side of God in the Old Testament." In *Ethical and Unethical in the Old Testament: God and Humans in Dialogue,* edited by Katharine Dell, 122–34. New York: T&T Clark, 2010.

Baumann, Gerlinde. *Love and Violence: Marriage as Metaphor for the Relationship between YHWH and Israel in the Prophetic Books*. Collegeville, MN: Liturgical, 2003.

Baumgartner, Walter. *Jeremiah's Poems of Lament*. Sheffield, UK: Almond, 1988.

Bautch, Richard J. "The Function of Covenant across Ezra-Nehemiah." In Boda and Redditt, *Unity and Disunity in Ezra-Nehemiah*, 8–24.

Bembry, Jason. *Yahweh's Coming of Age*. Winona Lake, IN: Eisenbrauns, 2011.

Bergen, Wesley. *Elisha and the End of Prophetism*. Sheffield, UK: Sheffield Academic, 1999.

Berlin, Adele. *Lamentations: A Commentary*. Louisville: Westminster, 2002.

———. *Poetics and Interpretation of Biblical Narrative.* Winona Lake, IN: Eisenbrauns, 1983.

Biddle, Mark E. *Polyphony and Symphony in Prophetic Literature: Rereading Jeremiah 7–20.* Macon, GA: Mercer University Press, 1996.

Blenkinsopp, Joseph. *Creation, Un-Creation, Re-Creation: A Discursive Commentary on Genesis 1–11*. London: T&T Clark, 2011.

———. *Ezra-Nehemiah: A Commentary* . Louisville: Westminster, 1988.

———. "The Structure of P." *CBQ* 38 (1976): 275–92.

Block, Daniel. *The Book of Ezekiel: Chapters 1–24*. Grand Rapids, MI: Eerdmans, 1997.

Bloom, Harold. *Jesus and Yahweh: The Names Divine*. New York: Riverhead, 2005.

Blumenthal, David. *Facing the Abusing God: A Theology of Protest*. Louisville: Westminster, 1993.

Boda, Mark J., and Paul L. Redditt, eds. *Unity and Disunity in Ezra-Nehemiah: Redaction, Rhetoric, and Reader*. Sheffield, UK: Sheffield Phoenix, 2008.

Brown, Robert McAfee. *Unexpected News: Reading the Bible with Third World Eyes.* Philadelphia: Westminster, 1984.

Brown, William P. *The Ethos of the Cosmos: The Genesis of Moral Imagination in the Bible*. Grand Rapids, MI: Eerdmans, 1999.

Brueggemann, Walter. *1 & 2 Kings*. Macon, GA: Smyth & Helwys, 2000.

———. *Hopeful Imagination: Prophetic Voices in Exile*. Philadelphia: Fortress Press, 1986.

———. *Jeremiah 1–25: To Pluck Up, to Tear Down*. Grand Rapids, MI: Eerdmans, 1988.

———. *The Prophetic Imagination*. Philadelphia: Fortress Press, 1978.

———. "2 Samuel 21–24—An Appendix of Deconstruction?" In *Old Testament Theology: Essays of Structure, Theme, and Text*, edited by Patrick D. Miller, 235–51. Minneapolis: Fortress Press, 1992.

———. "A Shape for Old Testament Theology I: Structure Legitimation." *CBQ* 47 (1985): 28–46.

———. "A Shape for Old Testament Theology II: Embrace of Pain." *CBQ* 47 (1985): 395–415.

———. *The Theology of the Book of Jeremiah*. Cambridge: Cambridge University Press, 2007.

———. *Theology of the Old Testament: Testimony, Dispute, Advocacy*. Minneapolis: Fortress Press, 1997.

Burnett, Joel S. *Where Is God? Divine Absence in the Hebrew Bible*. Minneapolis: Fortress Press, 2010.

Carr, David M. *The Formation of the Hebrew Bible: A New Reconstruction*. Oxford: Oxford University Press, 2011.

———. *Writing on the Tablet of the Heart: Origins of Scripture and Literature*. Oxford: Oxford University Press, 2009.

Childs, Brevard S. *Biblical Theology of the Old and New Testaments: Theological Reflection on the Christian Bible*. Minneapolis: Fortress Press, 1992.

———. *Old Testament Theology in a Canonical Context*. Philadelphia: Fortress Press, 1985.

Christenson, Duane L., ed. *A Song of Power and the Power of a Song: Essays on the Book of Deuteronomy*. Winona Lake, IN: Eisenbrauns, 1993.

Cogan, Mordechai. *I Kings: A New Translation with Introduction and Commentary*. New York: Doubleday, 2001.

Cohen, Margaret. "Leave Nehemiah Alone: Nehemiah's 'Tales' and Fifth-Century BCE Historiography." In Boda and Redditt, *Unity and Disunity in Ezra-Nehemiah*, 55–74.

Cohn, Robert C. *2 Kings*. Collegeville, MN: Liturgical, 2000.

Collins, John J. *The Apocalyptic Imagination: An Introduction to the Jewish Matrix of Christianity*. New York: Crossroad, 1984.

———. *Daniel: A Commentary on the Book of Daniel*. Minneapolis: Fortress Press, 1993.

Comstock, Gary. "Truth or Meaning: Ricoeur versus Frei on Biblical Narrative." *JR* 66 (1986): 117–40.

———. "Two Types of Narrative Theology." *JAAR* 55 (1987): 687–717.

Conrad, Edgar. *Reading Isaiah*. Minneapolis: Fortress Press, 1993.

Copan, Paul. *Is God a Moral Monster? Making Sense of the Old Testament God*. Grand Rapids, MI: Baker, 2011.

Cox, Dorian G. Coover. "The Hardening of Pharaoh's Heart in Its Literary and Cultural Contexts." *BSac* 163 (2006): 292–311.

Crenshaw, James L. *Education in Ancient Israel: Across the Deadening Silence*. New York: Doubleday, 1998.

Cross, Frank Moore. "The Song of the Sea and Canaanite Myth." In *Canaanite Myth and Hebrew Epic*, 112–44. Cambridge: Harvard University Press, 1973.

Davies, Gordon F. *Ezra and Nehemiah*. Collegeville, MN: Liturgical, 1999.

Dawkins, Richard. *The God Delusion*. Boston: Houghton Mifflin, 2006.

Day, John, ed. *Prophecy and Prophets in Ancient Israel: Proceedings of the Oxford Old Testament Seminar*. New York: T&T Clark, 2010.

deClaissé-Walford, Nancy L. *Reading from the Beginning: The Shaping of the Hebrew Psalter*. Macon, GA: Mercer University Press, 1997.

Dempsey, Carol J., and Mary Margaret Pazdan, eds. *Earth, Wind, and Fire: Biblical and Theological Perspectives on Creation*. Collegeville, MN: Liturgical, 2004.

Diamond, A. R. *The Confessions of Jeremiah in Context: Scenes of a Prophetic Drama*. Sheffield, UK: Sheffield Academic, 1987.

Dietrich, Walter, and Christian Link. *Die dunklen Seiten Gottes: Willkür und Gewalt*. Neukirchen-Vluyn: Neukirchner, 2000.

Douglas, Mary. "The Abominations of Leviticus." In *Purity and Danger: An Analysis of Concepts of Pollution and Taboo*. New York: Routledge, 1970.

Eichrodt, Walther. *Theology of the Old Testament*. Translated by J. A. Baker. 2 vols. Philadelphia: Westminster, 1961–67.

Eskenazi, Tamara Cohn. *In an Age of Prose: A Literary Approach to Ezra-Nehemiah*. Atlanta: Scholars, 1988.

Eslinger, Lyle. "Freedom or Knowledge? Perspective and Purpose in the Exodus Narrative." *JSOT* 52 (1991): 43–60.

Even-Shoshan, Abraham. *A New Concordance of the Bible*. Jerusalem: Kiryat Sefer, 1990.

Exum, J. Cheryl. *Fragmented Women: Feminist (Sub)Versions of Biblical Narratives.* Sheffield, UK: JSOT Press, 1993.

———. *Tragedy and Biblical Narrative: Arrows of the Almighty*. Cambridge: Cambridge University Press, 1992.

Feldmeier, Reinhard, and Hermann Spieckermann. *God of the Living: A Biblical Theology*. Translated by Mark E. Biddle. Waco, TX: Baylor University Press, 2011.

Fishbane, Michael. *Biblical Myth and Rabbinic Mythmaking*. Oxford: Oxford University Press, 2003.

Forster, E. M. *Aspects of the Novel.* London: Arnold, 1927.

Fox, Michael V. *Proverbs 1–9: A New Translation with Introduction and Commentary.* New York: Doubleday, 2000.

Freedman, David Noel. "The Song of the Sea." In *Pottery, Poetry, and Prophecy*, 179–86. Winona Lake, IN: Eisenbrauns, 1980.

Frei, Hans. *The Eclipse of Biblical Narrative: A Study in Eighteenth and Nineteenth Century Hermeneutics*. New Haven: Yale University Press, 1974.

———. *The Identity of Jesus Christ: The Hermeneutical Bases of Dogmatic Theology.* Philadelphia: Fortress Press, 1975.

Fretheim, Terence E. *God and World in the Old Testament: A Relational Theology of Creation.* Nashville: Abingdon, 2005.

———. *Jeremiah: A Commentary.* Macon, GA: Smyth & Helwys, 2002.

Fried, Lisbeth S. "Who Wrote Ezra-Nehemiah—and Why Did They?" In Boda and Redditt, *Unity and Disunity in Ezra-Nehemiah*, 75–97.

Friedman, Richard Elliott. *The Disappearance of God: A Divine Mystery*. Boston: Little, Brown, 1995.

Frye, Northrop. *The Great Code: The Bible and Literature*. New York: Harcourt Brace Jovanovich, 1982.

Gadamer, Hans Georg. *Truth and Method.* London: Sheed & Ward, 1975.

Geller, Stephen. "The Struggle at the Jabbok: The Uses of Enigma in Biblical Narrative." *Journal of Ancient Near Eastern Studies* 14 (1982): 37–60.

Gerstenberger, Erhard S. *Theologies in the Old Testament.* Translated by John Bowden. Minneapolis: Fortress Press, 2002.

Gottwald, Norman K. *The Tribes of Yahweh.* Maryknoll, NY: Orbis, 1979.

Grabbe, Lester. *Ezra-Nehemiah.* New York: Routledge, 1998.

Greenberg, Moshe. *Ezekiel 1–20: A New Translation with Introduction and Commentary*. New York: Doubleday, 1983.

Gunn, David M. *The Fate of King Saul: An Interpretation of a Biblical Story*. Sheffield, UK: Sheffield University Press, 1980.

———. "The 'Hardening of Pharaoh's Heart': Plot, Character, and Theology in Exodus 1–14." In *Art and Meaning: Rhetoric in Biblical Literature*, edited by David J. A. Clines, David M. Gunn, and Alan J. Hauser, 72–96. Sheffield, UK: JSOT Press, 1985.

Gutiérrez, Gustavo. *On Job: God-Talk and the Suffering of the Innocent*. Maryknoll, NY: Orbis, 1987.

Haak, Robert. "Mapping Violence in the Prophets: Zephaniah 2." In *The Aesthetics of Violence in the Prophets*, edited by Julia M. O'Brien and Chris Franke, 18–36. New York: T&T Clark, 2010.

Haas, Peter J. "The Book of Daniel: The Strange End of Biblical Theology." In *Jewish Bible Theology: Perspectives and Case Studies*, edited by Isaac Kalimi, 249–62. Winona Lake, IN: Eisenbrauns, 2012.

Hahn, Scott W. *The Kingdom of God as Liturgical Empire: A Theological Commentary on 1–2 Chronicles*. Grand Rapids, MI: Baker Academic, 2012.

Hamlin, E. John. *At Risk in the Promised Land: A Commentary on the Book of Judges*. Grand Rapids, MI: Eerdmans, 1990.

Hamori, Esther. *When Gods Were Men: The Embodied God in Biblical and Near Eastern Literature*. Berlin: de Gruyter, 2008.

Hanson, Paul D. *The Dawn of Apocalyptic: The Historical and Sociological Roots of Jewish Apocalyptic Eschatology*. Philadelphia: Fortress Press, 1979.

———. *The Diversity of Scripture*. Philadelphia: Fortress Press, 1984.

———. *The People Called: The Growth of Community in the Bible*. San Francisco: Harper & Row, 1986.

Hartley, John E. *Leviticus*. Waco, TX: Word, 1992.

Hartman, Louis Francis, and Alexander A. Di Lella. *The Book of Daniel*. Garden City, NY: Doubleday, 1978.

Hayes, John, and Frederick Prussner. *Old Testament Theology: Its History and Development*. Atlanta: John Knox, 1985.

Hillers, Delbert R. *Covenant: The History of a Biblical Idea*. Baltimore: Johns Hopkins University Press, 1969.

Holliday, William L. *The Psalms through Three Thousand Years: Prayerbook of a Cloud of Witnesses*. Minneapolis: Fortress Press, 1993.

Humphreys, W. Lee. *The Character of God in the Book of Genesis: A Narrative Appraisal*. Louisville: Westminster John Knox, 2001.

Japhet, Sara. "The Supposed Common Authorship of Chronicles and Ezra Investigated Anew." *VT* 18 (1969): 334–70.

Jellico, Sidney. *The Septuagint and Modern Study*. Oxford: Oxford University Press, 1968.

Jobes, Karen H., and Moisés Silva. *Invitation to the Septuagint*. Grand Rapids, MI: Baker Academic, 2005.

Kalimi, Isaac. *The Reshaping of Ancient Israelite History in Chronicles*. Winona Lake, IN: Eisenbrauns, 2005.

Kalmanofsky, Amy. *Terror All Around: The Rhetoric of Horror in the Book of Jeremiah*. New York: T&T Clark, 2008.

Kamionkowski, S. Tamar, and Wonil Kin, eds. *Bodies, Embodiment, and Theology of the Hebrew Bible*. New York: T&T Clark, 2010.

Knierem, Rolf P. *The Task of Old Testament Theology: Method and Cases*. Grand Rapids, MI: Eerdmans, 2000.

Knoppers, Gary N. "Democratizing Revelation? Prophets, Seers, and Visionaries in Chronicles." In Day, *Prophecy and Prophets in Ancient Israel*, 391–409.

Kraft, Robert A. "The Codex and Canon Consciousness." In *The Canon Debate*, edited by Lee Martin McDonald and James A. Sanders. Peabody, MA: Hendrickson, 2002.

Kugel, James L. *The Bible as It Was*. Cambridge, MA: Harvard University Press, 1997.

Kuhn, Karl Allen. *Having Words with God: The Bible as Conversation*. Minneapolis: Fortress Press, 2008.

Labuschange, Casper J. "Divine Speech in Deuteronomy." In Christenson, *Song of Power and the Power of a Song*, 375–93.

Lacocque, André. *The Book of Daniel*. Translated by David Pellauer. Atlanta: John Knox, 1979.

Lacocque, André, and Paul Ricoeur. *Thinking Biblically: Exegetical and Hermeneutical Studies*. Chicago: University of Chicago Press, 1998.

Launderville, Dale F. *Spirit and Reason: The Embodied Character of Ezekiel's Symbolic Thinking*. Waco, TX: Baylor University Press, 2007.

Levenson, Jon D. *Creation and the Persistence of Evil: The Jewish Drama of Divine Omnipotence*. San Francisco: Harper & Row, 1988.

———. *Sinai and Zion: An Entry into the Jewish Bible*. San Francisco: Harper & Row, 1985.

Levine, Yigal. "Nimrod the Mighty, King of Kish, King of Sumer and Akkad." *VT* 52 (2002): 350–66.

Lévi-Strauss, Claude. *The Savage Mind*. London: Weidenfeld & Nicolson, 1966.

Linville, James Richard. *Israel in the Book of Kings: The Past as Project of Social Identity*. Sheffield, UK: Sheffield Academic, 1998.

Lopez, Kathryn M. "Standing before the Throne of God: Critical Spatiality in Apocalyptic Scenes of Judgment." In *Constructions of Space II: The Biblical City and Other Imagined Spaces*, edited by Jon L. Berquist and Claudia V. Camp, 139–55. New York: T&T Clark, 2008.

Lothar-Hossfeld, Frank, and Erich Zenger. *Psalms 2: A Commentary on Psalms 51–100*. Translated by Linda M. Maloney. Minneapolis: Fortress Press, 2005.

McCarthy, Dennis J. "Covenant and Law in Chronicles-Nehemiah." *CBQ* 44 (1982): 25–44.

McEntire, Mark. "Being Seen and Not Heard: The Interpretation of Genesis 4.8." In *Of Scribes and Sages: Early Jewish Interpretation and Transmission of Scripture*, edited by Craig A. Evans, 1:4–13. London: T&T Clark, 2004.

———. *The Blood of Abel: The Violent Plot in the Hebrew Bible*. Macon, GA: Mercer University Press, 1999.

———. *Dangerous Worlds: Living and Dying in Biblical Texts*. Macon, GA: Smyth & Helwys, 2004.

———. *The Function of Sacrifice in Chronicles, Ezra, and Nehemiah*. Lewiston, NY: Mellen Biblical Press, 1993.

———. "The God at the End of the Story: Are Biblical Theology and Narrative Character Development Compatible?" *HBT* 33 (2011): 1–19.

———. "The Graying of God in Daniel 1–7." *RevExp*, forthcoming.

———. "Haggai—Bringing God into the Picture." *RevExp* 97 (2000): 69–78.

———. "Portraits of a Mature God: What Would a Theology of the Hebrew Scriptures Look Like if Ezra-Nehemiah Was at the Center of the Discussion?" *PRSt* 39 (2012): 113–24.

———. "A Prophetic Chorus of Others: Helping Jeremiah Survive in Jeremiah 26." *RevExp* 101 (2004): 301–14.

———. *Struggling with God: An Introduction to the Pentateuch*. Macon, GA: Mercer University Press, 2008.

Mendenhall, George. "The Hebrew Conquest of Palestine." *BA* 25 (1962): 66–87.

Michelson, Marty Alan. *Reconciling Violence and Kingship: A Study of Judges and 1 Samuel*. Eugene, OR: Pickwick, 2011.

Middlemas, Jill. *The Templeless Age: An Introduction to the History, Literature, and Theology of the "Exile."* Louisville: Westminster John Knox, 2007.

Milazzo, G. Tom. *The Protest and the Silence: Suffering, Death, and Biblical Theology*. Minneapolis: Fortress Press, 1992.

Miles, Jack. *Christ: A Crisis in the Life of God*. New York: Knopf, 2001.

———. *God: A Biography*. New York: Vintage, 1995.

Miller, Patrick D. "'Moses My Servant': The Deuteronomic Portrait of Moses." In Christenson, *Song of Power and the Power of a Song*, 302–3.

———. *The Way of the Lord: Essays in Old Testament Theology*. Grand Rapids, MI: Eerdmans, 2004.

Mobley, Gregory. *The Return of the Chaos Monsters and Other Backstories of the Bible*. Grand Rapids, MI: Eerdmans, 2012.

Moughtin-Mumby, *Sexual and Marital Metaphors in Hosea, Jeremiah, Isaiah, and Ezekiel*. New York: Oxford University Press, 2008.

Mowinckel, Sigmund. *He That Cometh*. Oxford: Blackwell, 1956.

Mudge, Lewis. "Paul Ricoeur on Biblical Interpretation." In *Essays on Biblical Interpretation*, edited by Lewis Mudge, 1–10. Philadelphia: Fortress Press, 1980.

Murphy, Roland. "Can the Book of Proverbs Be a Player in 'Biblical Theology'?" *Bulletin of Biblical Theology* 31 (2005): 4–9.

Nicholson, Ernest W. "Deuteronomy 18.19-22, the Prophets, and Scripture." In Day, *Prophecy and Prophets in Ancient Israel*, 151–71.

———. *Exodus and Sinai in History and Tradition*. Atlanta: John Knox, 1973.

Nickelsburg, George W. E. *Jewish Literature between the Bible and the Mishnah*. 2nd ed. Minneapolis: Fortress Press, 2005.

Niditch, Susan. *Judges: A Commentary*. Louisville: Westminster John Knox, 2008.

———. *War in the Hebrew Bible: A Study in the Ethics of Violence*. Oxford: Oxford University Press, 1993.

Nogalski, James. *Literary Precursors to the Book of the Twelve*. Berlin: de Gruyter, 1993.

Noth, Martin. *The Chronicler's History*. Translated by H. G. M. Williamson. Sheffield, UK: Sheffield Academic, 2001.

O'Brien, Julia. *Challenging Prophetic Metaphor: Theology and Ideology in the Prophets*. Louisville: Westminster John Knox, 2011.

O'Connor, Kathleen. *The Confessions of Jeremiah: Their Interpretation and Role in Chapters 1–25*. Atlanta: Scholars, 1988.

Oduyoye, Modupe. *The Sons of God and the Daughters of Men: An Afro-Asiatic Reading of Genesis 1–11*. Maryknoll, NY: Orbis, 1984.

Olson, Dennis T. *Deuteronomy and the Death of Moses: A Theological Reading*. Minneapolis: Fortress Press, 1994.

Pagels, Elaine. *Adam, Eve, and the Serpent*. New York: Vintage, 1988.

———. *The Origin of Satan*. New York: Random House, 1995.

Parker, D. C. "The Hexapla of Origen." In *The Anchor Bible Dictionary*, edited by David Noel Freedman, 3:188–89. New York: Doubleday, 1993.

Patrick, Dale. *The Rendering of God in the Old Testament.* Philadelphia: Fortress Press, 1983.

———. "The Translation of Job XVII, 6." *VT* 26 (1976): 369–71.

Patton, Corrine L. "'Should Our Sister Be Treated Like a Whore?': A Response to Feminist Critiques of Ezekiel 23." In *The Book of Ezekiel: Theological and Anthropological Perspectives*, edited by Margaret S. Odell and John T. Strong, 221–38. Atlanta: Scholars, 2000.

Perdue, Leo G. *Reconstructing Old Testament Theology: After the Collapse of History.* Minneapolis: Fortress Press, 2005.

———. *The Sword and the Stylus: An Introduction to Wisdom in the Age of Empires.* Grand Rapids, MI: Eerdmans, 2008.

Perdue, Leo G., Robert Morgan, and Benjamin D. Sommer, eds. *Biblical Theology: Introducing the Conversation.* Nashville: Abingdon, 2009.

Person, Raymond F., Jr. *The Deuteronomistic History and the Book of Chronicles: Scribal Works in an Oral World*. Atlanta: Society of Biblical Literature, 2010.

Petersen, David L. *The Prophetic Literature: An Introduction.* Louisville: Westminster John Knox, 2002.

Pixley, Jorge V. *On Exodus: A Liberation Perspective.* Translated by Robert R. Barr. Maryknoll, NY: Orbis, 1987.

Ricoeur, Paul. *Time and Narrative.* Vol. 1. Chicago: University of Chicago Press, 1984.

Roberts, Colin Henderson, and Theodore Cressy Skeat. *The Birth of the Codex*. Oxford: Oxford University Press, 1987.

Rogerson, John W. *A Theology of the Old Testament: Cultural Memory, Communication, and Being Human*. Minneapolis: Fortress Press, 2009.

Saebo, Magne. "Yahweh as *Deus absconditus*: Some Remarks on a Dictum by Gerhard von Rad." In *Shall Not the Judge of All the Earth Do What Is Right? Studies on the Nature of God in Tribute to James L. Crenshaw,* edited by David Penchansky and Paul L. Redditt, 43–55. Winona Lake, IN: Eisenbrauns, 2000.

Sanford, John A. *King Saul: The Tragic Hero*. New York: Paulist, 1985.

Sawyer, John F. A. "The Language of Leviticus." In *Reading Leviticus: A Conversation with Mary Douglas*, edited by John F. A. Sawyer, 15–20. Sheffield, UK: Sheffield Academic, 1996.

Schaefer, Konrad. *Psalms*. Collegeville, MN: Liturgical, 2001.

Schipper, Jeremy. "Hezekiah, Manasseh, and Dynastic or Transgenerational Punishment." In *Soundings in Kings: Perspectives and Methods in Contemporary Scholarship*, edited by Mark Leuchter and Klaus-Peter Adam, 81–108. Minneapolis: Fortress Press, 2010.

Schmid, Konrad. "The Late Persian Formation of the Torah: Observations on Deuteronomy 34." In *Judah and the Judeans in the Fourth Century B.C.E*, edited by Oded Lipschits, Gary N. Knoppers, and Rainer Albertz, 237–51. Winona Lake, IN: Eisenbrauns, 2007.

———. *The Old Testament: A Literary History*. Minneapolis: Fortress Press, 2012.

Schmidt, Werner H. *The Faith of the Old Testament: A History*. Translated by John Sturdy. Philadelphia: Westminster, 1983.

Schneider, Tammi J. *Judges*. Collegeville, MN: Liturgical, 2000.

Schwartz, Howard. "Does God Have a Body?" In Kamionkowski and Kin, *Bodies, Embodiment, and Theology of the Hebrew Bible*, 201–37.

Schwartz, Regina M. *The Curse of Cain: The Violent Legacy of Monotheism*. Chicago: University of Chicago Press, 1997.

Segal, Jerome. *Joseph's Bones: Understanding the Struggle between God and Mankind in the Bible*. New York: Riverhead, 2007.

Seibert, Eric A. *Disturbing Divine Behavior: Troubling Old Testament Images of God* Minneapolis: Fortress Press, 2010.

Seitz, Christopher R. *Prophecy and Hermeneutics: Toward a New Introduction to the Prophets*. Grand Rapids, MI: Baker Academic, 2007.

———. *Zion's Final Destiny: The Development of the Book of Isaiah*. Minneapolis: Fortress Press, 1991.

Sherwood, Stephen K. *Leviticus, Numbers, Deuteronomy*. Collegeville, MN: Liturgical, 2002.

Sherwood, Yvonne. *The Prostitute and the Prophet: Hosea's Marriage in Literary-Theoretical Perspective*. Sheffield, UK: Sheffield Academic, 1996.

Smith, Mark S. *The Laments of Jeremiah and Their Contexts*. Atlanta: Scholars, 1990.

———. *The Priestly Vision of Genesis 1*. Minneapolis: Fortress Press, 2010.

Smith-Christopher, Daniel L. *A Biblical Theology of Exile*. Minneapolis: Fortress Press, 2002.

Sommer, Benjamin D. *The Bodies of God and the World of Ancient Israel*. Cambridge: Cambridge University Press, 2009.

———. "Dialectical Biblical Theology: A Jewish Approach to Reading Scripture Theologically." In Perdue, Morgan, and Sommer, *Biblical Theology*, 1–54. Nashville: Abingdon, 2009.

Stephenson, Neal. *Snow Crash*. New York: Random House, 1993.

Sternberg, Meir. *The Poetics of Biblical Narrative: Ideological Literature and the Drama of Reading*. Bloomington: Indiana University Press, 1987.

Steussy, Marti J. *Samuel and His God*. Columbia: University of South Carolina Press, 2010.

Stiver, Dan R. *Theology after Ricoeur: New Directions in Hermeneutical Theology*. Louisville: Westminster John Knox, 2001.

Stulman, Louis, and Hyun Chul Paul Kim. *You Are My People: An Introduction to Prophetic Literature*. Nashville: Abingdon, 2011.

Sweeney, Marvin A. *Reading the Hebrew Bible after the Shoah: Engaging Holocaust Theology*. Minneapolis: Fortress Press, 2008.

———. *Tanak: A Theological and Critical Introduction to the Jewish Bible*. Minneapolis: Fortress Press, 2011.

Tamez, Elsa. *Bible of the Oppressed*. Translated by Matthew J. O'Connell. Maryknoll, NY: Orbis, 1982.

Terrien, Samuel. *The Elusive Presence: Toward a New Biblical Theology*. New York: Harper & Row, 1978.

Thomas, Matthew A. *These Are the Generations: Identity, Covenant, and the "Toledoth" Formula*. London: T & T Clark, 2010.

Tov, Emmanuel. *Textual Criticism of the Hebrew Bible*. Minneapolis: Fortress Press, 1992.

Trible, Phyllis. *God and the Rhetoric of Sexuality*. Philadelphia: Fortress Press, 1978.

———. *Rhetorical Criticism: Context, Method, and the Book of Jonah*. Minneapolis: Fortress Press, 1994.

———. *Texts of Terror: Literary-Feminist Readings of Biblical Narratives*. Philadelphia: Fortress Press, 1984.

Tullock, John H., and Mark McEntire. *The Old Testament Story*. 9th ed. Boston: Prentice Hall, 2012.

van Wolde, Ellen. "The Story of Cain and Abel: A Narrative Study." *JSOT* 52 (1991): 25–41.

Vassar, John S. *Recalling a Story Once Told: An Intertextual Reading of the Psalter and the Pentateuch*. Macon, GA: Mercer University Press, 2007.

Vogt, Peter T. *Deuteronomic Theology and the Significance of Torah: A Reappraisal*. Winona Lake, IN: Eisenbrauns, 2006.

von Rad, Gerhard. *Deuteronomy: A Commentary*. Translated by Dorothea Barton. Philadelphia: Westminster, 1966.

———. "The Form-Critical Problem of the Hexateuch." In *The Problem of the Hexateuch and Other Essays*. New York: McGraw-Hill, 1966.
———. *Holy War in Ancient Israel*. Translated by Marva J. Dawn. Grand Rapids, MI: Eerdmans, 1991.
———. "Offene Fragen im Umk einer Theologi des Alten Testaments." *TLZ* 88 (1963): 401–16.
———. *Old Testament Theology*. Translated by D. M. G. Stalker. 2 vols. New York: Harper & Row, 1962–65.
———. *Wisdom in Israel*. Nashville: Abingdon, 1970.
Walsh, Jerome T. *1 Kings*. Collegeville, MN: Liturgical, 1996.
Warning, Wilfred. *Literary Artistry in Leviticus*. Leiden: Brill, 1995.
Watts, James W. *Ritual and Rhetoric in Leviticus: From Sacrifice to Scripture*. Cambridge: Cambridge University Press, 2007.
Wenham, Gordon J. *Psalms as Torah: Reading Biblical Song Ethically*. Grand Rapids, MI: Baker, 2012.
Williamson, H. G. M. *Ezra-Nehemiah*. Waco, TX: Word, 1985.
———. *Israel in the Books of Chronicles*. Cambridge: Cambridge University Press, 1977.
Willis, Amy C. Merrill. "Heavenly Bodies: God and the Body in the Visions of Daniel." In Kamionkowski and Kin, *Bodies, Embodiment, and Theology of the Hebrew Bible*, 13–37.
Wilson, Gerald. *The Editing of the Hebrew Psalter*. Chico, CA: Scholars, 1985.
Wolff, Hans Walter. *Joel and Amos*. Philadelphia: Augsburg, 1977.
Wright, Robert. *The Evolution of God*. New York: Little, Brown, 2009.

Subject Index

Author Index

Scripture Index

2 Kings

1 Chronicles

2 Chronicles

Ezra